The Armenian
Revolutionary Movement

PUBLISHED UNDER THE AUSPICES OF THE NEAR
EASTERN CENTER UNIVERSITY OF
CALIFORNIA, LOS ANGELES

THE ARMENIAN REVOLUTIONARY MOVEMENT

The Development of Armenian Political Parties through the Nineteenth Century

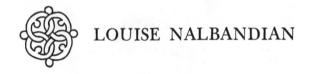 LOUISE NALBANDIAN

UNIVERSITY OF CALIFORNIA PRESS

Berkeley and Los Angeles, 1963

University of California Press
Berkeley and Los Angeles, California

Cambridge University Press, London, England

© *1963 by The Regents of the University of California*

Library of Congress Catalog Card Number: 63–13806

ISBN: 9780520303850

In Memory of My Parents

*Ziazan Hinaekian of Erzingan
Boghos Mugerditch Nalbandian
of Sinamoud-Kharput*

Preface

The need for a more comprehensive work in English dealing with the revolutionary activities among the Armenians during the nineteenth century has led to the writing of this book. I have endeavored to clarify the origins, objectives, activities, and achievements of the Armenian political parties that arose during the last half of the nineteenth century. These developments are shown in relation to similar national revolutionary forces that were already at work in Western Europe, Russia, and the Balkans.

This study covers in detail the armed struggle of the Armenian revolutionists against the Ottoman government, beginning with the first major disturbance in 1862 and extending to 1896. The latter year terminates this work for three major reasons. The year 1896 marked a national crisis in Armenian history by reason of the massacres of Armenians by the Turks; also, a definite shift took place within the ranks of the political organizations; and, finally, there was a reëvaluation by outside forces of what could or should be done in regard to the revolutionary movement in Armenia.

Small secret societies directed these uprisings from 1862 to 1885. In the latter year a maturity of political thought was evidenced by the formation of the first political party; and thereafter organized political parties assumed leadership of the Armenian revolutionary forces. These physical manifestations of revolution are narrated and analyzed within a framework of the political and intellectual history of the Armenians in chapters i and ii.

The year 1896 does not, of course, end the activities

of Armenian political parties. These same parties, with some changes, continue as active organizations to this very day. Accordingly, this study may be considered the first part of the history of modern Armenian political parties.

The source material for this work has been obtained mainly from private collections in the Near East, Europe, and the United States. The most important private collections utilized are those of the late Paul Julian, Fresno, California, and of Mr. Albert Nalbandian and Mr. Harry M. Tashinian, both resident in San Francisco, California. I am particularly indebted to the Libraries of the Armenian Mekhitharist Monasteries at Vienna and Venice; the Armenian Cultural Foundation in Boston; the Collections at the Armenian Revolutionary Federation in Boston; and the Hoover Institution and Library on War, Revolution, and Peace, at Stanford University, Stanford, California.

I am grateful for the pertinent suggestions and counsel of Harlan J. Swanson, the late Professor John Mills McClelland, Dr. A. O. Sarkissian, and Dr. Michael O'H. Lavin. At the Hoover Institution generous assistance was given by Mrs. Marina Stragus Tinkoff and Dr. Enver Ziya Karal. I am also indebted to Professor Gustave E. von Grunebaum for his assistance in arranging for the publication of the work, and to Mr. Robert Y. Zachary for his editorial suggestions and personal attention to the text.

In addition to the sources mentioned above, I have had the inestimable advantage of conferring both personally and by letter with numerous Armenians, both abroad and in the United States, who were involved in the revolutionary and political activities narrated in these pages. These include the former Prime Minister of the Armenian Republic, Mr. Simon Vratzian of Beirut, Lebanon, the late Archbishop Tirayre Der Hovhanisian, and the late Mushegh Seropian, former Archbishop of Cilicia. I have also had the fortunate opportunity of obtaining first-hand knowledge of the organizations dealt with in this study by attending meetings and functions sponsored by various Armenian political parties in the Near East, Europe, and the United States.

Louise Nalbandian

Contents

I

An Outline of Armenia's Struggle for Freedom

The Armenian Revolutionary Movement of the nineteenth century was the expression of a new nationalism, which embodied a fervent desire for individual freedom and political rights. At first the movement was only the inspired and inspiring response of a few patriotic individuals to those ideals. Through the stirring message of that handful of men, the Armenian people awoke from years of lethargy. First small groups, then organizations, and finally political parties came into existence to create from those ideals a social reality.

Before proceeding to the political and intellectual history of the nineteenth century, it is necessary to trace the historical development of the Armenian nation. The remote past reveals the deep roots which in later centuries helped the Armenian political parties to stand spiritually firm and strong. More than twenty-five centuries of cultural heritage, national consciousness, and political vicissitudes are woven into the revolutionary carpet on which stands the patriot of modern times. Let us briefly examine this

Armenian "carpet" and outline the struggles for freedom which it displays.

GEOGRAPHICAL AND HISTORICAL ARMENIA

Geographically, Armenia covers roughly that area of Western Asia which includes the highest and most rugged mountain ranges. On the north, the region is bounded by the Pontus and is separated from the Caucasus by the Kur and Rioni rivers. On the south, Armenia extends to the plain of northwestern Mesopotamia. On the west, the region is bounded by Asia Minor and on the east by the plateau of Azerbaijan and the southern extension of the Caspian Sea. Thus, the geographical area includes the territory situated between longitudes 37 and 47½ degrees East and latitudes 37 and 41½ degrees North. It is a natural geographic unit comprised of roughly 120,000 square miles.[1]

The mountain ranges of the Armenian Plateau act as fortresses and are the source of numerous rivers, notably the Tigris and the Euphrates. The land of the Armenians, which locally is called Hayastan,[2] is often identified by patriotic natives with the Garden of Eden. And according to Genesis 8:4, Noah's Ark landed "upon the mountains of Ararat." Mount Ararat is of singular importance to the Armenians. It marks the epicenter of their country and it is also at the present time a symbol of their national aspirations; for it is a fact that only in one period of Armenian history has the whole region been a united kingdom under a single ruler—in the first century B.C., under Tigranes the Great.

Historically, the country was divided into three distinct areas: Armenia Major (Greater Armenia), Armenia Minor (Lesser Armenia), and New Armenia (Armeno-Cilicia or Sissouan). Armenia Major and Armenia Minor date from ancient times, and were considered two separate states by

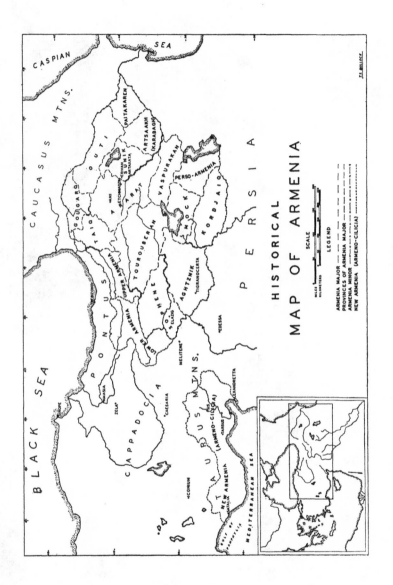

HISTORICAL
MAP OF ARMENIA

SCALE

MILES
KILOMETERS

LEGEND

ARMENIA MAJOR
PROVINCES OF ARMENIA MAJOR
ARMENIA MINOR
NEW ARMENIA (ARMENO-CILICIA)

the writers of the ancient world. Armenia Major was the largest of the three areas. It consisted of fifteen provinces, among which the most important were Sophene, Upper Armenia, Perso-Armenia, Vaspurakan (Van), Sunik, Karabagh, and Ararat with its historic cities of Armavir, Artaxata, Etchmiadzin, Ani, and Erivan. Armenia Minor was the region west of Armenia Major, south of the kingdom of the Pontus, and north of Cappadocia. After the period of Alexander the Great, Armenia Major and Armenia Minor were often considered to be one region.[3]

New Armenia belongs to the third historic area, which dates from the eleventh century. It was located southwest of Armenia Minor, and its northern boundary, which shifted from time to time, generally coincided with the Taurus Mountains. New Armenia occupied more than 250 miles of the Mediterranean coast from the Gulf of Alexandretta to the Gulf of Pamphylia near the town of Satalia.[4] Although New Armenia lies outside of the geographical boundaries of present-day Armenia, it is considered an important part of the homeland.

THE URARTU KINGDOM AND THE ORIGINS OF THE ARMENIANS

The origins of the Armenian people and the beginnings of their history remain obscure to this day. Nevertheless, some traces of their early history are found in ancient writings, and recent linguistic and archeological discoveries have thrown additional light on the Armenian past. In the ninth century B.C. the powerful Kingdom of Urartu or Ararat occupied the lands of Armenia. Its capital was located near Lake Van,[5] and the power of the Urartu state extended as far as Transcaucasia.[6] The Urartians maintained economic and cultural contacts with Assyria, Egypt, Crete, and other countries in the ancient Near East.[7] They vied for power with the Assyrian Empire, whose ruler

Shalmaneser (860–825 B.C.) caused to be depicted on the gates of his palace various conflicts with the Urartians.[8]

The Urartu Kingdom was not only a powerful military state but it also had a highly developed civilization.[9] Its people spoke a non-Aryan language, which has been deciphered,[10] and they believed in a single supreme god whom they named Khaldi. It is from their god that the people of Urartu derived the name Khaldians.[11] In the eighth and seventh centuries B.C. a new people invaded Urartu and conquered it. According to Herodotus, the people who overthrew Urartu were Phrygian colonists known as Armenians.[12] As time passed, the Armeno-Phrygian tribes imposed their Indo-European language on the Urartians, and the amalgamation of the two peoples resulted in the formation of the Armenian nation.[13]

ARMENIA UNDER PERSIAN RULE

Soon after taking over the former Kingdom of Urartu, the Armenians themselves fell victims to more powerful forces. In the sixth century B.C. they first became part of the Median Empire, and then their land was incorporated into Achaemenid Persia under Cyrus the Great (558–529 B.C.). The Armenians were not content to remain under foreign domination and found it opportune, after the death of Cyrus, to rise in a coalition with other subject peoples against the Persians. The severe battles that the new Persian king, Darius I Hystaspes, fought against the Armenians are narrated on the Rock of Behistun (521 B.C.). Subdued by the Persian forces, the Armenians were in 518 B.C. organized into a satrapy, possessing a great degree of political and administrative freedom. Some description of the life of the people during the Achaemenid period is given in the *Anabasis* of Xenephon, who relates the difficult "March of the Ten Thousand" through the rugged mountains of Armenia in 401–400 B.C.

Persian domination lasted nearly two centuries (518–330 B.C.) and brought about many changes in the life of the Armenians. It was a period of great material prosperity, during which the country's transportation facilities, industry, commerce, and agriculture improved and expanded. Although the Persian language was not forced on the people, it became very much used, especially among the upper classes. The Armenians adopted certain Persian customs, and the nobility, later followed by the lower classes, educated their children in Persian ways and religious customs. However, they retained their ethnic individuality and were not completely assimilated. Persian domination brought peace and prosperity, and no serious efforts were made to obtain political independence.[14]

HELLENIC INFLUENCES IN ARMENIA

The conquests of Alexander the Great in the East had a great effect on the Armenians, who, during nearly two centuries of Persian rule, had become orientated toward the Eastern world. Following Alexander's conquest of Persia in the fourth century B.C., Armenia became a province of the Macedonian Empire and came into contact with European civilization. Greek philosophic concepts were introduced into the country.

The Armenian nobility were noticeably influenced by the dissemination of Hellenic culture. They now spoke Greek rather than Persian and prided themselves on being Hellenophiles. Greek deities were added to previously accepted Persian religious traditions and they combined to become the basis of the Armenian religion of ancient times. However, to a great extent, the masses did not fully benefit from the new culture introduced by Alexander the Great. Armenia remained predominantly an oriental nation and continued to be politically and culturally directed toward the East until its adoption of Christianity, which sharpened the cleavage between Armenia and her eastern neighbors.

After the death of Alexander the Great, the Armenian territory fell under the rule of the Hellenistic Seleucid Empire, and in 312 B.C. its administration was entrusted to two native generals. Armenia Major was ruled by Artaxias or Artashes I, and the small area of Sophene was under the administration of Zariadras or Zareh. In the fall of 190 B.C. the Romans defeated the Seleucids at Magnesia, and the two rulers of Armenia seized the opportunity to revolt against the domination of the weakened Seleucid Empire. In 189 B.C. they declared themselves kings of their respective regions. Finally, after many centuries of foreign domination, Armenia became an independent nation under two separate kingdoms.

THE ARTAXIAN (OR ARTASHESIAN) DYNASTY

Artaxias I, who was of Armenian origin, became the first king of Armenia Major and was the founder of the Artaxian Dynasty, which gave eleven kings to the nation. The most notable of these were Artaxias I (189–145 B.C.), Tigranes II (95–56 B.C.), and Artavasdes III (56–34 B.C.).

All the kings of the Artaxian Dynasty worked to bring about the unification of Armenia. Artaxias I achieved Armenian independence, which lasted for nearly two centuries. Not only did he unite the country by military efforts, but he developed in his people a sense of unity and nationalism. He made the universal use of the Armenian language compulsory and strove to assimilate foreign elements in order to make a strong, homogeneous nation. The old capital of Armavir was replaced by a new capital, Artaxata, built on the banks of the Araxes River. The new capital was designed according to a plan attributed to the Carthaginian general Hannibal, who at that time had found refuge in the court of the Armenian king.

Artaxias I, a lover of Hellenic culture, encouraged intellectual pursuits and furthered economic progress. During his reign there was much commercial enterprise, and the period has been described as a time when ". . . there wasn't any land left uncultivated and there wasn't any need for men to roam idle and unemployed." [15]

As King of Armenia Major, Artaxias I could not tolerate another Armenian kingdom next to his, and he wished to unify the whole country under one ruler. This unification was brought about by one of his successors, Tigranes II or Tigranes the Great (95–56 B.C.), who acquired the title "King of Kings" and gave Armenia one of the most glorious periods of its history.

Tigranes II invaded Sophene, the region of the other Armenian kingdom, and succeeded in bringing it under his rule. Thereafter the adjoining state of Cappadocia could no longer use Sophene as a buffer state. The artificial barrier between the two Armenian kingdoms was dissolved, and the country was spared any future separation of national traditions. The territory was expanded through the military might of Tigranes II, who extended his domains from the Kur River in the north to Egypt in the south. He also formed an alliance with Mithridates Eupator, King of the Pontus, and waged war against the powerful Roman armies in the east. For the first and only time in history, the Armenians saw the whole geographical area of their country united under one ruler.

Military victories were not the only accomplishments of King Tigranes II. He was a lover of Hellenic culture and a patron of intellectual pursuits. His newly founded capital of Tigranocerta became a center of culture, to which he brought Greek philosophers, sculptors, and theatrical groups. His talented son Artavasdes III (56–34 B.C.), who succeeded him on the throne, composed Greek tragedies for the theaters of Tigranocerta and was well known as a poet and writer.[16]

The empire of Tigranes the Great was short-lived, however. It disintegrated in 69–66 B.C. under the stress of military defeats. After the death of Tigranes himself in 56 B.C., Armenia declined as a powerful nation, and the Artaxian Dynasty, which had striven for Armenian unification for nearly two centuries, came to an end in 2 B.C. The region then became a buffer state between the Parthians in the east and the Romans in the west. Both of these empires had economic interests in Armenia, which had one of the main trade routes to India and China, and both sought to extend their influences over and to control the country.

Internally, Armenia was torn asunder by conflicts between its own *nakharars,* or feudal lords.[17] The severe external and internal pressures caused the country to undergo a period of chaos and bloodshed, such as it was destined to witness so frequently in future centuries.

THE ARSACID DYNASTY

Out of the national turbulence emerged a new dynasty, the Arsacid, relatives of the Parthian family of Persia. These rulers came into power near the beginning of the Christian era and reigned for nearly four centuries (A.D. 53–429).[18] The Arsacid state was a decentralized feudalistic structure, whose effectiveness was largely nullified by the influence of the *nakharars,* members of princely families who formed the upper class of the Armenian feudal system.

During the nearly four centuries of Arsacid rule, Armenia became Christianized, witnessed a remarkable period of literature, and was invaded and partitioned by foreign powers.

In A.D. 301[19] Armenia became the first country in the world to adopt Christianity as an official religion. The adoption of Christianity marked a turning point in its history, both in terms of internal political and cultural development and of foreign influences and alignments. Christianity in Armenia dates from the time of the Apostles, and the Armenian Church derives Apostolicity from the five Apostles—Thaddeus, Bartholomew, Simon the Zealot, Andrew, and Matthias[20]—who evangelized there and became the founders of the Armenian Church. By the early part of the fourth century, the country had a large Christian population. In A.D. 301 King Tiridates III was converted to Christianity by Gregory the Parthian (Grigor Partev) and immediately declared Christianity the official religion of the land. Thus, Armenia became the first Christian nation, twelve years before Christianity was officially adopted in the Roman Empire.

Gregory, known to the Armenians as St. Gregory the Illuminator (Grigor Lusavoritch), became the Catholicos or Chief Pontiff of the Armenians and took up residence at Etchmiadzin, which became the Holy City. St. Gregory and Tiridates worked together to stamp out the pagan religion and its priesthood, which, however, lingered on as late as the first quarter of the fifth century.[21]

The Armenian Church was represented at and accepted the decisions of the first three Ecumenical Councils—Nicaea (325), Constantinople (381), and Ephesus (431)—and was desirous of establishing a spiritual communion between the Churches, but only on the basis of equality and liberty for each within its own sphere of activity.[22] The Armenian Church was headed by the Catholicos, as its supreme spiritual leader, and never recognized the supremacy of the Papacy or the Greek Orthodox Patriarchate of Constantinople. The Catholicoi, especially after the fourteenth century, acted not merely as religious leaders but as temporal leaders also. When the country later came under foreign domination and the Armenians were left without political rights, it was often from the ranks of the Catholicoi that men arose to work toward freedom and independence.

During the fourth century there were two major political factions among the Armenians. One had an Eastern and

the other a Western orientation. Those who looked toward
the East felt an economic and cultural affinity with the
Persians. They included certain segments of the royal
house and some of the nobility. The faction of the West
was inclined to favor Armenia's orientation toward Rome
and Byzantium, both economically and culturally. These
included the Catholicoi, who were spiritual descendants
of St. Gregory the Illuminator, as well as certain *nakharars,*
who were either under Byzantine rule or near the frontier
of the Byzantine Empire. These two factions played important roles in the fourth-century wars between the East
and the West.[23]

The Western faction was the stronger of the two Armenian political groups and, in the fourth century, repeatedly
brought the Armenians in on the side of the Byzantine
Empire in the latter's wars against the Sassanid Persians.[24]
With the adoption of Christianity, Armenia became more
and more attracted toward the Christian West rather than
toward its Zoroastrian and, later, its Moslem neighbors.
The Christian faith made the Armenians feel a certain
affinity with the European West, but this spirit of brotherhood was seldom reciprocated. In reality, the West looked
upon Armenia as belonging to a different faith, since it
had its own pontiff and would not recognize the spiritual
supremacy of any other. Also, though most Armenians
grew to look westward toward Byzantium and Europe,
there always remained certain political groups that were
orientated toward eastern neighbors such as the Persians,
Arabs, and Mongols.

In A.D. 387 Armenia was partitioned between the Byzantine West and the Persian East. About one-fifth of the
country fell under the Byzantine Empire; the remainder
came under the Persians and in this region the Arsacid
kings held only nominal power.

The Persians strove to stamp out Byzantine influences
in their territory and forbade the use in Armenia of the

Greek language.[25] The Christian Armenians had customarily used both the Greek and Syriac languages for their religious services. Now, in the fourth century, they found themselves forced to move into a closer relationship with the Syriac Church. The Armenian leaders of the late fourth and early fifth centuries strove to do away with both Greek and Syrian influences,[26] but wishing to insure the autonomy of their church and to eradicate the last remnants of paganism from the country,[27] as well as to create a stronger nationalism, continued to draw upon Greek and Syrian sources so far as it suited their purpose. The aim of the Armenian leaders of the time was to establish an Armenian alphabet and to encourage Armenian literature, hoping that these measures would secure the Armenization of the country. One of the major results of this undertaking was the fifth-century golden age of literature.

King Vramshapuh (392–414) coöperated with Catholicos Sahak I and a monk, Mesrop Mashtots, in bringing about the literary renascence. Mesrop, after years of research, devised the Armenian alphabet in 404. Sahak and Mesrop, along with a selected body of scholars, called "Translators," translated the Bible into the Armenian language for the first time. Inspired by their Christian faith and their newly created alphabet, these two eminent men[28] and their students left for posterity a rich nucleus of original works and translations. Nearly every well-known work then existing in the Greek and Syriac languages was translated into Armenian.[29]

Many of the students of Sahak and Mesrop had received their higher education in the West and had returned to Armenia with a greater zeal to further the interests of their native land. A similar movement was to occur in the nineteenth century when Armenian students studying in Western institutions returned to their homeland and worked toward its enlightenment.

The golden age of literature served not merely to further

the Armenian Church but also helped to instil in the people a consciousness of their national identity and a pride in their own culture. These educators were the torch-bearers of Armenian cultural development. The literary renascence of the fifth century, like that of the nineteenth century, awakened the more enlightened members of society to a greater love for their fatherland and a desire for freedom.

The Armenians demonstrated their love for freedom and their devotion to the Christian faith in the famous Battle of Avarair,[30] which took place in A.D. 451. Refusing to comply with the demands of the Persian king, who wanted them to give up their Christian religion and adopt Zoroastrianism, they went to war against the overwhelming forces of the Persians, who now dominated their country. Although they lost the Battle of Avarair, the Armenians won a spiritual victory in that they continued to hold to their faith. Their leader in this conflict was the famous general Vardan Mamikonian, whose memory is honored to this day by the Armenians, who call him St. Vardan the Brave.

The Armenians suffered immeasurably in defense of their Christian faith during the fifth century and the centuries that followed. But their persistence in adhering to the Christian religion helped to harden them in their struggle for survival. Located between Persia and Byzantium, Armenia was frequently devastated during the unceasing wars between the two empires. These conflicts continued to take place on Armenian soil until the seventh century. In the meantime the Arsacid Dynasty, after nearly four centuries of rule (A.D. 53–429), had come to an end. Most of Armenia had become part of Sassanid Persia and was ruled by *marzpans* (Persian governors-general).

In A.D. 639 Armenia was conquered by the Arabs, who dominated the country for over two centuries. The region now became the battleground of the Byzantine-Arab conflicts. At times part of the country came under the rule of the Byzantine Empire, but the Armenians were treated just as despotically by the Christian Greeks as by the Moslem Arabs. Under such conditions, it is not surprising that the Armenians, during more than two centuries of Arab domination, cherished the hope of regaining their independence.[31]

THE BAGRATID DYNASTY

In the ninth century the desire for independence was at last realized by the establishment of the Bagratid Dynasty (886–1045), founded by Ashot the Great. Before receiving the Armenian crown, Ashot had been appointed by the Arabs as the governor-general of Armenia, and in 862 the Caliph had awarded him the title of "Prince of Princes" for his faithful service. In 886,[32] with the waning of Arab and Byzantine interest in Armenia, the title of "King of Kings" was bestowed upon Ashot by Caliph Motamid, and his crown was also recognized by the Byzantine Emperor Basil I, who was also as it happened an Armenian. Thus, after over four centuries of foreign domination, Armenia in the ninth century regained her political independence.

The Bagratid Dynasty initiated a policy of peaceful diplomacy with foreign nations. For centuries the Bagratids and Mamikonians, two prominent princely families, had opposed one another in regard to the country's political attitude toward foreign rule. The Mamikonians had believed in revolting against the foreign powers who dominated Armenia and they had led Armenian soldiers to the battlefields. In the ninth century the Mamikonian policy of revolt and bloodshed was superseded by the Bagratid policy of prudence and caution.[33] For a time this policy resulted in good relations between Armenia and its powerful neighbors, the Arabs and the Byzantine Empire, both of whom wished to have the Bagratids as an ally in their wars with one another.[34]

During the Bagratid period, which lasted nearly 160 years, there was cultural and material prosperity. As a neutral territory Armenia regained its importance in international commerce. Industry and agriculture were restored; monasteries and churches were built; towns and villages became repopulated. Under the Bagratids there were great architectural accomplishments;[35] Ani, the capital, was later described as the City of a Thousand and One Churches. The glory of Ani, as the very heart and essence of Armenia, was evoked by the nineteenth-century Armenian poets, and their laments over its ruin were a poignant expression of their nationalistic feelings and their longing for freedom.[36]

The Bagratid state encompassed only a very small part of Armenian territory, mainly the province of Ararat. Bagratid power was decreased by rival *nakharars,* especially by the princely family of Ardzruni, who had established the Kingdom of Vaspurakan in the ninth century. Rivalry among various *nakharars* was increased and encouraged by both the Byzantine Greeks and the Arabs, with the result that in the tenth century as many as seven kingdoms divided the country.[37]

Independence under the Bagratids came to an end in 1045 when the Byzantine Empire annexed the country and imposed terrible suffering on the population. A few years later the region was dealt an even heavier blow by the coming of the Seljuk Turks. In 1048 the Turkish tribes invaded the regions north of Lake Van, and in 1064 they captured and destroyed Ani. They burned and sacked villages and massacred men, women, and children. Agriculture, the basis of Armenian economy, was temporarily disrupted. Economic and cultural development ceased and the country lay in ruins. Nonetheless, the Armenians preserved their Christian faith and ethnic identity. Even though political freedom for Armenia Major[38] ended with the Seljuk invasion, the majority of the Armenians remained in their homeland and endured the hardships that a cruel destiny had inflicted upon them.

NEW ARMENIA: ITS RISE AND FALL

In the late eleventh century an Armenian nobleman, Ruben I, founded an independent principality called New Armenia,[39] which lasted nearly three centuries (1080–1375). This new Armenian homeland was first established as a barony in 1090; in 1196 it was raised to the status of a kingdom, when Leo II, later called Leo I, received the crown from the German Emperor Henry VI and Pope Celestine III.

New Armenia, with its capital first at Tarsus and later at Sis, was not landlocked as was Armenia Major. It stretched across the Mediterranean coast and exercised an important role in international commerce. Although New Armenia was materially prosperous, and cultivated music, architecture, painting, and literature, it enjoyed little peace. Conflicts took place with the Seljuk Sultans of Iconium, and the region was often invaded and partially devastated by the Mamelukes. During the thirteenth century the Mongols arrived in Armenia. At first they allied themselves with the Armenians, but later, on becoming Moslems, they turned against their former friends and allies.

New Armenia came into direct contact with Europeans when the Crusaders of the West crossed their territory en route to the Holy Land. Centuries afterward, Pope Gregory XIII paid tribute to the Armenians in his Bull *Ecclesia Romana* (1584):

Among the other merits of the Armenian nation as regards the Church and Christendom, there is one that is outstanding and deserves particularly to be remembered, namely, that when in times past the Christian princes and armies went forth to recover the Holy Land, no nation, no people came to their aid more speedily and with more enthusiasm than the Armenians, giving them assistance in men, horses, food, supplies, and counsel; with all their might and with the greatest bravery and fidelity, they helped the Christians in those holy wars.[40]

Internally, New Armenia was torn by a religious strife that involved Roman Catholicism and the Armenian Church. The Rubenian Dynasty, which had been of Armenian origin, had married into European nobility, and the throne had been transferred to the French noble house of Lusignan. These Catholic Lusignans attempted to impose Catholicism on their Armenian subjects.

During the reign of Leo IV Lusignan (1320–1342) there were two political parties. The larger party, called Nationalists, was led by the Catholicos and was anti-Papal and anti-European; the other was the pro-Catholic party of the King. Hostility toward the throne grew to even larger proportions on the succession of the Catholic Guy de Lusignan (1342–1344), who was not an Armenian at all but a member of the French aristocracy. The new king believed that his subjects should adopt Roman Catholicism to encourage much-needed assistance from Europe, and he entered into negotiations with the Pope. The people's dislike of Guy de Lusignan was only increased by this foreign king's attempt to impose an alien religion. The clergy and nobility believed that he was disregarding the national customs and that his successors would do likewise. The brief reign of Guy de Lusignan ended with his assassination in 1344, but the Lusignan dynasty continued to reign ineffectually for three more decades. When the last king of New Armenia, Leo V (1374–1375), also a Catholic and a Lusignan, ascended the throne, opposition toward the pro-Catholic royal house continued, and but few Armenians changed allegiance from the Catholicos to the Pope during this period.

In the later fourteenth century the external enemies of New Armenia had gathered strength, and the country, weakened by religious strife, fell to the powerful forces of the Mameluke Sultan of Egypt. The fortress of Sis fell in 1375 and the kingdom of New Armenia came to an end after a history of nearly three centuries. King Leo V was captured after bravely defending his country.[41] After his release, he spent his last years in Europe, where he tried in vain to regain his lost kingdom with the aid of the European nations and the Pope.

While the kingdom of New Armenia fell to the Mameluke Sultans of Egypt in the latter part of the fourteenth century, Armenia Major was being overrun by a new wave of Mongolians. These were the Tartars, led by Tamerlane, who spread death and destruction. After the death of Tamerlane in 1405, Armenia came under the domination of the Turkoman tribes of Ak-Koyunli and Kara-Koyunli. In 1514 the region fell to another Turkish tribe, the Ottoman Turks, who, under Sultan Selim I (1512–1520), conquered Armenia and added it to the Ottoman Empire. The area that remained under the domination of the Ottoman Turks was to be the focal point of the revolutionary movement of the nineteenth century.

In the late sixteenth and early seventeenth centuries the eastern part of Armenia became the area of conflict between the Ottoman Turks and the Safavid Persians. During one of his campaigns against the Turks, Shah Abbas the Great (1586–1628) transplanted a large population of Armenians from the province of Ararat to Persia. He settled them adjacent to his capital of Isfahan, where he founded the Armenian city of New Julfa[42] in 1605.

The Turkish-Persian rivalry in Armenia subsided in 1639, when a treaty was signed designating the frontier

between the two Moslem countries. The smaller area of
Armenia, which included the Holy City of Etchmiadzin,
went to the Shah and was known as Persian Armenia.
Amid continuing invasions, large numbers of the population, especially among the aristocracy, left the country,
and Armenian history flowed into two channels: the homeland and the Diaspora. The place of the original population was gradually filled by Turks, Kurds, and Turco-
man tribesmen who abused and exploited the native
Armenians.

MOVEMENTS FOR INDEPENDENCE FROM THE FIFTEENTH CENTURY TO THE NINETEENTH CENTURY

There is little definite information about the movement
for emancipation that took place during the interval between the fall of Sis in the latter part of the fourteenth
century and the activities of the Persian Armenians in the
sixteenth century. However, mention is made of an Armenian nobleman of the fifteenth century named B. Sem-
pat, who declared himself King of Armenia. Scant information is available about this man except that he had received
outside aid to achieve his purpose and his grandson became
Catholicos Grigor Aghtamartsi.[43] The next definite steps
toward emancipation were centered in Persian Armenia.

Under Shah Abbas the Great (1586–1628), the Armenians of Persia were concentrated in the plateau of
Karabagh and were ruled by five Armenian *meliks* who
had been recognized by the Shah. These *meliks*, whose
position was usually hereditary, were the governors, judges,
and commanders-in-chief of five contiguous provinces.[44]
Although Shah Abbas had granted the Armenians many
political rights, his successor was so tyrannical that the
Armenians desired to escape the Persian rule. In the sixteenth century they appealed to Europe by sending missions on two different occasions.

Stepanos Salmastiants, who was well acquainted with European thought, became the Catholicos of Etchmiadzin in 1541. Finding his position under Persians impossible, he resigned. In 1547 he called a secret meeting at Etchmiadzin to discuss a way to relieve his people of their suffering. The delegates, who were Persian Armenian lay and clerical leaders, decided to send Catholicos Salmastiants on a mission to Europe. He was to ask the Christian nations and the Pope for assistance in delivering the Armenians from the Moslem yoke. The Catholicos proceeded to Europe and applied to the Pope and to various European nations for assistance, but all his efforts on behalf of his nation were in vain.[45]

Catholicos Mikael Sebastatsi, who had succeeded Salmastiants, also found it necessary to resign from his position because of the arbitrariness of the Persians. He had been present at the secret meeting at Etchmiadzin in 1547 and called a similar secret meeting at Sebaste in 1562. In contrast to the meeting of 1547, those present at this second meeting were predominately clerics. The plan envisaged by this body was the liberation not only of Persian Armenia but of Turkish Armenia as well. They again decided to send a mission to the European states and the Pope to request Western intervention and assistance in carrying out their plans. The mission was headed by Abgar Tbir (Abgar Tokattsi), who was said to be a descendant of the kings of New Armenia. In May, 1562, Abgar with his son Sultanshah and a priest, Aleksander, journeyed to Europe. These delegates were cordially received by Pope Pius IV, who promised to send Abgar Tbir back to Armenia as "king." The Pope was interested in bringing about a religious union between the Armenian Church and Rome, and he sent a priest to Etchmiadzin for this purpose. The Roman Catholic priest died on the way to Armenia, and the plans laid by the delegates of Sepaste came to an unsuccessful end.[46]

The plans for liberation espoused by the Armenians of Persia were followed by a comparable move on the part of their brothers under Turkish rule. In the seventeenth century the power of the Ottomans declined and the European nations began to take the offensive against the Turks. As part of their plan to extend French control in the East, Cardinal Mazarin and King Louis XIV wished to utilize the unusual qualifications of the Dominican friar Father Dominique de Saint-Thomas. This man was actually Osman, the eldest son of Sultan Ibrahim. As a boy Osman had been one of the passengers aboard a galleon that was seized by Maltese pirates while en route to Alexandria from Constantinople in 1644. At the age of twelve he was placed in a Dominican Monastery in Malta and two years later was baptized and given a Christian name.

At the request of the French government, Father Dominique, also called "Père Ottoman," came to Paris in 1665. In the following year two foreign emissaries, a Greek and an Armenian, conferred with him. The Armenian was a prince named Shazi Murat[47] who had come to Father Dominique to plead the cause of his people. Shazi Murat and the Greek emissary declared that the discontented Armenians and Greeks under Turkish rule were ready to revolt and requested that Father Dominique head the movement for the liberation of their people. They assured the Father that if he headed the future revolt, the Russians and Walachians would give him material assistance. Father Dominique agreed to assume the leadership. Shazi Murat, not content with the Father's assurances, continued to pursue his mission. Besides carrying on a correspondence with Father Dominique, he made contacts with Colbert, Mazarin's successor as France's chief minister.

Meanwhile, Father Dominique's plans received the support of the kings of France and England, of the Venetian Republic, and of the Pope. Father Dominique was treated with great dignity and on occasion was addressed as "Your Majesty," perhaps indicating his possible position as the future king of Ottoman Christians. He proceeded to organize the discontented Christians of the Balkans against their Ottoman rulers. He wished to go to Armenia for the same purpose, but was unable to do so because of ill-health. He died on March 28, 1676, at the age of thirty-four, on the island of Malta.[48] With the death of Father Dominique de Saint-Thomas, Shazi Murat's mission for the liberation of Armenia from Ottoman rule came to an end.

Persian Armenian leaders had not ceased to pursue a way of throwing off foreign domination. In 1678 Catholicos Hakob Tjughahetsi called a secret meeting in Etchmiadzin to lay plans for the liberation of his people from Moslem rule. The six clerics and six lay leaders who were present decided to send a mission to the Pope asking his assistance. The mission was also to confer with the Pope concerning the religious aspect of the two churches. There was, however, no wish on the part of the Catholicos to give up the independence of the Armenian Church in exchange for papal support.[49]

The delegation headed by the Catholicos had only reached Constantinople when the Catholicos died, and the group forthwith abandoned its plans. Only one of its members, Israel Ori, a boy of twenty who had taken the place of his father in the delegation, decided to continue the journey to Europe. A sketch of his career will illustrate the tenacity of the Armenian patriot whose best efforts are doomed to failure. He became a soldier in the British army and for twenty years continued to make contact with European dignitaries in furtherance of the liberation of his country; he went so far as to offer the crown of Armenia to Prince Johann-Wilhelm of the Palatinate, whom he had interested in the Armenian situation. In April, 1699, Ori, long since forgotten and thought dead, returned to his homeland. On reaching Etchmiadzin, he found that the new Catholicos refused to accept Roman Catholicism, which was a vital factor in Ori's plans for Armenian freedom. He returned to his native village in Karabagh and began making new connections with clerics and lay leaders in the country. In 1699 Ori returned to Europe once again, where Prince Johann-Wilhelm assisted him in communicating with the Roman Emperor Leopold I, from whom he attempted to obtain military assistance. From the Pope, Ori received a letter concerning political affairs which he was to deliver to the Shah of Persia. While fulfilling this mission, he went to Russia and was received by Peter the Great. The Tsar endorsed his plans, promised to aid the Armenians, and sent Ori on a mission to Persia. Soon after Ori arrived in Persia in 1707, his secret plans were revealed to the government, and he was asked to leave the country. With his death in 1711, Ori's efforts toward the liberation of Armenia, which had begun in 1678, came to an end without tangible result.[50]

With the accession of Peter the Great to the Russian throne, the Armenians had entertained great hopes for possible Russian aid and deliverance from the Moslems. Catholicos Yessai appealed to the Tsar in an official bull, dated August, 1716. It soon became apparent, however, that Peter the Great was not interested in freeing Christians from Islam, but only in furthering his own foreign and domestic policies. These two objectives happened at times to coincide.

Peter the Great's expedition against Persia in 1722 momentarily served the interests of the Armenians. Hope of liberation by Russia ended, however, with the conclusion of a Russo-Persian treaty of peace; and when Peter gave up Georgia and Karabagh to the Turks in 1723 the Armenians felt abandoned by the Tsar. With little choice left, they began making preparations for their own protection. In Persia they formed small self-defense groups. Among the leaders of such groups in Karabagh was a man named David Beg, who was to play an important though brief role in the movement for Armenian freedom. He defeated the Turks who attacked the Armenians and Persians, and the Shah bestowed honors on him. The district of Karabagh, commanded by David Beg, was permitted in 1727 to become a semi-independent state under Persian suzerainty. Unfortunately, David Beg died in the following year, and the semi-independence of Karabagh came to an end in 1730.

During the eighteenth century another national figure emerged in the movement for emancipation. This was Joseph Emin, an Armenian from the Diaspora, whose life was dominated by the desire to liberate Armenia. At the age of eighteen Emin left his home in India and arrived in England in 1751. Like Israel Ori, Emin considered it necessary to obtain military experience before pursuing his plans to free his country; and he too believed that the freedom of Armenia must be sponsored by a Christian nation. Whereas Ori had directed his attention toward the Prince of the Palatinate, Emin chose King Heraclius I of Georgia to head the emancipatory struggle. Emin pursued his objective with the aid of his friends the Duke of Cumberland and Edmund Burke.[51]

After obtaining military experience in Europe and making certain valuable connections, he went to Armenia and to Georgia. He presented his plans to local leaders, but encountered opposition and indifference in the native Armenians. Returning to London, he became acquainted with the Russian Ambassador, Golitsyn, and thereafter went to Russia, where he won the support of prominent Russian officials. Here he also met Hovhannes Lazarian, a wealthy and patriotic Armenian, who supported him financially and otherwise encouraged him.[52]

Emin arrived in Tiflis in 1763 and related his plans to the King of Georgia, who at first supported him but later refused aid, after being discouraged by Catholicos Simeon of Etchmiadzin, who was absolutely opposed to rebellion. Emin, however, was determined to carry out his life's dedication. He next went to India, where he tried to obtain financial assistance from the Armenian community to raise a small army. This, like all of Emin's plans, was destined to fail; nonetheless, he remains notable among the precursors of the nineteenth century movement for the liberation of Armenia.[53]

In the early part of the nineteenth century the desire of the Persian Armenians to achieve Russian protection was fulfilled, following two major wars (discussed below) in which Russia conquered Transcaucasia. One of the chief exponents of Russian policy was Nerses Ashtaraketsi, the Prelate of the Georgian Armenians, who actively supported and encouraged this policy among them. He firmly believed that the Russians were coming to liberate his people. By the Treaty of Turkmen-Tchai (February 10, 1828) following the Russo-Persian War (1826–1828), in which the Armenians gave invaluable assistance to the Russians, the provinces of Nakhichevan and Erivan went to Russia. At last, the dream of Armenians from Israel Ori to Nerses Ashtaraketsi to be under Russian rule seemed close to realization.

The dream of the Armenians was to form an autonomous "Russian Armenian Province" under the suzerainty of the Tsar. But the Armenians soon discovered that the aim of their northern neighbor had not been so altruistic as they had naïvely believed. To their bitter disappointment, Tsar Nicholas, in the *ukaze* of March 21, 1828, announced the annexation to the empire of the new territories, which were called "Armenian Provinces," and added to his imperial title that of "King of Armenia."[54] By a statute (*Polozhenie*) announced on March 11/23, 1836, the Armenians were allowed a nominal degree of self-government in ecclesiastical and educational matters.[55]

TURKISH ARMENIA AND THE ARMENIAN QUESTION

Russia in the meantime continued her conquest of Transcaucasia, and after the Russo-Turkish War (1828–1829), which was concluded by the Treaty of Adrianople in 1829, Armenia was divided among Russia, Turkey, and Persia. The largest number of Armenians lived in Turkey and were concentrated in the six vilayets (provinces) of Turkish Armenia: Van, Bitlis, Erzerum, Diarbekiar, Sivas, and Mamuret-ul-Aziz (Kharput). There are no statistics available on the Armenian population after the wars in the early nineteenth century. The number of Armenians in Turkey fluctuated as a consequence of centuries of continual migration. However, it is estimated that there were approximately three million Armenians in Turkey in 1878.[56]

With the close of the Russo-Turkish War and the Treaty of San Stefano (1878), the "Armenian Question" appeared in international politics. Turkish Armenia had been part of the Ottoman Empire since 1514. In this Moslem state, the non-Moslem subjects were given the name *"rayah,"* meaning flock or herd, and were organized into *millets* or communities. The Armenian community, or *Ermeni* millet, was headed by the Armenian Patriarch of Constantinople, who was considered to be the head of the nation and was a recognized official of the Ottoman government. The patriarch held the position as head of the Armenian community until the nineteenth century, when Armenian Catholics and Protestants fell within the jurisdiction of the two newly established Catholic (*Katolik*) and Protestant millets. The Armenian Patriarch was given certain privileges and prerogatives, but these were voluntary and unilateral and could be withdrawn at any time.[57]

As Christians, the Armenians under Turkish rule were discriminated against. They were not allowed to carry or possess arms; they were taxed more heavily than the Moslems; they were liable to taxes from which the Moslems were exempt; they were barred from positions in government military and naval services; their testimony was not acceptable in courts; and they were exposed to the brutality of neighboring nomadic tribes.[58] In spite of this oppression and persecution, they lived in relative peace during nearly four centuries of corrupt Ottoman rule and did not rise in insurrection against their overlords until the later half of the nineteenth century.

In the nineteenth century a new era of reforms appeared in Turkey, but this did not alleviate the misery of the Armenians. In 1839 Sultan Abdul Medjid introduced a Charter of Reforms called *Hatti-sherif*. Except as they pertained to the military, these reforms were a dead letter, and Christians were not treated as equal before the law.[59] On February 6/8, 1856, Sultan Medjid issued the *Hatti-humayun*, the so-called Magna Charta of Turkey. Shortly after this document was issued, guarantees for internal reforms in the Ottoman Empire were incorporated in the Treaty of Paris (March 30, 1856) following the Crimean War, but these assurances were of little avail. The provisions in the *Hatti-humayun* regarding religious liberty, for example, were constantly violated.[60]

The Armenian General Assembly at Constantinople, which had come into existence in 1860 and was sanctioned by the Sultan in 1863 as a result of the Armenian National Constitution of Turkey, was besieged with complaints from the provinces and requests for the alleviation of mistreatment from the Kurds, Turks, and Circassians. It was hoped that the liberal Ottoman Constitution, which was issued in December, 1876, a few months after the accession of Sultan Abdul Hamid II to the throne, would relieve the burden of the Christians. Unfortunately, the Constitution was replaced by the absolute rule of the Sultan after it had been in force only a few months.[61] The lot of Turkish Armenia was unimproved, and early in 1877, when hostilities broke out between Russia and Turkey, the situation became critical.

At the beginning of the Russo-Turkish War (1877–1878), the Russian troops were able to make rapid advances on Turkish territory. The victorious Russian army included many Russian Armenians, some of high rank. The Turks believed that the Turkish Armenians had afforded valuable assistance to the advancing Russian forces; and these suspicions led the Turks to seek vengeance on the Armenians. When the Russian troops were driven back, the Turks found it opportune to allow hordes of Kurds and Circassians to pillage Armenian villages.[62]

The Russo-Turkish War concluded early in 1878 with a decisive victory for the Russians. The Armenians hoped to benefit from this favorable political situation. Hitherto, four principal political factions existed among the Armenians. These groups were unorganized, but included a large number of Russophiles; the Anglophiles, who were anti-Russian; the Catholics, who were also anti-Russian and who had hopes that Italy and France would come forth as the protectors of the Turkish Armenians; and the Turkophiles, whose number was greatly diminished after the Russian victory. These differences in orientation were now put aside and the several factions united with one another for the protection of national interests and the solution of the Armenian Question.[63]

In the sixteenth article of the Treaty of San Stefano (March 3, 1878), which concluded the Russo-Turkish War, the Sublime Porte agreed ". . . to carry out, without further delay, the ameliorations and reforms demanded by local requirements in the provinces inhabited by the Armenians, and to guarantee their security against the Kurds and Circassians." [64]

A few months after the signing of the Treaty of San Stefano, it was submitted, under the pressure of Great

Britain, Austria-Hungary, and Germany, to a congress of European Powers, who revised it. At the Congress of Berlin the promises of reforms in Armenia, which had been stipulated in Article XVI of the Treaty of San Stefano, became Article LXI of the Treaty of Berlin (July 13, 1878). Thus the reforms previously guaranteed by the Sublime Porte to Russia alone were now guaranteed also to the European Powers, who were to superintend their application.[65] Before the Berlin Congress adjourned, the provisions of the secret Cyprus (Anglo-Turkish) Convention signed on June 4, 1878, were announced. In it the Porte promised England to introduce reforms into Armenia.[66] While this Convention was taking place, the Kurds had been taking advantage of the evacuation of the Russians from Turkish Armenia and had resumed their pillaging.[67] The prevalent lawlessness and personal insecurity caused by the Kurds and Circassians induced thousands of Armenians to emigrate to Russia.[68]

The Armenians soon learned that the promises of reforms made at the Congress of Berlin and the Cyprus Convention existed only on paper. They listened with anxiety to one of their Berlin spokesmen, Archbishop Khirimian, who had just returned from the Congress. During a sermon to a large crowd gathered in the Armenian Cathedral in Constantinople, the Archbishop described in a striking metaphor the bitter outcome of his mission. He had gone to Berlin with a petition for reforms which in itself was merely a piece of paper. There, in the council chamber, were the diplomats of the European Powers, who had placed on the table before them a "Dish of Liberty." One by one the Bulgarians, Serbians, and Montenegrins strode into the chamber, and with their iron spoons, scooped into the delicious dish, taking out a portion for themselves. When his turn came, the Armenian was armed only with the fragile paper on which the petition was written. As he dipped into the dish on the table, his paper spoon gave way and crumpled, leaving him deprived of any share of the luscious treat.

This historic sermon by Archbishop Khirimian was an indirect appeal for the use of arms—"iron spoons"—the means successfully adopted by Balkan revolutionaries. The results of the Congress of Berlin showed that "Christian" and "civilized" Europe had abandoned the Armenians and had left them to their own resources. This was not a new experience. For centuries they had appealed their cause to Europe without avail. Dominated by overlords and crushed by invaders throughout their history, they had survived to continue their struggle. In the latter part of the nineteenth century the Armenians, who had passively tolerated Ottoman misgovernment for centuries, broke into insurrection; their desire for individual freedom and political rights became an outcry. Secret political organizations were formed, which no longer tolerated the oppressive regime. The members of these organizations had been influenced by the ideas of the Armenian awakening, which had come into maturity in the nineteenth century and were a vital factor in molding the mind of the patriot. We turn to this "awakening" before proceeding to the activities of the revolutionaries.

II

The Ideological Background and Sources of the Armenian National Awakening

The fall of the kingdom of New Armenia in the fourteenth century was followed by many centuries of cultural and intellectual apathy. From time to time, however, individuals or groups endeavored to maintain the awareness of the Armenian people in their historical past and to prepare them to struggle for freedom and equality. The most important role in these nationalistic efforts was played by the Armenian Church, which functioned both as a religious and as an intellectual force through certain distinguished leaders and in its major monasteries.

THE ROLE OF THE CHURCH IN THE NATIONAL STRUGGLE

Since the official adoption of Christianity in the early part of the fourth century and the extirpation of paganism, the Armenian Church had become the stronghold of religious and cultural life in Armenia. During centuries of foreign domination, the church tried to preserve the ancient traditions and language of the Armenians. From the church the people derived not only spiritual and moral strength but the inspiration for literary and artistic expression.

The administration of the Armenian Church was shared by both the laity and the clergy. The clergy, unlike that in many other countries, did not form a separate estate, and they intimately understood the sentiments of the people.[1] In the absence of political independence, the Catholicos embodied the aspirations of his people and became the link between the Armenians in the Diaspora and those of the homeland.[2] The contribution to the movement for liberation by a number of these pontiffs has already been discussed in chapter i.

Following the invasions of Armenia Major (eleventh century) and the kingdom of New Armenia (fourteenth century), the monasteries of the church were the centers of learning. Among the monasteries that played an important educational role were those in Armenia Major: Kailatzor, Datev, Etchmiadzin, and Amirdolou. The activities of these monasteries and of the Armenian Church in Constantinople, St. Petersburg, and Nor Nakhichevan[3] were extremely significant in preparing the way for the new nationalism of the nineteenth century.

MISSIONARY ACTIVITIES

The work of the Roman Catholic missionaries during the fourteenth and seventeenth centuries helped in bringing about an interchange of thought between Armenia and the West. In the fourteenth century Pope John XXII sent Franciscan and Dominican missionaries to Armenia. Bartholomew, one of the emissaries of the Pope, arrived in the country in 1316. He then organized the *Fratres Unitores* group for the purpose of bringing about a union between the Armenian Church and that of Rome. This group established its headquarters at the Monastery of Maragha; it organized schools and translated books from Latin into Armenian. Such intense competition forced the Armenians to take countermeasures. The Monastery of Datev led in the resistance to the missionary efforts.

The direct influence of the Roman Catholic missionaries was negligible and their knowledge of the Armenian language was inferior to that of the native schools. However, their indirect contributions were more significant. The Armenians were encouraged to use the more rigorous methodology and to draw on the erudition that their Latin adversaries had brought with them from the West. The foreign missionaries also indirectly helped in strengthening and improving the Monastery of Datev.[4]

In the seventeenth century Jesuit missionaries visited Armenia. They were financed by King Louis XIV of France, who also requested that the Shah give protection to these missionaries as well as to the Armenian Catholics under his domination.[5] The Jesuits were at first well received because the Armenians respected Latin erudition.[6] However, their proselytizing activities soon created conflict between the Armenian and Roman churches. The native monasteries of Datev in Sunik, Amirdolou in Bitlis, and Amenaperkitch in New Julfa, which were the centers of learning during this century, took the lead in opposing the Jesuits.[7] Native leaders came to the realization that they must be armed with knowledge to combat their adversaries. An active reaction on the part of the Armenians resulted in the opening of more native religious schools and in better training of clergymen.[8] Seventeenth-century Jesuit activity also furthered cultural interchange between Europe and Armenia.

The eighteenth century was a turning point in the awakening of the Armenian people. This was the result of the work of Mekhithar of Sebaste (1676–1749) and the

Mekhitharist Congregation. Mekhithar, an Armenian, founded the congregation at Constantinople in 1701 as a Benedictine order[9] (after his death the congregation was named after its founder); in 1703 the seat of the order was moved from Constantinople to Modon (Methone) in the Morea, and in 1715 Mekhithar went to Venice where, two years later, the Venetian Republic gave him the Island of St. Lazarus. The monastery of the Mekhitharist Congregation still exists on this small Venetian island. A branch of the order was established in Trieste in 1773 and moved to Vienna in 1811, where it remains to this day.

The contributions of this small group of Armenian Catholic monks completely overshadowed those of the *Fratres Unitores* and the Jesuits. The order was devoted to educational and literary pursuits. Mekhithar stressed the need for European enlightenment and strove to bring his nation into closer contact with the West without losing any of the cultural heritage or national spirit of his people. He wished to take from Europe only those elements which would be beneficial to his country.[10] Mekhithar also stressed the study of the Armenian past—its history, language, and literature. Thus, he ensured a continuity between the ancient literature and that of the literary renascence of the nineteenth century.[11]

Among the large number of works written by Mekhithar are a Classical Armenian grammar,[12] which treats of the literary language of the eighteenth century, and a grammar of the vernacular.[13] In writing this grammar of the Armenian vernacular, Mekhithar was a forerunner in realizing the importance of using the common speech rather than the classical language in writing, since it was primarily the vernacular language that was used in the literary works of the nineteenth century.

The Mekhitharists enriched Armenian literature by scores of scholarly publications, which included literary, historic, linguistic, archeological, and geographical works as well as a great number of translations from Greek, Roman, and European authors.

The Mekhitharists occupy a singular place among the educators of the Armenian people. In stressing the study of national history, language, and literature, they sowed the seeds of the new nationalism which was to find expression in the nineteenth century. Also, by recognizing the need for a closer contact between Armenia and Europe and in furthering such a relationship, they were forerunners in directing their people toward European thought, which, a century later, was to have a marked effect on their country.

EXPATRIATES AND THEIR ACTIVITIES

The Armenian communities in the Diaspora were the first to show evidence of a reawakening. It was in these communities that printing was first utilized. The first book printed in the Armenian language was published in 1512, in Venice, and in the following year four more books were published there.[14] In 1565 a Psalter (*Saghmosaran*) was published in Venice by Abgar Tbir,[15] who had headed the liberation mission to Europe on behalf of the Armenians. By moving his press from Venice to Constantinople in 1567,[16] Abgar Tbir established the first Armenian press in the Ottoman Empire. Catholicos Hakob Tjughahetsi, who was active in the liberation movement, realized the educational importance of printing. He commissioned Father Vosgan of Erivan to go to Europe to secure the printing of the Bible in Armenian. The mission was accomplished in 1666, when the Armenian Bible was first printed in Amsterdam.[17] In the seventeenth century 126 books[18] were printed on presses in the Armenian communities abroad.

In the eighteenth century the printing press helped in disseminating both national culture and European thought among the Armenians. Community leaders became the first lay representatives in presenting the ideas of the "Age of Enlightenment" to their people. They introduced the ideas of the Encyclopedists, Voltaire, Locke, Montesquieu, Rousseau, and the Russian intellectuals to the Armenians, and the printing press facilitated this activity. The Madras community in India was notable for instructive publications with the purpose of liberating the Armenians in the homeland.

The Armenian community of Madras was composed primarily of wealthy merchants who carried on a lucrative trade with Europe and the Far East. Many of these merchants were notable for their philanthropy and patriotic zeal.[19] Such a one was Joseph Emin, for example, who successfully appealed to the Madras colony for assistance in his quest for the liberation of Armenia. He also left behind him ideas of independence that prompted other men in Madras to follow in his footsteps during the latter part of the eighteenth century.

One important Madras group was led by a wealthy merchant, Shameer Shameerian,[20] and included Shameer's son Hagop (Hakob), a wealthy merchant, Grigor Khodjadjian, and an intellectual named Movses Bagramian, who was Hagop's tutor. To reach their objective these men decided to use the printed page as a means of propaganda.[21] in 1772 they published the *New Pamphlet Called Exhortation* (*Nor Tetrak Vor Kotchi Hordorak*), written by Bagramian and addressed to the Armenians, for the special purpose of ". . . awakening Armenian youth from the weakness of idle sleep . . .";[22] it was printed at the press of Hagop Shameerian, in Madras.

In this *Exhortation* Bagramian declared that the honor, progress, salvation, and happiness of the Armenians could not be obtained without political freedom. He affirmed the necessity of educating the Armenians and having them follow in the footsteps of the European nations; he criticized them for not fighting for the independence of their enslaved country and demanded that they arise and unite for the realization of this goal. The author stressed the need for the Armenians of the Diaspora to return to their native land and willingly make sacrifices in the fight for freedom. Bagramian, like Joseph Emin, believed that Heraclius, the King of Georgia, should sponsor the movement for Armenian independence; but, at the same time, the *Exhortation* opposed monarchical government. It stated that among the causes of the downfall of the kingdom of New Armenia was the despotic rule of the monarchy as well as the lack of unity, obedience, industry, and intellectual pursuits of the people. In his conclusion Bagramian called for a republican state and a constitution.[23]

In 1773 the Madras group published a book, entitled *Snare of Glory (Vorogait Parats)*, the authorship of which is uncertain. Under this unusual title, a detailed constitution was set forth for the proposed independent Armenia. In the preface of this book, which was published three years before the American Revolution, reference was made to George Washington and the aspirations of the American colonists toward freedom from England. Like the American Constitution, the *Snare of Glory* reflected the influence of the philosophies of Locke and Montesquieu.[24] Both the *Snare of Glory* and the *Exhortation* were sent to Armenians of prominence and to foreign dignitaries.[25]

In such publications, the Madras group expressed what might be called Utopian ideas in regard to the future of their beloved homeland. However immature and visionary were the plans set forth, these men played an important part in the political education of the Armenians and in pointing out the path for future work. The Madras community was the earliest and most active publisher of political propaganda for the Armenian cause; and, significantly, was the home of the first Armenian journal, the *Intelligencer (Aztarar)*, which began publishing in 1794.

THE IMPACT OF THE FRENCH REVOLUTION AND
NAPOLEON ON THE ARMENIANS

It was also from the colonies of the Diaspora that voices were heard uttering hopes for the liberation of Armenia by the armies of Napoleon Bonaparte. In a letter from Paris dated January 8, 1800, an Armenian cleric, Jacques Chahan de Cirbied (Hakovb Tjerpetian Shahaniants), wrote to Catholicos Ghukas of Etchmiadzin concerning various church matters. In this same letter he also spoke of possible political relations between his country and France. Chahan de Cirbied said that France respected Armenia and knew of her glorious past. He went on to suggest that the Armenians make contact with Napoleon's armies in Egypt or in Syria, since these armies were moving toward Cilicia and Armenia Major and Minor. He believed France would be more helpful to the Armenians than it had been toward other Oriental nations.[26]

The thoughts of this lone cleric in Paris showed once again the influence of European ideas and history on the Armenians in the Diaspora. Here was an example of how patriots abroad strove to relieve the misery of their subjugated people in the ancestral home and their determination to continue the struggle for the liberation of Armenia.

It has been suggested that Napoleon had both political and cultural interests in the Armenians. He was acquainted with their history and saw in them a possible agent for the furtherance of his policies. After defeating Russia, he perhaps had the intentions of invading India via the Caucasus. It has been said that at Tiflis he planned to assemble a French army with Armenian and Georgian auxiliaries for his future campaign.[27] Napoleon indicated a desire to lay the groundwork for Armenian support. On October 18, 1802, he had written to one of his generals: "The Ambassador of France at Constantinople wished to take the

Christians of Syria and Armenia under his protection." [28]
Further evidence of his interest in the Armenians is a
decree issued in 1810. By it the emperor suppressed the
monasteries in the kingdom of Italy, but excluded the
Armenian Catholic Mekhitharist Monastery of Venice, and
even posed as its protector.[29] In Paris Napoleon created an
Armenian chair at the School of Living Oriental Languages
and appointed the aforementioned Chahan de Cirbied to
head it.[30]

THE ROLE OF KHATCHATUR ABOVIAN
IN THE ARMENIAN AWAKENING

Armenia was not destined to be liberated by the armies
of Napoleon, however, and its people continued to endure
the yoke of Turkey and Persia. In 1828, following the
Russo-Persian War, the Armenian provinces of Nakhichevan and Erivan became part of Russia. The events of
this time and the reaction of the Armenians to their new
rulers are described by Khatchatur Abovian, the patriot
and writer, who contributed to the cultural, literary, and
political development of the Armenians.

Khatchatur Abovian was born 1804–1810[31] in Kanaker,
a small village near Erivan, then under Persian rule. He
was an eye-witness of the Russo-Persian War of 1826–1828
and saw his birthplace fall to the Russians. In his important historical novel *Woes of Armenia (Verk Hayastani)*[32]
he portrays the anarchy resulting from these events as well
as the centuries of suffering his countrymen endured under
foreign domination. The plot of this book deals with events
during the war period. Here he tells how joyous the Armenians were at the prospects of having a "Christian"
power rule their country. However, this dream was to
prove a delusion and the Armenians were faced with the
bitter disappointment of living under the tyrannical rule

of the Russian Tsar. Indirectly, the author reveals these disappointments and the lack of improved conditions under the new regime,[33] and describes so vividly the ravages that had taken place in the homeland that the reader wonders if any other country has suffered as much as Armenia.[34] Abovian made an emotional appeal to his countrymen to be mindful of the sorrows of their native land and to mourn its martyrs. He drew the mind and heart of his readers toward their fatherland and, in doing so, awakened in them the desire for revolution.[35]

Abovian's life was dedicated to the welfare of his people and the desire to direct them toward the advantages of European education which he himself had the opportunity of obtaining. He received his early education at the Monastery of Etchmiadzin and studied at the Nersessian Seminary in Tiflis. At the request of the Catholicos of Etchmiadzin, he became a deacon and the personal aid of the pontiff at the monastery.[36] In 1829 a German scholar from the University of Dorpat, Dr. Friedrich Parrot, came to Armenia on a scientific expedition to Mount Ararat. This event was a turning point in the life of the young deacon. The Catholicos appointed him as the interpreter and guide for the scientists, and he thus became a member of the first recorded party to scale Mount Ararat. Abovian himself made an indelible impression on Professor Parrot, who wrote: "He established a claim on our respect and gratitude by his earnest thirst after knowledge, his modesty, self-denial, and pious feelings, no less than by his penetration, his courage, and his perseverance." [37]

In 1830, through Parrot's efforts, Abovian received a scholarship to the University of Dorpat, where he studied philosophy and history. Here he lived with the Parrot family, met and studied under learned European scholars, and became well acquainted with European languages and thought. After eight years of study and teaching at the university, he was glad to return to his native land and bring to it his newly acquired learning.[38]

Unfortunately, on his return in 1836, he was faced with bitter opposition from conservative leaders, especially among the clergy, who were against any kind of Europeanization. Being unable to open a school in Etchmiadzin, as he had long desired to do, Abovian went to Tiflis in 1837 and became a teacher in one of the state schools; in 1843 he became the principal of a village school in Erivan.[39]

Abovian was greatly disillusioned by the political events of his time and his inability to carry out adequately his desire to acquaint the youth of his nation with Western ideas. He struggled against the reactionary forces within his people as well as against the Tsarist regime[40] which had completely failed to improve conditions. Grieved by the tortured existence of the Armenian masses in their fatherland, and unhappy in his married life besides, he vanished mysteriously on April 2, 1848,[41] and was not heard of again. The circumstances surrounding his disappearance have never been clarified.

Abovian is considered to be the father of modern Armenian literature. He wrote in the vernacular, the language of the common people, which was to become the accepted vehicle of literary expression. To acquaint his people with foreign thought, Abovian wrote prolifically and made translations from the works of Homer, Schiller, Rousseau, Goethe, Karamzin, Zhukovsky, and Krylov.[42] Abovian is the symbol of the modern nationalism that was to emerge in the following decades. He inspired and influenced Russian Armenian writers, glorified the revolutionists, and tried to incite his downtrodden countrymen to act. His patriotic dedication set the groundwork and became the inspiration of the political parties of the nineteenth century. The new spirit of the age, as exemplified in Khatchatur Abovian in Russian Armenia, was to become evident in Turkish Armenia by the mid-century.

CATHOLIC AND PROTESTANT MILLETS
IN TURKISH ARMENIA

The impact of the French Revolution did not make any notable changes within the ranks of the Armenians in Turkey during the early decades of the nineteenth century. While other subjects of the Ottoman regime, especially in the Balkans, were rising in revolt, the Armenians remained loyal subjects. The Turkish Armenians were so absorbed in a religious conflict among themselves that little attention was given to the international scene and the political and intellectual changes that were taking place in other parts of the world. The community was torn from within by bitter controversies between the Armenian Church and the Catholic and Protestant groups.

The activity of the Roman Catholic missionaries, which had begun centuries before, had its culmination in the early period of the nineteenth century. It was evident by 1820 [43] that unity between the Armenian Church and that of Rome could not be attained. The religious conflict during this period resulted in putting Armenian Catholics, who were legally within the jurisdiction of the Patriarch, in a very precarious position. The Turkish Sultan also became hostile to these Catholics because of alleged friendly relations with the European fleet which had given the Turks a decisive defeat at Navarino (October 20, 1827).[44] However, these troubles subsided when on January 5, 1831,[45] the Porte issued an imperial edict establishing a separate papal civil community, known as the Catholic (*Katolik*) millet in Turkey. Under this edict, Armenian Catholics in Turkey became politically separated from the centuries-old *Ermeni* millet, which was headed by the Patriarch.

Religious difficulties continued with the coming of the Armenian Protestant mission to Turkey. In 1831 this mis-

sion was established in Constantinople,[46] and in 1836 a
secret Evangelical Union was organized.[47] Unsuccessful in
converting Moslems to the Christian faith, these missionaries remained active among the Armenians. Protestant
activity caused a bitter counter-reaction by the Armenian
Church, and in 1846 the Patriarch issued a bull of perpetual excommunication and anathema against all Protestants.[48] These Armenian Protestants, who considered themselves church reformers, were now placed outside of their
traditional church and soon became part of a separate
church and administrative organization. By 1846 more than
one thousand Armenians had withdrawn from the national
church.[49] In the following year the Protestants of Turkey
were recognized by the Porte as a separate community, and
in 1850, by an imperial *firman,* their rights and privileges
were permanently defined and they were allowed to elect
a civil head.[50]

The establishment of the Catholic and Protestant millets
placed these groups on a legal basis in the Ottoman Empire. Although this separation had certain positive effects
on the Armenian community, the negative aspects of this
religious dissension were evident among the Armenians
of Turkey throughout the first half of the nineteenth century.[51]

TURKISH REFORMS AND THE ARMENIAN QUESTION

Another internal problem held back the Armenians
from revolutionary activity against Ottoman rule. This
was the struggle for democratic representation within the
framework of the *Ermeni* millet. Beginning in the thirties
and lasting over two decades, the struggle culminated in
the victory of the liberal elements by the establishment
of the Armenian Constitution in 1860. This dispute, which
will be discussed later, stemmed from various intellectual
and political changes that had taken place in Europe as

an aftermath of the French Revolution. Among the Armenians in Turkey, it was led by groups within the community which had been nurtured by liberal European ideas and wished to put these into practical effect.

The reforms of Sultan Abdul Medjid (1839–1861) were evidence of the influence exerted by the currents of change in Europe upon the Ottoman Empire. Although the reforms were not permanent and did not better the inferior position of the Christian Armenians, they were symptoms of progress, of an awareness, at least, on the part of the Turkish leaders of the new European liberalism. Thus Abdul Medjid's edicts began to excite the hopes and dreams of the Christians in Turkey.

AMIRAS, ESNAFS, AND THE PATRIARCHATE

According to the system set forth in the fifteenth century by Sultan Mohammed II, the Armenian Patriarch of Constantinople was recognized as the leader of the *Ermeni* millet; and the Patriarch was, in fact, the administrator of the religious, educational, and social life of the Armenians of the Ottoman Empire. By the nineteenth century, this Patriarchal office had become so weakened that the real power was not in the hands of the Patriarch but was held by an oligarchy comprised of wealthy conservative elements among the Armenians of Constantinople.

This oligarchy was drawn from the *amira* class, which consisted of bankers, rich merchants, and government officials. By controlling the Patriarch, the amiras dominated the national and much of the religious activity of the Armenians of Constantinople. The public passively submitted to this domination until the 1830's, when new forces began to demand a voice in the activities of the community. These were intellectuals and the more dynamic representatives of the organized guilds or *esnaf* class.[52] The conflict over representative government within the community turned into a class struggle which at first involved the esnafs, amiras, and the Patriarchate, and afterward the vast majority of the people.

The immediate event that brought this conflict into the open was a dispute over the funds for the Armenian National College of Scutari in 1838. The amiras, who controlled the Patriarchate, refused to give financial support to the school. This act incited the esnafs to form a separate organization, the Union, in order to collect and distribute funds for the school. Thus, the esnafs were assuming a function that ordinarily was in the hands of the Patriarchate and its dominating amiras. Although the powerful amiras did not have any confidence in the ability of either the masses or the esnafs to rule, they at first remained silent, but soon took steps to halt the activities of the esnafs.[53]

The class struggle between the esnafs and the amiras increased to such an extent that both the Patriarchate and the Ottoman government intervened in order to bring about harmony. As a result, a new National Committee was officially established on December 12, 1841,[54] and its twenty-seven members were drawn mainly from the esnaf class and consisted entirely of common folk. However, this victory for the esnafs and the masses did not last long: interference from the amiras soon brought about the complete breakdown of communal activity.

The newly elected Patriarch Mattheos Tchukhadjian (1844–1848), who was known for his leanings to the side of the masses,[55] intervened and brought about an agreement between the amiras and esnafs, who previously had been bitter enemies. A National Assembly was organized with sixteen amiras and fourteen esnafs, who were appointed by the Patriarch.[56]

When later the Patriarch tried to act independently of the Assembly an odd coalition of forces occurred: the amiras and esnafs joined against the Patriarch. At the same time, the vast majority of the people, who were neither of the amira nor of the esnaf class, did not have legal representation on the National Assembly. To remedy this situation a plan was devised to have the affairs of the *Ermeni* millet administered by elected "national assemblies." The government confirmed the plan, elections took place on May 20, 1847, and two new assemblies convened. One was the Spiritual Assembly for religious affairs, composed of fourteen clergymen. The other was the Supreme Assembly for secular affairs, composed of twenty laymen.[57] Unfortunately, this election was actually a defeat for the democratic forces, since the amiras were influential enough to select the members of both assemblies. Intrigues and dissensions followed, and Patriarch Mattheos, finding that he did not have the power to remedy the situation, was prepared to resign.

THE DEMONSTRATION OF 1848

In 1848, for the first time in centuries, the Armenians of Constantinople rose up in protest against the resignation of the Patriarch. They held a demonstration in the district of Kum Kapu, where the two assemblies met and demanded that the Patriarch continue his fight for the cause of democracy and freedom from amira domination. The Patriarch resigned, nonetheless, but in favor of Hakobos Serobian, another popular leader.[58]

The demonstration was remarkable in the history of the Armenians of Turkey. For the first time in centuries, the masses, recognizing their rights as individuals, had come together to voice their protest and thus accomplished what was in effect the Armenian counterpart of the European revolutions of 1848. Although small by comparison, this outburst in Constantinople was a giant step toward democracy. It indicated that the Armenians were ready to resort to revolutionary methods in order to achieve political freedom.

ARMENIAN STUDENTS AND THE NATIONAL CONSTITUTION

Numerous groups were beginning to play a part in the Armenian scene and were eventually to lead the people to a victory over oligarchy in 1860 by the establishment of a National Constitution for the *Ermeni* millet.

The most outstanding of these groups were composed of students who had received their higher education in European institutions of learning and who, like those of the fifth century, had returned to their homeland to further the welfare and the national awakening of their people. They brought with them not only scientific knowledge but also ideas about democracy and nationalism. These students were mainly the sons of wealthy families of Constantinople which had prospered from the prevailing favorable economic conditions, particularly in the field of trade.[59] They were members of a small but growing middle class.

The first group of students to study abroad went mainly to Italy, which was the home of the Mekhitharist Monastery.[60] Later, most students went to Paris for their education. Here they lived in an atmosphere filled with echoes of the French Revolution and the ideas of Lamartine, Chateaubriand, Victor Hugo, De Musset, Auguste Comte, Michelet, Guizot, and Quinet.[61] Some students witnessed the revolutions of 1830 and 1848, and almost all returned to Constantinople with an ardent love for freedom.

The growth of the young Armenian intelligentsia and the ideas they espoused were not to the liking of the older leaders, and a rivalry ensued between the new and the old leaders within the Armenian community. Those liberals who championed the ideas of freedom and democracy were called *Illuminati*. Those who wanted the affairs of the Armenian community to be governed by the old system of oligarchic rule were the conservatives known as the *Non-*

Illuminati. The struggle of these forces was particularly evident in the two assemblies of the *Ermeni* millet. The Illuminati wished to free the affairs of the nation from the domination of the amiras and the Patriarch. This contest between democracy and oligarchy, which continued for decades, finally resulted in the victory of the liberals through the codification of the Armenian National Constitution, which was adopted by the Supreme Assembly on May 24, 1860,[62] then revised and confirmed by the Sultan on March 17, 1863.[63] Notable in the work toward the formation of this new Constitution were some members of the Educational Council, which had been established by the Spiritual and Supreme Councils on October 21, 1853: Dr. Nahabed Rusinian, Nikoghos Balian, Grigor Odian, Dr. Servichen (Serovbe Vitchenian), and Karapet Utudjian.[64]

The Constitution provided for a General Assembly which was vested with the highest legislative power in the Armenian community of the Ottoman Empire. These powers pertained to the religious and cultural aspects of the community—for example, opening schools, building new churches—but did not, of course, extend to political rights and obligations, which were under Ottoman government jurisdiction. During the life of the General Assembly only one party came into existence, the *Ghalathyo Odjakh,* whose object was to protect the interests of the people from those elements in positions of control which were still inclined to the amira philosophy.[65] This party was not related to the political parties of the later decades, which were to be devoted to the Armenian Question.

The Armenian National Constitution of 1860 was the answer of the enlightened elements of the community to the domination of the Armenian oligarchy. Among the Fundamental Principles of the Constitution is the following:

Each individual has obligations toward the nation. The nation . . . has obligations toward each individual . . . duties of the individual are the rights of the nation . . . obligations on the part of the nation are the rights of its members. . . . the Administration . . . must be representative. . . . the principle of RIGHTS and DUTIES . . . is the principle of *justice*. Its strength is to be found in the plurality of voices, which is the principle of legality.[66]

This victory may be compared to the success of the liberal elements of Europe over the reactionary forces of Metternich. Although the new constitution had many shortcomings and was unable to settle Armenian communal affairs, it ushered in a new era of progress for the Armenians. Its establishment very likely influenced and encouraged liberal Turkish elements of the Ottoman Empire in their efforts toward reforms and the Turkish Constitution of 1876.[67] The Armenian Constitution laid the groundwork for a system of public education for the Armenians of Turkey and, in doing so, helped bring about a literary renascence that disseminated liberal ideas and thus led to stiffer opposition to Ottoman rule.

EDUCATION

After 1860 the number of Armenian schools and philanthropic and patriotic organizations multiplied; as a result, literary publications and the press changed their character. The nation was turning from a complacent into an awakened society. This change was described by the journalist Grigor Ardzruni, who wrote in an editorial in the *Mushak* (*Laborer*) in 1872: "Yesterday we were an ecclesiastical community, today we are patriots, tomorrow we will be a nation of workers and thinkers." [68]

The significance of education had been recognized prior to this time by the pontiff of the Armenian Church, Catholicos Nerses, when he declared in the early part of the nineteenth century that "The preparation of the spirit and the development of instruction are the preliminary conditions for the elevation of the Armenian nation." [69] But after 1860 it accelerated its pace and became an important key to national advancement.

A major factor that helped combat illiteracy and subsequently encouraged new writers was the new form of literary expression. The Armenian language had passed through many changes during the past centuries. The spoken language or vernacular known as modern Armenian (*ashkharabar*) now differed greatly from the written or classical language (*grabar*) that had been used by writers of the fifth century. People were ashamed to write in the vernacular, and the literary efforts of the nation were in the hands of scholars and clergymen.[70] The vast majority of the population, who understood only the spoken language and had little opportunity to secure a formal education, remained illiterate.

As mentioned earlier, the first grammar of the modern language was written by Abbot Mekhithar in the eighteenth century, and Khatchatur Abovian's *Woes of Armenia,* dating from the first half of the nineteenth century, was the first major work written in the vernacular for the common people. The use of the modern language was further facilitated by the American missionaries, who, under the direction of Dr. Elias Riggs, translated the Bible into Modern Armenian in 1853.[71] During the nineteenth century there was a constant conflict between conservatives, who wished to continue the use of the classical language as the literary form of expression, and the modernists, who advocated the use of the modern idiom. Leaders in this modernist movement were those students who had been educated in European and Armenian institutions and had worked toward the establishment of the National Constitution. It was this new generation that took the helm in the nation's educa-

tional efforts and paved the way toward the creation of a
new literature.

Until 1790 the Armenians of Turkey were not allowed
to have community schools; only seminaries were tolerated
by the Ottoman government. Under Sultan Selim III, conditions changed and in 1790 the first Armenian community
schools were established in Constantinople. These schools
were founded by the amira Shnork Mekertitch, who, like
many individual members of his class, was interested in
the welfare of the people. The educational institutions
founded by this generous amira were financially supported
by him, by the Armenian Church, and by students' tuition
fees. From 1790 to 1800 numerous other parochial schools
were opened. In the capital in 1830, the first school for girls,
a trade school, was established by another amira, Bezdjian.
By the time of the adoption of the Armenian Constitution,
there was a network of elementary parochial schools established in Constantinople. Yet, there still remained a great
need for educational facilities in the interior provinces.

In the nineteenth century the first Armenian secondary
schools were established. These produced a large propor-
tion of the intellectuals who dominated Armenian life in
the late nineteenth and early twentieth centuries. Outstanding among these institutions were the College of Scutari, the Nupar-Shahnazarian, Central, and Berberian Colleges in Constantinople, the Sanassarian College at
Erzerum, the Normal School of Van, and the seminaries of
the monasteries of Varag and Armash.

To this list of national schools should be added the numerous educational institutions founded by the Mekhitharist Congregation, especially their Murat-Raphaelian
colleges in Venice, Padua, and Paris. Also, the American
Protestant missionaries were instrumental in elevating the
educational standards of the Armenians of Turkey with
their various schools and their colleges in Constantinople,
Marsovan, Aintab, Kharput, Marash, and Tarsus.[72]

A parallel development occurred in Russian Armenia, where a unified system of education had been introduced by the *Polozhenie* of 1836. Since Armenians under Tsarist rule were far more prosperous than their brothers on the other side of the frontier, they had more opportunity for educational advancement. The first important institution that served the Armenians of Russia was the Lazarian Institute of Moscow, founded in 1816 with funds bequeathed for this purpose by Hovhannes Lazarian, who had been a privy counselor to the Russian state.[73] The Institute had a school of oriental languages, a seminary, and a press. It attracted the Armenians not only of Russia but of the Near East and India as well.[74] Other significant Armenian institutions in Russia were the Nersessian Seminary in Tiflis (1823) and the Gevorgian Academy of Etchmiadzin. Russian Armenian students completed their higher education in European institutions. These students were particularly attracted to Russian institutions and to the German University of Dorpat, which became the alma mater of many revolutionary leaders of the nineteenth century.

To aid and encourage education, societies were formed which collected and distributed funds. These were particularly numerous in Turkey, where they aided national schools. Russian Armenians not only helped the institutions in their own area but also contributed to the educational needs of their less fortunate compatriots in the Ottoman Empire.

The most outstanding of these educational societies was the United Societies, which had come into existence in 1880 by the union of three separate organizations: *Ararathian, Tebrotzasiratz Arevelian,* and *Cilician.* The *Ararathian* was organized in 1876 with the purpose of opening schools in the provinces of Van, Erzerum, and Kharput. The *Tebrotzasiratz Arevelian* (Oriental School Society), also founded in 1876, was active in Moush, Bitlis, and Tigranakert. The third was the *Cilician,* which had been founded by students and alumni of the Nupar-Shahnazarian College in 1871. Another important educational society was the *Andznever* (Altruistic Society) which was founded in Constantinople in the 'sixties. It was active in teaching the Armenian language to those in the capital who had recently arrived from the provinces.

THE PRESS AND JOURNALISM

Along with schools, the press played an important educational role and pointed the way to insurrection. In the past, as noted earlier, the press had been used for this dual purpose by the Armenian colony of Madras. However, it was not until nearly a century later that journals that were primarily devoted to revolutionary propaganda appeared. Before 1840 journals had been mainly in the hands of the clergy and devoted little space to the Armenian customs and ancient history. In general these publications did not have any particular policy and scarcely seemed to address themselves to Armenians,[75] but in succeeding decades journals multiplied and become more and more nationalistic.

In the 'fifties of the nineteenth century there were three outstanding organs. These were the *Massis (Ararat)*, the *Hiusissapile (Aurora Borealis)*, and the *Ardzvi Vaspurakan (Eagle of Vaspurakan)*.[76]

The *Massis* was published in Constantinople from 1852 to 1893 by Karapet Utudjian (1823–1904), whose aim was to bring together the old and the new without provoking radical social changes or endangering the Ottoman Empire. Under his guidance many young journalists were trained.[77]

The *Hiusissapile* was published in Moscow from 1858 to 1864 by Stepanos Nazariants (1812–1879). Nazariants had graduated from the Nersessian Seminary, attended the University of Dorpat, and received his doctor's degree at the University of Lausanne; he had also been a teacher at the Lazarian Institute. The object of his paper was to help establish an intellectual bridge to Europe so as to spread knowledge to all classes of Russian Armenians for their material and spiritual benefit. A staunch proponent of nineteenth-century progressivism, the paper advocated the use of Modern Armenian for literary purposes and fought against ignorance and indifference among the clergy. The *Hiusissapile* was published mainly for the Russian Armenian public and did not show much interest in or knowledge about the situation in Turkish Armenia.[78]

Representative of the interests of Turkish Armenia was the third of these important journals, the *Ardzvi Vaspurakan (Eagle of Vaspurakan)*, which was published from 1855 to 1863. It was founded in Constantinople by Bishop Mekertitch Khirimian (1820–1907), known to the Armenians as Khirimian Hairig,[79] who ranks as one of the most noteworthy personalities in Armenian history. He was a native of Van, where he received his education under the guidance of his uncle. After the early death of his wife and daughter, he entered the priesthood. He rose to the rank of Patriarch of the Armenians of Turkey (1869–1873), was the spokesman of the Armenians at the Congress of Berlin (1878), and later became the pontiff of the Armenian Church, the Catholicos of All Armenians at Etchmiadzin (1893–1907). Zealous in the cause of education and realizing the importance of printing in this undertaking, he established in Van the first press in the Armenian provinces of Turkey. In 1858 he moved his press from Constantinople to the Monastery of Varag in Van, where he continued the publication of the *Ardzvi Vaspurakan* and also established a school. A few years later, he also held the position of Abbot at the Monastery of St. Karapet in Moush. Here, too, he set up a press, where in 1863 he started to publish the journal *Ardzvik Darono (Eagle of Daron)* with the assistance of Bishop Garegin Servandstiants.[80]

Khirimian Hairig lived among his people in the remote provinces and witnessed their suffering at the hands of the oppressive regime. The *Ardzvi Vaspurakan* described these miseries and lamented the fate of the people, but, at the same time, always brought words of optimism and encouragement. In this journal there were passages written by contemporaries which actually advocated rebellion against oppression: "Let us stop crying, let us be courageous, and let us fight . . . we are not chickens, we are also men and children of men. . . . Let us wipe our tears, not shed them. . . . Those that cried, cried and passed on. They were the old. We must follow the new. . . ." [81]

Khirimian Hairig was representative of the new fighting spirit of the age. He was ". . . the Armenian Bossuet, Pius IX and Garibaldi all in one." [82] It was he who helped educate a generation of young men who wanted to participate in the nation's struggle for freedom—which eventually led to uprisings and the formation of the political parties.

The 'sixties was a period of transition socially and politically. In Turkey the National Constitution opened a new era of optimism, and in Russia the liberal reforms of the Tsar brought about a period of greater freedom in the ranks of the Russian Armenians. A flood of short-lived journals were established, but it was not until the 'seventies that journalism reached its maturity. Nationalistic feeling and the hope for reforms and a better future became the standard of the day. The downfall and dismemberment of the Ottoman Empire seemed close to realization during the Russo-Turkish War (1877–1878) and after the Treaty of San Stefano (1878). The Armenians had always nurtured the thought of freedom during the centuries of foreign domination, but now they believed they could move effectually against it. Even after the great disappointment at the Congress of Berlin, this hope for a brighter future did not die.

The journals of the 'seventies and 'eighties reflected the thought of the times. Unrest was in the air and liberal ideas became more and more popular. One of the most outstanding of these journals was the *Mushak* (*Laborer*). Published in Tiflis (1872–1920),[83] this paper carried on the crusade for intellectual advancement started by Nazariants, and was destined to play an important role in the lives of the Armenians of the Caucasus.[84] The *Mushak* was founded by Grigor Ardzruni (1845–1892), who played an important role in molding the mind of the revolutionary through his own writings and the writings of the group of intellectuals who contributed to his paper. He was born in Moscow and attended school in Tiflis. He continued his education at the universities in Moscow, St. Petersburg, Zurich, and Geneva, and received a degree from the University of Heidelberg in 1870. Wishing to further his knowledge of the Armenian language and to become better acquainted with his nation's past, he studied at the Mekhitharist monasteries of Vienna and Venice. He returned to Tiflis in 1871 eager to utilize his knowledge and energies for the benefit of his people, and commenced publication of the *Mushak* the following year.

Under Ardzruni's editorship, the pages of the *Mushak* were filled with revolutionary propaganda. During a critical period of the Russo-Turkish War, as the Russian armies were marching into Turkey, he wrote:

If Turkey vanishes from the face of the earth as a nation, the Armenians of Turkey must try every means to join Russia. But, if subjugation is against Russian policies and ideals, the Armenians must try every means not to fall under the exploiting and oppressive hands of the insidious, selfish British. . . . Then the only thing left for the Armenians of Turkey to do is to strike out for independence and in this situation, too, our only hope is the help of Russia. And for Russia, too, it is better to have a small independent Armenia as a neighbor— always faithful and grateful to Russia—than an insidious, selfish, oppressive, and always enemy neighbor like the British.[85]

Ardzruni, writing from the Russian Caucasus, was able to express freely his pro-Russian viewpoint. Such bold and daring words could not be written in journals on Turkish soil. Nevertheless, the *Arevelian Mamul (Orient Press)* of Smyrna showed evidences of liberal ideas.

This journal, founded by Mattheos Mamurian (1830–1901) in 1871, became the first successful Armenian monthly.[86] Its editor was a man of great ability and was much esteemed by the Armenians. He was born in Smyrna, where he received his elementary education. He continued his studies at the Mekhitharist school in Paris (1846–1850) where, upon his graduation, he received his diploma from the hands of Alphonse Lamartine, a man who made an indelible mark on Mamurian throughout his lifetime. He returned to Turkey where he won recognition as an educator, publicist, writer, translator, and editor. His journal, the *Arevelian Mamul,* became a forum for public opinion on current topics and encouraged discussions on politics, history, economics, and philosophy. Mamurian was well acquainted with ancient and modern history and European literature. Being a linguist, he translated many foreign works, among them Goethe's *Werther*. His journal carried, in serial form, selections from Mazzini and from Buckle's *History of Civilization in England;* from the biographies of Washington and Franklin; from Scott's *Ivanhoe,* and from Macaulay's *Historical Essays;* and it made frequent references to the writings of Jean-Jacques Rousseau.

Mamurian was a fighter against ignorance, and his *Arevelian Mamul* made an important contribution to the lives of a generation of men who lived in a critical time that was shot through with nationalistic fervor.

Other journals that contributed to the distribution of information and became depositories for nationalistic literature during the 'seventies and 'eighties included *Portz (Endeavor), Meghu Hayastani (Armenian Bee), Nor Tar (New Century), Artzagank (Echo), Ararat, Aghpur (Foun-*

tain), and *Gords* (*Work*)—all of which were printed in the Russian Caucasus—and the *Hairenik* (*Fatherland*), *Yergrkound* (*Globe*), and *Dzaghik* (*Flower*), which were printed in Turkey. To these must also be added the numerous newspapers and periodicals issued by Armenians in foreign countries.

In the 'eighties there occurred a reëvaluation of the new ideas coming from the West, and the press showed marked changes. Previously, Western ideas had been accepted indiscriminately as good and Oriental ones as bad. Now, these foreign concepts were being scrutinized and there was a change in the attitude toward Eastern ideas.[87]

Intellectuals, especially during the 'sixties, had been leaning toward atheism and agnosticism, and the Armenian Church was under constant attack. Their attitude toward the national church now underwent a significant shift. The church began to be recognized as the focus of Armenian life and the embodiment of the nation. The idea of reform within it was looked upon with disfavor. In general, the leaders of the times thought that Western ideas should be approached carefully and that, if possible, these should be harmonized with Armenian institutions in order to yield most benefit to the people.[88]

THE LITERARY RENASCENCE

The writers of the latter half of the nineteenth century reflected both the new ideas and the traditional ones for the nation. Their contributions combined to make a literary renascence whose like had not been seen since the fifth century. Romanticism became the response of an awakened society and contributed to building a new nationalism which was to turn the people toward unrest and insurrection.

Khatchatur Abovian (1805–1848) is considered the founder of this modern Armenian literature. After him there followed a host of writers, some of whom have already been mentioned. Others included Mesrop Taghiadiants (1803–1858), who was both a poet and prose writer, and members of the Mekhitharist Congregation—Father Bagratuni (1790–1866), Father Hurmuz (1797–1876), and Father Alishan (1820–1901). The patriotic poetry of Father Alishan had a powerful effect on the youth of his day. Others of major importance were the poets Beshiktashlian (1829–1868), Nalbandian (1829–1866), Tourian (1851–1872), Patkanian ("Kamar Katiba") (1830–1892), Archbishop Narbey (1831–1892), Terzian (1840–1909), and Shahazizian (1841–1907); the essayist Demirjibashian (1851–1908), the publicists Odian (1834–1887) and Arpiarian (1852–1908); and several novelists—"Dzerents" (Hovsep Shishmanian) (1822–1888), Berhoshian (1837–1907), and "Raffi" (Melik-Hakobian) (1835–1888). No list of Armenian writers can omit Bishop Servandstiants (1840–1892), an authority on Armenian folklore and collaborator with Bishop Khirimian (Khirimian Hairig) on his journal; the humorist Baronian (1842–1891); and the dramatist Sundukian (1825–1912), who contributed to the Armenian theater, which became an important medium for the development of nationalism.

REVOLUTIONARY PROPAGANDA

Among those writers who followed Bishop Khirimian as outstanding propagandists for revolutionary activity were Mikael Nalbandian, Rafael Patkanian ("Kamar Katiba"), and "Raffi" (Hakob Melik-Hakobian). For an understanding of their impact on Armenian society, it is necessary to give short biographies of these three men.

Mikael Nalbandian (1829–1866) was a personal friend and comrade of Herzen, Bakunin, Ogariev, Turgeniev, and Dobrolyubov and became a link between the revolutionary movement in Russia and that of Armenia. He had great admiration for Owen, Proudhon, and Fourier and was influenced by their works as well as by the ideas of his contemporary Russian revolutionaries.

Mikael Nalbandian was born on Russian soil, in the Armenian city of Nor Nakhichevan on November 2, 1829,[89] and here received his elementary education. He first came into prominence in connection with Armenian parochial schools, of which he remained a staunch supporter—a seemingly odd fact in view of his materialistic philosophy and the widespread anticlericalism of native and foreign intellectuals of his time.

Nalbandian became a teacher at the Lazarian Institute in Moscow in 1853 and also studied at universities in St. Petersburg and Moscow. While attending the University of Moscow, he formed a personal friendship with Stepanos Nazariants and became a member of the staff of the latter's new journal, the *Hiusissapile* (*Aurora Borealis*), which was founded in 1858. In 1860 Nalbandian was commissioned by the lay and religious leaders of his native city to go to India to receive some money that had been willed to their city. This trip gave him the opportunity to visit Europe, where he had previously gone for his health in 1859, and especially Constantinople, which was an important Armenian intellectual center. He visited the capital on two occasions, on his way to India, from November 20 to December 21, 1860, and on his return, from November 20 to December 27, 1861.[90]

On these visits, he was able to better acquaint himself with the Turkish Armenians and to spread his socialistic and radical ideas. He was received with favor by the younger generation, but was looked upon with suspicion by the older people. In Constantinople he spread a certain unrest that was to develop into the Zeitun Rebellion which will be discussed later.

Before returning to Russia in 1862, he spent some time in London where he met Herzen Ogariev, and Bakunin.[91]

His contacts with these Russian revolutionaries aroused the suspicion of the Tsarist authorities. He was arrested and imprisoned at the Fortress of Petropavlovskaya (July 27, 1862–May 13, 1865)[92] and was then exiled under heavy guard to Kamyshin, where he died of tuberculosis on March 31, 1866. In accordance with his last request, his body was returned to his native city of Nor Nakhichevan where it was buried in the courtyard of the Armenian Monastery of the Holy Cross.[93]

Mikael Nalbandian was notable both as a poet and as a sincere patriot, devoted to the purpose of freeing his countrymen from their overlords. He was concerned with the plight of the Armenian peasant and in his *Agriculture as the Just Way* (*Yerkragordzuthiune Vorbes Ughigh Djanaparh*) (1862),[94] he displayed his socialist viewpoint and his conviction that only the equal distribution of land could bring prosperity and happiness to the people.

He advocated freedom not only for the Armenians but for all peoples.[95] He rejoiced on hearing of the independence of Italy and believed that the Armenians should follow in the footsteps of the Italian liberation movement.[96] The miserable conditions in his own fatherland were to him a source of great sorrow and in his poem *Days of Childhood* he wrote:[97]

> There never could be joy for me,
> While speechless, sad, in alien hands,
> My country languished to be free.

His love for freedom also finds expression in his popular poem *Liberty* in which he writes:[98]

> "Freedom!" . . .
> I will be true to thee till death;
> Yea, even upon the gallows tree
> The last breath of a death of shame
> Shall shout thy name, O Liberty!

In order that the Armenians might obtain political independence, he advocated that they take up arms against their oppressors rather than rely on nonviolent methods and a waiting policy. The influence of Mikael Nalbandian was keenly felt by the people of his day and helped to motivate future revolutionaries.

Rafael Patkanian (1830–1892) was another nationalistic poet who encouraged rebellion through his writings. He was born on November 8, 1830, in Nor Nakhichevan, and was first educated by his father, Gapriel Patkanian, a noted priest and man of letters. He attended the Lazarian Institute and then went to Tiflis to be near his father, who had started the publication of the journal *Ararat*. It was in this publication that Patkanian's poems first appeared. While in Tiflis he taught at the Nersessian Seminary, which for a time was directed by his father.

Patkanian's education was continued at the University of Dorpat where he stayed for one year (1851–1852). Unable to continue his studies because of financial need, he went to Moscow where he helped organize an Armenian students' literary club in 1854. This group was called "Kamar Katiba,"[99] which later became Patkanian's pen name. The object of this literary club was to spread learning and patriotic feeling among the Armenians by means of published material. Patkanian was assigned the poetry section and this gave him the opportunity to develop his literary talents. In 1855 he moved to St. Petersburg, where he continued his studies and received a degree in 1860. During these years he was in close contact with his Moscow friends and together they published five pamphlets. The Kamar Katiba club was later dissolved, but Patkanian continued to write under this name. As Kamar Katiba he made contributions to the journals *Hiusissapile* (*Aurora Borealis*) and *Groung* (*Crane*), and for one year (1863–1864) he published his own paper, the *Hiusiss* (*North*), in St. Petersburg.

In 1866 he returned to Nor Nakhichevan. There he engaged in educational activities, work that took him to Rostov and Bessarabia. Patkanian continued to publish literary works and became an extremely popular writer, whose works were read by Armenians all over the world. He visited Constantinople in 1890, where he was received with great honor by the community. He died two years later, on August 22, 1892, in his native city of Nor Nakhichevan.

This famous poet aroused in his readers a love of country and a deep desire to redeem their enslaved homeland. In his poem *The Armenian Youth Speak* (1861), Patkanian advocated that the Armenians forget the past and be born again to a new life. He also speaks of a Young Armenia movement.[100] This brings to mind the Young Russia circle which had been formed at that time by students of Moscow University, but what relationship existed between the two is not clear.

Always profoundly concerned with the miserable conditions of his people, Patkanian strongly voices the aspirations of his compatriots during the Russo-Turkish War, when it appeared that the Armenians would be freed from their Ottoman overlords. In *The Song of the Van Mother* he wrote:[101]

Awake! The happy fortune of Armenia has begun.
Lo, it is fallen, dashed to bits, the Sultan's golden throne!
From under it the liberty of many lands hath shone.
Now he who speedily shall rise shall find his liberty:
Will my fair son alone remain fast bound in slavery?
Yet Europe says, "No strength, no power have they,"

The unfortunate aftermath of the war and the anger of the Armenians were expressed in a *Complaint to Europe*. Here the poet proclaimed Armenia's sacrifices, which had now been completely forgotten by the West. For and about an oblivious Europe he wrote:[102]

My hands, my feet, the chain of slavery ties,
Yet Europe says, "Why do you not arise?
Justice nor freedom shall your portion be;
Bear to the end the doom of slavery!"

Six centuries, drop by drop, the tyrant drains
The last remaining life blood from our veins;
Yet Europe says, "No strength, no power have they,"
And turns from us her scornful face away.

In spite of the great disappointment following the Congress of Berlin, which was a disillusion for many of his countrymen, Patkanian never lost hope for the eventual emancipation of his fatherland. He believed that the Armenians from all over the world should join together to fight for the common purpose.[103]

Rafael Patkanian's life was one of absolute dedication to his nation, and at his death, ". . . he left nine children orphaned, four million brothers unconsoled, and a name that will never be forgotten as long as the Armenian language is spoken."[104]

Armenia's foremost novelist is Raffi, born as Hakob Melik-Hakobian (1835–1888). Raffi's writings served as a guide for organized revolutionary action. He was born in the small village of Bayajouk in Salmast, Persia, and he received there his elementary education. In Tiflis he attended an Armenian school (1847) and then a Russian government school (1852–1855), but did not graduate because he was obliged to return home to help his father. Raffi, therefore, had little formal education, but he read extensively from translations and original works in the Russian and Armenian languages. His knowledge was further enhanced by travels in Turkish Armenia, where he visited such important centers as the monasteries of Varag, Aghtamar, and St. Karapet. During his stay at the Monastery of Varag, he came to know and admire the work of Khirimian Hairig.[105] So impressed was he with this man's activity that he became inspired to take part in the mission to emancipate his distraught brothers. He also had the opportunity of visiting Armenian centers in Persian Armenia. Thus he became closely acquainted with his people living under three different flags. Bringing together this rich experience, Raffi began his writing career in 1860. His first work appeared in the *Huisissapile,* to which, it will be remembered, Nalbandian and Patkanian had also made important contributions.

In 1868 Raffi moved to Tiflis where, because of business failures, he became destitute. Fortunately, in 1872, he was somewhat relieved of economic burdens by being invited by Grigor Ardzruni to join the staff of the *Mushak.* Ardzruni recognized Raffi's great talent and encouraged him in his literary endeavors. Many of Raffi's historical and romantic novels first appeared in serial form in the pages of *Mushak.* After serving twelve years as a member of the staff, he was obliged to resign because of failing health; he died in Tiflis in 1888 to the deep sorrow of the nation whose respect he had so rightfully earned.

Raffi's novels depict the life of his oppressed nation and are filled with examples of bravery, fortitude, and triumph. Such famous novels as *Jellaledin, Khente (The Fool), David Beg, Kaitzer (Sparks), Samuel,* and *Khamsayi Melikuthiunnere (The Meliks of Khamsay)* inflamed the nationalist feeling of his readers and moved them to desire freedom from despotic rule.

Raffi believed that man is born free and has a right to remain so. If man is enslaved, he becomes morally weak and intellectually stagnant—and all the more so as his condition is more oppressed. Raffi argued that a free atmosphere was needed for the Armenians to develop to their utmost capacity, and education was essential for arousing the people to the realization of the need for freedom; and since only an educated and informed public could serve the national struggle, a new, enlightened generation must take up the task of spreading education.[106]

Raffi recalled Vardan the Brave, who had personified Armenia's protest against force, injustice and servility. He asserted that it was the united strength of all the people, under Vardan's leadership, which had brought victory on the battlefield of Avarair in the fifth century.[107] Raffi saw the same need in the nineteenth century and therefore advocated unified, armed action against the regime in power. He also contended that the Armenians must rely on their own powers and that assistance from foreign countries could not be expected, since the latter had clearly proved that their actions were motivated solely by selfish interests.[108]

Raffi was optimistic and believed that a new Golden Age would again arise in his homeland.[109] In *Khente* (*The Fool*) his hero dreamed of Armenia's future in two hundred years—a peaceful land of happy, industrious, educated people who no longer lived under persecution, domination, and fear; a united Armenia with a representative government and socialization of important industries.[110]

Raffi wished to plant the seeds of this new freedom which, he trusted, would grow and be harvested by future generations. He had hopes and plans for a successful revolutionary movement; for he believed that "Patriotism and nationalism are holy duties for every individual and the war for freedom and protection of the fatherland is a holy war." [111]

In the nineteenth century the Armenians began treading the sanguinary road toward revolution. The success of the three writers Mikael Nalbandian, Rafael Patkanian ("Kamar Katiba"), and "Raffi" (Hakob Melik-Hakobian) indicated the popularity of literature that encouraged the use of armed force against the Ottoman government. Indeed, the Armenians were awakening to a new nationalism that brought forth a fighting spirit. The conditions and the preparations for this state of affairs had gone on slowly in Armenia during the course of several centuries, though its cumulative effect was demonstrated only in the last half of the nineteenth century. This change was produced by political, social, and economic forces that were at work both in foreign lands and in the homeland. Among the media through which these forces communicated themselves to the Armenian people were the Armenian monasteries, foreign missionary activities, the printing press, the activities of Armenians in the Diaspora, Western enlightenment through literature and direct contact, student activities, vernacular literature, schools, societies, journals, writers, and the Armenian theater.

The nineteenth-century revolutionary movement manifested the same dedication to freedom as had the fifth-century battlefield of Avarair. The love of liberty, which had burned in the hearts of the Armenian people even during the darkest centuries of their history, now became a blaze. The desire to be treated with justice and humanity had become an ultimatum. The masses realized their oppressed condition and knew that they, too, deserved what other peoples at least to some degree now possessed. They were no longer willing to tolerate complacently the despotic regime under which they lived. They recognized their past glories and were convinced that they had the moral and physical strength once again to strike out for freedom. There was a feeling of hope and a conviction that they would eventually be victorious in their righteous demand. What had at one time been a remote dream now appeared as a victory on the horizon.

Thus it was that the more active and enlightened Armenians began organized action for self-protection, for human rights, and eventually for political independence. The Zeitun Rebellion of 1862 was to be the first major blow in this struggle.

III

Revolutionary Activity in Turkish Armenia, 1860–1885

The centers of revolutionary activity in Turkish Armenia were Zeitun, Van, and Erzerum. The Zeitun Rebellion of 1862 was the beginning of extensive uprisings directed against the Ottoman government. A decade later a secret society, the Union of Salvation, was formed at Van to free the Armenians from their ruthless overlords. In 1878 the Black Cross Society followed in the footsteps of the Union of Salvation. An underground society called Protectors of the Fatherland was established at Erzerum in 1881. This society was short-lived, and its leaders were placed on trial by the government. The revolutionary activities in Turkish Armenia during the nineteenth century culminated in 1885 with the establishment of the first political party, the Armenakan Party. Before proceeding to the history of the Armenakans, the activities in Zeitun, Van, and Erzerum will be described.

THE ARMENIANS OF ZEITUN

Zeitun[1] was an Armenian town hidden in the crests of the Taurus Mountains of Cilicia and seldom visited by outsiders. Zeitun or Oulnia was likewise the name of the whole district, which comprised many villages with a preponderantly Armenian population.[2] According to tradition, the original settlers of this district had been refugees from the Bagratid capital of Ani,[3] which had fallen to the Seljuk Turks in A.D. 1064. In the following centuries Zeitun had been part of the kingdom of New Armenia and later had been conquered by the Ottoman Turks. Sultan Murad IV, by the edict of February 17, 1618, gave these mountaineers nearly complete independence for the payment of a yearly tax.[4]

For centuries Zeitun, under the rule of four barons, or *ishkhans,* successfully maintained its semi-independence. To retain this unusual status, it fought perhaps as many as fifty-seven battles[5] against the Ottoman regime. The heroic deeds of this little Montenegro became well known to Armenians all over the world, for they cherished this glimmer of freedom still remaining in their ancient kingdom.[6]

After the first half of the nineteenth century, the causes of rebellion in Zeitun were more than the results of local discontent. A new nationalistic zeal was manifested, which changed the direction of the revolutionary activity in Zeitun from merely a local disturbance to a national movement.[7]

In 1853 the first "ideological preacher," Melikian Ardzruni Hovagim, came to Zeitun from Constantinople and acquired a very important administrative position. Hovagim, among other things, took steps to strengthen the defenses of the town. To secure additional funds for this purpose, he planned a journey to Russia in 1854. The *ishkhans,* the local rulers, tried to discourage him from making the trip because of the dangers he might encounter as a result of the Crimean War then in progress. Disregarding these warnings, Hovagim started on his unsuccessful mission. In Erzerum he was arrested and hanged by the Turkish authorities.[8]

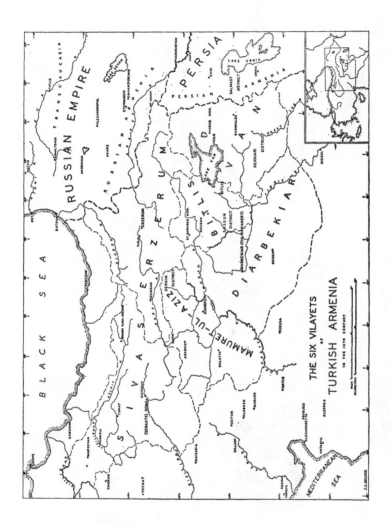

THE SIX VILAYETS
OF
TURKISH ARMENIA
IN THE 19TH CENTURY

Hovagim's presence in Zeitun, together with his contemplated journey to Russia, indicates the national character of his activity. It implies that as early as the 1850's Armenians in Constantinople had direct interests in Zeitun and that the Armenians in Russia were concerned with the political situation in Turkish Armenia. Since Zeitun still remained semi-independent, it was probably considered a suitable center for political agitation by the Armenian intellectuals of Constantinople and Russian Transcaucasia. Very likely this was the reason Hovagim went to Zeitun and then to Russia.

After the Crimean War the Armenians of Zeitun were faced with new problems, when the Turkish government proceeded to confiscate some of their lands to settle Moslem Tatars there.[9] The latter had been compelled to abandon Russia and seek refuge in Turkey.[10] The confiscatory measure was in violation of the liberal *Hatti-humayun*, which had been promulgated by the Sultan in 1856, and the Zeitunlis resisted this unjust encroachment on their lands. Although they lacked legal documents proving their rightful ownership, they had, by virtue of long-continued use of the land, a hereditary claim to it.[11] But the Turkish authorities ignored this claim and, moreover, imposed higher taxes on the Zeitunlis. The real purpose behind the measures taken in Zeitun was to snuff out the freedom of the Zeitunlis and prevent them from becoming a source of inspiration for future Armenian uprisings against the Turks. The Armenians resisted a Turkish force sent into the Zeitun district on June 8, 1860, to compel the people to pay higher taxes.[12] The resistance marked the beginning of full-scale warfare that came to a head two years later.

On the political front in Zeitun the situation was further complicated in the winter of 1861 by the arrival of Levon, who claimed to be the descendant of the Lusignian Dynasty and the heir of the kingdom of New Armenia. Levon remained in the area four months and made preparations for presenting a petition to Napoleon III in which he requested that the French emperor pressure the Turkish government into granting independence to Zeitun and appointing an Armenian prince as ruler. The petition stated that the Zeitunlis were ready for independence and had 70,000 men who could bear arms.

Levon went to Paris and personally presented the petition to Napoleon III, who referred it to his ambassador in Constantinople for transmittal to the Turkish government. Subsequent investigation revealed that the petition had greatly exaggerated the population figures of Zeitun, and the French government disregarded Levon's request. The Porte, on the other hand, interpreted the petition as a direct threat to its authority and set out to crush the Zeitunlis.[13]

In the summer of 1862 a dispute that flared up between the Armenian village of Alabash and the Turkish village of Ketman served as a pretext for the government's plans against Zeitun. Aziz Pasha of Marash, with an army of 40,000 men,[14] marched on Alabash and reduced it to ruins.[15] His forces then moved toward Zeitun, burning and pillaging villages en route. On August 2, 1862,[16] the large Turkish army laid siege to the town of Zeitun, which was defended by a small fighting force of about 5,000 men.[17] In spite of the great strength of the invaders, the Armenians, with the aid of loyal Zeitunli Moslems,[18] were able to route Aziz Pasha's troops. The victory had an electrifying effect among Armenians everywhere and inspired them in their struggle for liberation.

The Turkish government desirous of avenging this humiliating defeat, planned to send a new and much larger army against the Zeitunlis.[19] In order to avert further Turkish military expeditions, the mountaineers sent a delegation to Constantinople to ask the influential Armenian leaders of that city to intervene with the Porte on their behalf. The delegates arrived in the capital on September

27, 1862,[20] and were greeted with great enthusiasm by their compatriots, who were appreciative of Zeitun's recent victory against the Turks.[21] Even before the delegation had arrived, an Armenian representative from Constantinople had been sent to Paris to plead the Zeitunli cause with Napoleon III. This representative and an Armenian priest residing in Paris were successful in their mission and the Emperor intervened on behalf of the Zeitunlis. French pressure, combined with that of influential *amiras,* forced the Porte to recall the large army advancing toward Zeitun.[22]

The Zeitun Rebellion of 1862 became the first of a series of insurrections in Turkish Armenia against the Ottoman regime which were inspired by revolutionary ideas[23] that had swept the Armenian world. The Zeitunli insurgents had had direct contacts with certain Armenian intellectuals in Constantinople who had been influenced by Mikael Nalbandian, a visitor from Russia to the Turkish capital during 1860 and 1861. These intellectuals were members of an organization called the Benevolent Union which had been established in Constantinople for the purpose of "improving the financial and social conditions of the nation." [24] The Benevolent Union stressed the need for founding schools in Cilicia[25] and improving the economic development of the Armenians through better agricultural methods. This special interest in agriculture was no doubt due to the influence of Nalbandian.[26] Members of the Benevolent Union included such prominent leaders of the community as H. Shishmanian (Dzerents), M. Beshiktashlian, H. Sevadjian, S. Tagvorian, and Dr. H. Kaitibian. The organization as such did not indulge in secret revolutionary activity, but some of its members did.

The writer Hovsep Shishmanian was a representative of the Benevolent Union in Cilicia at the time of the uprising at Zeitun; it is supposed by some writers that he participated in the revolt. The poet Mekertitch Beshiktashlian had prior contacts with the Zeitunli delegates who came to Constantinople in 1862.[27] Shortly after the rebellion he had conferred with a Polish prince regarding possible joint revolutionary activity between the Armenians and the Poles.[28]

A letter, partly written in cipher, dated May 14/28, 1862,[29] from the Benevolent Union member Serobe Tagvorian in Constantinople, to Mikael Nalbandian in St. Petersburg indicates that there were revolutionaries in the Turkish capital who had direct contacts with the Zeitun insurgents. The letter has been partially deciphered with the aid of Nalbandian's secret list of code words and phrases,[30] yet many parts of the message still remain vague. Tagvorian states that he is conferring with a priest from Zeitun for the purpose of increasing nationalism among the Zeitunlis. He and his friends in Constantinople had given some "textbooks" to the priest, who was to take them back to Zeitun. The men at Constantinople had promised the priest to continue helping the Zeitunlis. It might be inferred that these "textbooks" were munitions and that the "nationalism" at Zeitun really meant the cause of liberation through rebellion.

Tagvorian mentions the Benevolent Union, speaks of a letter that is to be sent to the Italian revolutionist Mazzini, and states that a secret committee is going to be formed in Constantinople. After mentioning the proposed secret committee, the letter describes at length a new lodge that will be formed shortly. The name of the lodge was to be "Haik" or "Orion" and it was to be a branch of the Odd Fellows Lodge of England. The Porte had already given permission to the future lodge to hold secret meetings. The members were to pay a designated sum which would be used as a fund for helping members in need. If the Haik-Orion Lodge did not have adequate funds, the mother lodge in England was to give financial assistance.

Tagvorian's letter indicates that preparations for the

Zeitun Rebellion (August, 1862) were probably begun as early as May, 1862. The letter shows that Nalbandian had close relations with certain men in Constantinople just prior to the rebellion in Zeitun. Not only did he know and have correspondence with Tagvorian,[31] but also with Dr. Kaitiban[32] and with Sevadjian, the editor of the *Meghu* (*Bee.*)[33]

It is not clear from the Tagvorian letter whether or not the "secret committee" and the "Haik" Lodge were the same, were related, or were two separate organizations. It is a fact, however, that the lodge mentioned in the letter came into existence only a few months after the letter was written.

The first meeting of the Haik Lodge took place in the Pera Quarter of Constantinople on August 21, 1862.[34] It had been officially approved as a branch of the Odd Fellows Lodge of Manchester, England. Although the Constantinople branch was named "Haik," it was referred to as the "Haik-Orion" Lodge. The president of the organization was Serovbe Aznavur, who published the bylaws of the new lodge in the pages of the *Massis* newspaper of Constantinople.[35] The president also wrote numerous other articles in the *Massis* which described the fraternal principles of the Masonic order. He stated that another branch of the order, called Aram, was to be established in the Kum Kapu Quarter of Constantinople and that in a short time branches would be formed in all parts of the Ottoman Empire. He predicted that Moslems, Christians, and Jews would join together under the fraternal, benevolent banner of the Odd Fellows Lodge.[36]

Although the Haik Lodge outwardly appeared as a purely fraternal order, it is highly probable that the lodge had carefully concealed political objectives. The details of the interrelation among Nalbandian, the Benevolent Union, and the Zeitun Rebellion are still lacking,[37] and the role of the Haik-Orion Lodge in the revolutionary activities of the Armenians of Constantinople remains obscure. It is certain, however, that Nalbandian's political influence was felt in Constantinople by a group of revolutionaries who had direct relations with the Zeitun insurgents.

RESULTS OF THE ZEITUN REBELLION OF 1862

The results of the victory at Zeitun encouraged revolts in other cities in the Ottoman Empire. In Turkey and abroad Armenians were stirred to new and more vigorous discussion as to the ways and means of achieving Armenian independence. Various plans for independence were proposed. Some Armenian spokesmen, like Levon, hoped to win the independence of Zeitun through French support; and negotiations in this direction took place between the Armenians and the French government. But before committing themselves, the French asked that the Zeitunlis change their allegiance from the Catholicos to the Pope.[38] This the Zeitunlis apparently refused to do and thereby did not secure a status comparable to that held by the Maronites of Lebanon.[39]

Another plan for independence encompassed not merely Zeitun but all of Cilicia. An independent state was to be created in Cilicia, which was to coincide roughly with the one-time kingdom of New Armenia. This plan became popular among the intelligentsia of Constantinople, who were encouraged by the Zeitun victory and by the liberal spirit of the early 'sixties, reflected in the Armenian National Constitution.[40]

As early as 1851 Mekertitch Khirimian, later known as Khirimian Hairig, had been sent to Cilicia from Constantinople.[41] Among other things, he was to organize a religious organization called Ser (Love), to be used as an instrument of furtherance of the proposed independence of Cilicia. Later, Nerses Varzhabedian, who became the Patriarch of Constantinople, also went to Cilicia to strengthen this organization. Contrary to the purpose for which it was formed, the Ser society, with branches in the region of Zeitun and in Hajjin, Kokison, and Yarpus[42] became strictly religious in nature.[43]

Although the Ser society was established in Cilicia during the 1850's, no records are available concerning such an organization in Constantinople at that time. A Masonic lodge named Ser was established in Constantinople on May 7, 1866, by seven Armenian intellectuals: Serovbe Aznavur, Serapion Hekimian, Serovbe Tagvorian, Ekeshian, Mikael Alishan, Mattheos Mamurian, and Haruthiun Sevadjian.[44] This Masonic order was established because of disillusionment with the Armenian National Constitution, which lacked political force in regard to reforms for the Armenians of Asiatic Turkey. The enthusiasm with which many intellectuals had at first greeted the Constitution gave way to disappointment. The National Assembly, provided by the Constitution, did not give enough attention to the plight of the Armenians in the provinces.

The object of the Ser Lodge was to bring about solidarity and a feeling of brotherhood among the Armenians. Strong fraternal ties were to be established between those of different economic status and religious denominations. Armenians who lived in the far-off Asiatic provinces were to be united with their compatriots in Constantinople and other major cities. The fraternal association of Armenians through the facilities of the Ser Lodge would be linked with world Masonry. The Ser Lodge had been officially approved by the Grand Orient Lodge of France,[45] and the Armenians of Turkey were thereby to gain the international support of a powerful organization.

Within a few months the Ser Lodge enlisted nearly forty members, most of them coming from the intelligentsia of Constantinople. Included in its membership were such notables as the poet Mekertitch Beshiktashlian, the painter and architect Romanos Setefdjian, and the editors Karapet

Utudjian and Stepan Papazian.[46] The emblem of the lodge
bore the motto "Union, Love, Enlightenment, Toil, and
Freedom." The members prepared oral and written reports
on various social, economic, political, and philosophic subjects.[47] The precise connection between their activities and
the Armenian revolutionary movement is not known, nor
is their understanding of the word "freedom" quite clear.
Although one cannot determine whether the members actively worked for political independence, it is evident that
they advocated important political and economic changes
for the Armenians in Asiatic Turkey.

The ideas of the revolutionary Mikael Nalbandian had
certainly impressed the Ser members, and their admiration
for him was further shown at a special meeting in his memory in 1866, after the news of his death reached Constantinople,[48] but since documents pertaining to the Ser Lodge
are few, one cannot precisely determine what effect Nalbandian's influence had upon the activities of the lodge.

Certain questions have never been fully answered. What
was the connection between the Haik-Orion Lodge and the
Ser Lodge of 1866? Had the idea and encouragement for a
Ser organization in Cilicia during the 'fifties come from the
same Armenian intelligentsia who later formed the Ser
Lodge in Constantinople? What political motivations were
present in the Ser Lodge of 1866? Was their connection
with international Masonry, through their affiliation with
the French Grand Orient Lodge, a method of obtaining
stronger support for possible political intentions in Cilicia?
A lack of documentary evidence prevents any fully adequate answers to these questions; yet it can be assumed
with certainty that the Ser Lodge had a special interest in
the Armenians of the provinces and that many of its members had close connections both with Nalbandian and with
the Zeitun insurgents.

The Armenians of the Diaspora also manifested much interest in Cilicia. In 1865 Karapet Vardabet Shahnazarian,

who lived in Egypt, bequeathed a large sum of money for the "intellectual, moral, and spiritual awakening of Cilicia . . . in preparation for the expected political rebirth" [49] of the region. During the following year this fund, together with another donation, was used to establish the Nupar-Shahnazarian College in Constantinople. The alumni of this institution, aware of the purpose for which their alma mater had been founded, formed the Vardanian Society in 1871 with the aim of improving the educational facilities of Cilicia.[50] Educational improvement within the region was considered the groundwork for the anticipated political independence. Another step taken in preparation for the eventual freedom of Cilicia was to encourage Armenian immigration into Cilicia. In 1863 Rafael Patkanian (Kamar Katiba) wrote an article in the journal *Hiusiss* (*North*), published in St. Petersburg, in which he advocated the movement of Persian Armenians into the Zeitun region.[51] An independent Zeitun might become the nucleus around which the rest of Cilicia could be eventually united. Mikael Nalbandian's secret list of code words and phrases indicates that he had an interest in Cilician immigration. He used the words "the cultivation of cotton" as the code expression for the phrase "to establish immigration in Cilicia."[52]

A third plan for independence envisioned the unification not only of Zeitun and Cilicia but of all Armenian lands. This plan was advocated in a letter written by Hakobik Noradounghian, who was friendly with the Ser Lodge of Constantinople.[53] The letter, which was written in Rome and dated October 21, 1863,[54] was addressed to Khirimian Hairig, a high-ranking clergyman of the Armenian Church.[55] Noradounghian urged Khirimian Hairig to take the initiative in forming a committee of three to five persons, which should be responsible for directing the foreign affairs of the Armenian nation. The main objective of the committee was to "break the chains of Armenia."[56]

Noradounghian's letter pointed out the path successfully

followed by other nations in attaining freedom: The united efforts of the patriotic committee or "triumvirate" must ultimately result in the establishment of an independent Armenia, provided they used their financial resources wisely, distributed literature to the best effect, maintained political contacts so as to gain the sympathy of foreign powers—and worked at this task for some years with prudence and dedication.[57] However, Khirimian Hairig's ideas regarding Armenian national objectives were not in harmony with those of Noradounghian, and for this reason, among others, the letter was ignored.[58]

As indicated above, the favorable outcome at Zeitun encouraged various programs for the freeing of Turkish Armenia from Ottoman rule. Journalism played an important role in disseminating and maintaining this spirit of independence represented by the Zeitunlis. Numerous articles and poems[59] were written in celebration of the heroic mountaineers. European states became more aware of the Armenian Question through newspaper reports on the Zeitun Rebellion and through the writings of such French Armenophiles as Victor Langlois and J. Saint-Martin.[60] New ideas were spreading, and a spirit of patriotic enthusiasm prevailed. The rebellion at Zeitun had its counterparts in the provinces of Van and Erzerum.

THE UPRISINGS IN VAN AND ERZERUM

An uprising took place in the city of Van in the early part of 1862. Although it preceded the Zeitun Rebellion of that year, it seems not to have had the same lasting impact on the discontented Armenian community. The Armenians in the city, numbering 20,000, allied with Kurdish peasants of the outlying areas and rose against their Turkish rulers. The fighting resulted in heavy casualities on both sides.[61]

Alliances between Armenians and Kurds were the exception rather than the rule. Kurdish bands frequently attacked Armenians; they were encouraged to do so at times by the Turkish authorities. Occasionally whole villages were terrorized unless they submitted to the arbitrary demands of Kurdish chieftains and bands.[62] Frederick Millingen, a military employee of the Ottoman government and an eyewitness of provincial injustices, observed that the Armenians were virtually "the serfs of their ferocious neighbors." [63]

The province of Erzerum[64] was a center of Kurdish pillaging. The sanjak[65] of Moush, in particular, was the scene of barbarity,[66] and there, in 1863, the Armenians rose against the Kurds. They had sent a delegation to Constantinople, but it had no success in presenting its grievances to Fuad Pasha, the Grand Vizir. When the delegates threatened that if the conditions in their homeland were not improved, their people would immigrate to Russia, the angered vizir bade them to do just that if they were not satisfied with the Turkish regime.[67]

In 1864 the Moush residents protested to the governor at Erzerum against the prevailing conditions, but again to no avail. During the following year the Armenians of Charsanjag (in the sanjak of Moush) underwent another terroristic attack by the Kurds. This time the Armenians sent to Constantinople a delegation of twenty-four, representing twenty-four towns, to appeal for protection. On March 31, 1865, the delegation presented its petition to the Sultan, who referred it to Fuad Pasha. Instead of offering a solution, the Turkish rulers saw fit to imprison the delegation for a week, then order them home.[68]

Another attempt to gain imperial assistance was made in 1867. Complaints from the village of Bulanik (in the province of Erzerum) came before the Grand Vizir. But the vizir dismissed the complaints by declaring: "If the Armenians do not like things as they are in these provinces, they may leave the country; then we can populate these places with Circassians." [69]

THE UNION OF SALVATION

Because the equality that the Porte promised in various legal documents from time to time remained a dead letter,[70] the Armenians of the province of Van decided to organize for self-protection. In 1872 they founded the Union of Salvation (Miuthiun I Perkuthiun), which became the first organized revolutionary society in Turkish Armenia. It is not surprising that a society of this kind should have emerged in the province of Van, for it was here that Khirimian Hairig and Bishop Servandstiants had endeavored to create a new generation of revolutionary thinkers. At the Monastery of Varag, Khirimian Hairig had established the first printing press in Turkish Armenia and began to publish his liberal journal *Ardzvi Vaspurakan* (*Eagle of Vaspurakan*).

Certain geographical and ethnic factors also favored Van as a center for revolutionary organization. The province was near the frontiers of Russia and Persia, where outside assistance might be readily obtained. Ethnically, Van (excluding the sanjak of Hekkiari) was the only province in the Ottoman Empire in which the Armenians outnumbered the Moslems.[71] All of these conditions helped induce an atmosphere of resistance to the Turkish administrators, who had become "birds of prey" [72] at the expense of the rest of the population.[73]

On March 3, 1872, forty-six persons in the city of Van met and took a pledge to dedicate themselves to winning freedom for their people. In thus forming the Union of Salvation, the Armenian spokesmen declared: ". . . gone is our honor; our churches have been violated; they have kidnapped our brides and our youth; they take away our rights and try to exterminate our nation . . . let us find a way of salvation . . . if not, we will soon lose everything." [74]

Other villages near Van sought admittance into the newly formed organization. On April 26, 1872, the villages of Anggh and Kerds addressed a letter to the Union in which they asked if they could join the Union for the common cause. The letter further said:[75]

> In order to save ourselves from these evils, we are prepared to follow you even if we must shed blood or die. We are ready to go wherever there is hope for our salvation.
>
> If the alternative to our present condition is to become Russified, let us be Russified together; if it is to be emigration, let us emigrate; if we are to die, let us die; but let us be freed. This is our desire.

Similar requests were made by the villages of Hortents, Khekkegh, Huntstan, Nor Gugh, and Haregh. From the signatories of the declaration at Van as well as the various letters written to the Union, it can be concluded that the Union represented all sections of the Armenian population. Merchants, artisans (e.g., cloth-weavers, tailors, soapmakers), and the clergy, all endorsed the movement.

The details of the organization and activity of the Union of Salvation are not known. It is probably this organization that was instrumental in bringing about diplomatic communications between the city of Van and the Russian government. An appeal that bore the seal of the Armenian community of Van was addressed to the Viceroy of the Caucasus on May 9, 1872. As fellow Christians, the Russians were asked to assist and protect the Armenians. The community requested that a consul be sent to Van so that the Russian government would be in closer contact with the conditions there. A similar request had been made some seven or eight years previously and although the Russians had promised to assign a consul, nothing further had occurred. But a second promise had been made by the Russians with respect to the consulate only a few months before the request made by Van in 1872. The Armenians of Van were now anxious to have this promise fulfilled. As an escape from their insecure position, they also asked to become Russian subjects.[76]

Two prominent men of Van, Hakob agha Galoian and Neshan Shirvanian, both members of the Union of Salvation, were commissioned to deliver this appeal to the Viceroy of the Caucasus. While in Russia they also made a similar appeal to the Governor of the province of Erivan.[77]

It would appear that the Union of Salvation had direct contact not only with the Russian government but with certain Russian Armenian organizations: the Goodwill Society (Barenepatak Enkeruthiun) (1868–1876) and the Devotion to the Fatherland Bureau (Kontora Haireniats Siro) (1874–1875).[78] Both of these organizations had secret political motives and were particularly interested in the liberation of the Armenians from Turkish rule. The Goodwill Society concentrated its efforts on the province of Van, and posted an agent there. It collected money for buying arms. These were probably sent to the Armenians of Van, who were prohibited from bearing arms—a privilege extended only to the Moslem population. The proximity in time, the uniformity of objectives, and the contiguous area of operation of the Union of Salvation and the two organizations on the Russian side of the frontier all lead to the conclusion that they coöperated with one another.

The Union of Salvation served as a major step toward the formation of the first Armenian political party, the *Armenakan,* founded in Van in 1885. In the meantime, there had been certain important developments. As noted earlier, the Armenians enthusiastically welcomed the announcement in 1876 of the liberal Ottoman Constitution. The problem of the Armenian people in the Ottoman Empire was recognized in Article XVI of the Treaty of San Stefano, which concluded the Russo-Turkish War of 1877–

1878. During the Congress of Berlin (1878) the hopes of the Armenian people all over the world rose, with dreams of freedom and justice. At Berlin, Article XVI of the Treaty of San Stefano was revised by the Great Powers (Great Britain, Austria-Hungary, France, Germany, Italy, and Russia), and became Article LXI of the Treaty of Berlin (July 13, 1878). It now read:[79]

The Sublime Porte engages to realize, without further delay, the ameliorations and the reforms demanded by local requirements in the provinces inhabited by the Armenians and to guarantee their security against the Circassians and the Kurds. She will periodically render account of the measures taken with this intent to the Powers, who will supervise them.

The Armenians had hoped that the Congress of Berlin would give them autonomy and stronger guarantees for reforms than those set forth in Article XVI of the Treaty of San Stefano, but the outcome was otherwise. By the Treaty of San Stefano, reforms in Turkish Armenia were connected with the eventual withdrawal of Russian troops in the Armenian provinces; the Treaty of Berlin, on the other hand, merely required Russian troops to evacuate Ottoman territory, and the Great Powers failed to secure a positive guarantee for carrying out the provisions for Armenian reforms.

In spite of their disappointment in Article LXI of the Treaty of Berlin, however, the Armenians continued to retain strong hopes that in the not too distant future they might secure a victory over Ottoman despotism.

THE BLACK CROSS SOCIETY

In 1878, while diplomatic negotiations were taking place in regard to Turkish Armenia, the difficult conditions in the country led to action on the part of the natives. The

Russo-Turkish War had brought chaos, terror, and famine to both the Moslem and Christian inhabitants, and organized efforts were made to alleviate this suffering.

One of the organizations formed in 1878 was the small, secret revolutionary Black Cross Society (Sev Khatch Kazmakerputhiun) at Van. It was composed of a group of young Armenians whose aim was to protect their unarmed compatriots. They wished to put an end to the looting, violence, and extortion of tribute to which the Armenians were subjected by the armed Turks and Kurds. This society was organized to combat such injustices by the use of armed force. Its members were sworn to secrecy and those who broke their oath were marked with a "Black Cross" and immediately put to death.[80]

Within a short time the necessity for reforms in Turkish Armenia grew increasingly urgent. The Great Powers sent to the Porte an "Identic Note" dated June 11, 1880,[81] and a "Collective Note" dated September 7, 1880,[82] both requesting the enforcement of Article LXI of the Treaty of Berlin. The Armenians were especially encouraged in 1880 by the victory of the Liberals in England and the prime ministry of Gladstone, whose memorable words, "To serve Armenia is to serve civilization," continue to be echoed to this day. On January 12, 1881, the English government sent a Circular on Armenia to the other Powers, drawing their attention to the need for the implementation of the reforms in Turkish Armenia.[83]

The European Powers issued statements, made promises, and urged reforms, but they never took firm action to force the Porte to carry out its obligations under the Treaty of Berlin. Armenian hopes and expectations were in vain. No recourse remained but to depend on their own resources and to resort to revolutionary activity. In the early 'eighties Erzerum became the focal point of protest against Ottoman misgovernment.

THE PROTECTORS OF THE FATHERLAND

A secret revolutionary society, Protectors of the Fatherland (Pashtpan Haireniats), was formed in 1881 at Erzerum.[84] Its purpose was to arm the inhabitants for defense
against any future attacks by Turks, Kurds, and Circassians.[85]

Preliminary organization of the Protectors of the Fatherland began in 1880 and indeed preceded its Constitution,
which went into effect in the beginning of May, 1881.[86]
Although H. M. Nishkian does not give a special name for
the society during its formative period, secondary sources
do. Leo[87] and Seropian[88] say that the organization was at
first called the Supreme Council (Geragun Khorhurd) and
later its name was changed to Protectors of the Fatherland.
Both sources declare that the latter society was directed by
Dr. Bagrat Navasardian from his headquarters in Tiflis.
Seropian[89] adds that it is probable than an organization
called the "Agricultural Society" (Yerkragordzakan Enkeruthiun), founded by Khatchatur Kerektsian, had merged
with the Supreme Council and that the name "Protectors
of the Fatherland" was given to the new society. H. M.
Nishkian makes no reference to either the Agricultural Society or the Supreme Council, but Nersessian[90] says that
"Agricultural Society" was merely another name given to
the Protectors of the Fatherland so as to eliminate suspicion
by the government.

The two principal leaders of the secret Protectors of the
Fatherland at Erzerum were Khatchatur Kerektsian and
Karapet Nishkian. They and four others—Hakob Ishgalatsian, Aleksan Yethelikian, Hovhannes Asturian, and Yeghishe Tursunian—were its founders. H. M. Nishkian was
asked to become one of the founders, but he refused. However, he agreed to serve in the capacity of advisor to the

group. By virtue of this position he was able to acquire an intimate knowledge of the workings of the Protectors of the Fatherland. Although H. M. Nishkian was not officially one of the six founders, he became the seventh member of the central committee that formulated the plans for the society.[91]

The constitution and bylaws of the Protectors of the Fatherland were not written; they were memorized by the members. This was done as a protective measure in the event of possible government investigation. The name of the society indicates the purpose for which it was founded: the protection of the Armenian population. Guns and other munitions were bought by the organization and sold at low cost, or, whenever possible, given free of charge to the members.[92]

The Protectors of the Fatherland was essentially a decentralized organization, wherein the membership was organized into groups of ten, each having its own leader. Admission to the organization was accomplished in such a fashion that no single person would know all the members of the central committee.

The following was the procedure for gaining admission. One of the founders would sponsor an able and reliable candidate who would then be approved by the other members of the central committee. The sponsor would orally relate to the new member the workings of the society, and the new member would then be in a position to become a group leader. He would be free to choose ten men who desired to work with him. A new group could be formed under the leadership of a member with the approval of his own group leader and a member of the central committee. In this manner the membership of the Protectors of the Fatherland rapidly increased in the city of Erzerum and in the villages of the province. Within three months hundreds of persons swore allegiance to the secret society.[93]

Plans were made to expand the organization, to collect

more funds for much-needed arms, and to get the advice and counsel of important members of the Armenian community. Bishop Ormanian, the highest-ranking church official at Erzerum, was informed of the existence of the society. In 1881 the Bishop notified the Patriarch of Constantinople, Nerses Varzhabedian, about the organization of the Protectors of the Fatherland and the Patriarch approved of it.[94]

In the autumn of 1881 Kerektsian was commissioned to go to Van and then to Russia to solicit support for the newly formed society. At Van he conferred with Khirimian Hairig and in Russia he made contacts with Grigor Ardzruni, the editor of the *Mushak*.

The need for funds also caused Karapet Nishkian to make two trips to Russia in quest of financial aid from the Russian Armenians. His first trip was in November, 1881, and extended over three months. He left Erzerum for the second time at the end of August, 1882, and remained in Russia three months. On his second journey he took with him an official certificate, especially prepared for the purpose of impressing prospective donors with the importance of the secret society. The certificate was an artistically decorated lithograph print on which appeared the emblem and oath of the society. The name "Protectors of the Fatherland" was inscribed at the head of the certificate, and at the end the words "Liberty or Death." [95] Numerous copies of this oath, the only official document prepared by the organization, found their way into circulation. Prior to Nishkian's return to Erzerum, a copy of the print unfortunately fell into the hands of Turkish government officials, on November 25, 1882.[96]

This discovery of the printed oath hastened the dissolution of the underground organization. A series of arrests followed immediately. The London *Times*[97] reported that four hundred persons in Erzerum had been arrested and that the leaders of the Protectors of the Fatherland were believed to be in Tiflis. The Russian Consul in Erzerum gave preferential treatment to the Armenians, which further aroused Turkish suspicions.[98] In the meantime, the Armenian Patriarch of Constantinople tried to persuade the Porte to mitigate the severe police action taken at Erzerum and urged the government to carry out the reforms agreed to in the Treaty of Berlin. This procedure, he asserted, would be the best way of eliminating internal unrest.[99]

The Turkish press tried to minimize the importance of these latest events. It repudiated the European newspaper reports and even denied that the Porte had made any arrests for political reasons.[100] The Porte wished to hush up the situation to prevent any possible interference in the domestic affairs of the Ottoman Empire by the Great Powers of Europe.

The trial of seventy-six persons arrested in the conspiracy took place in Erzerum in 1883. The decision of the court at Erzerum came before the Court of Appeal in Constantinople and a new trial was granted.[101] The retrial took place in Erzerum in June 1883, and the court rendered a verdict of guilty against forty persons. Khatchatur Kerektsian, a leader of the society, was sentenced to fifteen years in prison, and the others were given prison terms of thirteen, ten, seven, six, and five years.[102] Through the efforts of Patriarch Nerses and Bishop Ormanian, the majority of the prisoners were pardoned by the Sultan[103] and released on June 22, 1884.[104] Kerektsian, Hakob Ishgalatsian, and Hovhannes Asturian, three of the founders[105] of the society, were set free in the beginning of September, 1886.[106] The sentences of these convicted conspirators had not been severe, and this leniency can probably be attributed to the Porte's desire to eliminate possible European pressure in regard to Armenia.

The trial of the members of the Protectors of the Fatherland was the first of its kind among the Armenians of the

Ottoman Empire in the nineteenth century. Never before had so large a group of men, coming from various ranks of the Armenian population,[107] been placed on trial for political reasons. Those tried were predominantly young men.[108] The secret organization that they founded in Erzerum sent its agents to Russian Transcaucasia to effect coöperation with Armenian leaders there. Undoubtedly, these agents also made connections with Russian revolutionaries, who were organized in Transcaucasia in the early 'eighties.

The Protectors of the Fatherland existed only a year and a half (May, 1881–November, 1882), but its influence was far more enduring. It served to encourage the Armenians to an organized resistance against Ottoman oppression. The events at Erzerum during this period later served as the inspiration for the revolutionary song "The Voice Re-echoed from the Armenian Mountains of Erzerum" ("Dsaine Hunchets Erzumi Hayots Lerneren").

The call to revolution echoed in other parts of Armenia. Insecure living conditions and administrative mismanagement contributed to bringing about more organized action. Armenian discontent, which had expressed itself in the revolutionary uprisings in Zeitun, Van, and Erzerum, now found articulation in the formation of a larger political unit, the Armenakan Party.

IV

The Armenakan Party, 1885–1896

The Armenakan[1] Party was the first Armenian political party in the nineteenth century to engage in revolutionary activities. It was organized at Van in 1885 by the students of one of Armenia's foremost educators, Mekertitch Portugalian. Before discussing the history of the party, it is essential to give a brief biography of this inspiring schoolmaster.

MEKERTITCH PORTUGALIAN

Mekertitch Portugalian (1848–1921) was born in the Armenian Quarter of Kum Kapu in Constantinople.[2] He received his formal education in various Armenian institutions in the capital, and his interest in learning was further encouraged by his banker father, who possessed a fine private library. At an early age the boy became very conscious of the political alignments within the Armenian community. Young Mekertitch would listen to the debates among the delegates of the Armenian National Assembly, whose sessions took place in the same school building in which

he attended classes. He soon learned the difference in political viewpoint between the *Illuminati* and the Non-*Illuminati* representatives in the Assembly.[3] These political
factions had a direct bearing on Portugalian's education,
since he transferred in 1862 to the Sahakian Gymnasium
where the trustees were *Illuminati,* the faction favored by
his family.

After he had graduated from the Gymnasium, the talents
of Portugalian as an educator, organizer, and administrator
combined to make him one of the leaders of the Armenian
community. He became a private tutor, worked for a
French publisher in Constantinople, and then organized
a publishing society. For the new society he translated
Dumas' *La Dame de Monsoreau* into the Armenian language. In 1867[4] he was given the opportunity to use his
knowledge and abilities in raising the educational standard
of the less fortunate Armenians in the Asiatic provinces of
Turkey. He enthusiastically accepted an offer to go to the
town of Tokat (Yevdokia) as a teacher. While there he
worked to educate both the young and old in the community.

In 1869[5] Portugalian founded in Tokat a branch of the
Altruistic Society, whose object was to hold Sunday classes
in the Armenian language for Turkish-speaking Armenians. So successful was this endeavor that Khirimian Hairig,
who was at the time the Armenian Patriarch of Constantinople, sent a note of congratulations to the Altruistic Society of Tokat. The people of the town were very pleased
with Portugalian's work, but their satisfaction was not
shared by the wealthy Armenian *aghas.* The latter bitterly
opposed the pedagogue and had him arrested by the Turkish authorities.[6]

After being released, he returned to Constantinople. In
the Turkish capital he edited the journal *Asia,* but again
encountered opposition. Because of its severe criticism of
certain religious and political matters in the community,

the journal was forced to discontinue publication. Portugalian's journalistic work did not stop there, however. He became a member of the staff of the journal *Manzume,* which was published in Constantinople, and also contributed to the *Meghu Hayastani (Armenian Bee),* published in Russian Transcaucasia;[7] nor was there any abatement of his personal concern with the educational progress of the Armenian people.

Portugalian became a prominent member of the Ararathian society in 1876. His connections with this educational society helped bring him into closer contact with the inhabitants of the provinces. The society appointed him to direct their educational program at Van, the center of Ararathian operations. He journeyed there in 1876, at the time of the insurrections and turmoil in the Balkans. En route he visited other areas of Turkish Armenia, including Samson, Tokat, Sebaste, Mamuret-ul-Aziz (Kharput) and Tigranakert.[8] Through such travels he became even more familiar with the condition of the Armenians in Turkey. Before establishing his educational program in the city of Van, he went on a tour of investigation to the villages of the region. The outbreak of the Russo-Turkish War (1877–1878) interrupted his researches and he left Van for Russia as the representative of the Ararathian Society. In Tiflis he conferred with the Russian Armenian leader Ardzruni in regard to the plans of the society.[9] This was the second such meeting in Tiflis, the first having occurred two years previously, in 1876.[10] Having obtained the support of Ardzruni, Portugalian returned to Constantinople.

The Russo-Turkish War had ended, and the Armenians of Turkey were anxiously awaiting the results of the Russian victory. Portugalian left the capital during this period of uncertainty and arrived in Van in the autumn of 1878. He set to work immediately, establishing a school called the Normal School (Varzhapetanots).[11] Armenians as well as

Nestorian Christians and Moslem Kurds and Turks were invited to enroll at the institution.[12]

Because of the hostility of certain groups within the community toward Portugalian's educational program, the Normal School lasted only a short time. These opponents were chiefly from the reactionary political faction of Van known as the Boghosians, a group that opposed liberal ideas, advocated coöperation with the government, and were consequently hostile to Portugalian and Khirimian Hairig. The Boghosians in turn were challenged by the Aboghosian faction, which represented the liberal ideas of the young generation. These intercommunity conflicts[13] focused the suspicions of the government upon the Normal School. The school was soon closed by Turkish officials, who believed that Portugalian was promoting revolutionary ideas under the guise of education.

The teacher himself was forced to return to Constantinople in 1881.[14] After a brief stay he went back to Van with the purpose of continuing his educational program. The United Societies now aided him in founding another school, the Central Gymnasium (Kedronakan Varzharan).[15] Besides directing this educational institution for young people, Portugalian was again active in promoting adult education, but his efforts were once more disrupted. For political reasons the government banished him from Van on March 16/28, 1885.[16] The Central Gymnasium was ordered closed, and its students were dispersed on June 3, 1885.[17] During the same year Van was the scene of many political arrests;[18] and governmental restrictions caused a steady flow of Armenian émigrés outward from the Ottoman Empire, especially to Western Europe and the United States.

Portugalian left Turkey for France in 1885, never to return to his beloved Armenia, but the example of his life and his work in the provinces was enduring. He had been instrumental in educating the youth who gathered in his schools in Van from all parts of Armenia. It was he who ". . . blew a breath of freedom over all of Van. Without pronouncing the word revolution . . . he prepared a revo-tutionary generation." [19]

THE JOURNAL *Armenia*

Exile did not diminish Portugalian's personal interest in his native land. Marseille became his headquarters and here he started publishing the newspaper *Armenia*, July 20/August 1, 1885.[20] The journal, later identified with the Armenakan Party, had a four-fold objective:[21]

1. To draw the attention of the world toward the conditions in Turkish Armenia;

2. To aid the homeland through the assistance of the Armenians of the Diaspora;

3. To disseminate the ideas of the editor among the Armenian people; and

4. To use the experience and knowledge of the editor for the benefit of the Armenian people.

In the beginning the journal was devoted to promulgating the idea of reform for Turkish Armenia in conformity with the peaceful methods laid down in the Treaty of Berlin. At first the editor presented himself as a faithful citizen of Turkey,[22] but his views rapidly changed in the direction of revolution. Portugalian came to believe that freedom could not be won without bloodshed. This attitude was dictated by the experiences of other Ottoman subjects, such as the Greeks, Montenegrins, and Bulgarians.[23]

In the pages of *Armenia*, Portugalian praised the Irish abroad who were generously contributing to the revolutionary movement in their native land.[24] He envisaged a plan for united action on the part of thousands of Armenians in the Diaspora. The plan included the establishment of a large, strong, and wealthy organization that would work for the interests of the homeland and the solution of the Armenian Question. Already, various separate Armenian groups scattered in different countries had been organized for this purpose. Portugalian advocated that a General Congress be held for the purpose of combining and coördinating the efforts of these groups.[25] It was suggested that the Congress be held under the presidency of G. Hagopian,[26] who was the leader of the Armenian Patriotic Society of Europe (Hairenasirats Enkeruthiun Hayots Yevropai) which had been formed in London, December 23, 1885.[27]

A general Congress of Armenian groups in the Diaspora took place in June, 1886,[28] but instead of bringing about coöperation among them, the meeting caused much dissension and a disruption of united efforts. Nonetheless, Portugalian did not give up the idea of an international organization and decided to form a society under his own leadership. Accordingly, he established, on April 5/17, 1889,[29] the Armenian Patriotic Union (Hayots Hairenasirakan Miuthiun). Contrary to his expectations, it never became the powerful organization first outlined in the pages of *Armenia* in 1885. By the time the Union was formed in 1889, new revolutionary groups had already been organized in Turkish Armenia, Geneva, and Russian Transcaucasia.

THE ARMENAKANS

Although Portugalian was unsuccessful in establishing a powerful Armenian front, his work was instrumental in the formation of the first political party in the provinces. The journal *Armenia* now became the rallying point for his former students, who were becoming teachers and community leaders. A group of graduates from Portugalian's Central Gymnasium began discussing the need for a revolutionary organization. The discussions took place in an informal manner since Van was heavily policed and gatherings of any kind, either in public or in private dwellings, were prohibited by the government.

A secret meeting place was needed for this group. After much thought the graduates decided to hold a meeting in a small burrow called the *hundzan,* where grapes were pressed. The *hundzan,* which was situated in the vineyard of the brothers Mekertitch and Grigoris Terlemezian, remained deserted most of the year. The only furnishing in the damp burrow was a straw mat or *khesir,* from which the secret meeting place came to be called the "House of the Straw Mat" ("Khesri Tun").

At the first meeting in the House of the Straw Mat, which took place in the autumn of 1885, the former students of Mekertitch Portugalian founded the Armenakan Party, the first Armenian revolutionary political party in the nineteenth century. The name was derived from the journal *Armenia,* and the members of the party were called Armenakans (Armenakanner). There were nine young men present at the founders' meeting: Mekertitch Terlemezian (Avetisian), Grigoris Terlemezian, Ruben Shatavorian, Grigor Odian, Grigor Adjemian, M. Parutdjian, Ghevond Khandjian, Grigor Beozikian (Shikaher), and Garegin Manukian (Bagheshtsian). Three other graduates, Yeghiche Gontaktchian, Gabriel Natanian, and Dr. Galust Aslanian, who had been among those who had initiated the idea of an organization, had left Van and were not present at the founders' meeting.[30]

The journal *Armenia* was identified with the Armenakan Party, but never became the official organ of the organization. The journal was sent to subscribers in Van from France, where it was published without censorship. Its encouraging pages gave further impetus to the revolutionary drive of its readers. The journal was banned in August, 1885,[31] from entry into Turkey, but its influence continued, since copies were illegally circulated.[32] Additional encouragement was given to the Armenakans by Portugalian in

Marseille through secret correspondence with party members.[33]

The objectives of the Armenakan Party were formulated in Van and were written in a document called the *Program*. Only seven or eight handwritten copies were available and these were read aloud at the request of members.[34] The *Program* was not published until after World War II.[35] This informative document consists of seven parts, which may be summarized as follows:

I *Purpose*. The Armenakan Party was to ". . . win for the Armenian the right to rule over themselves through revolution. . . ." The organization was to restrict itself to the Armenian people, regardless of denomination. To include non-Armenians in the movement would only serve to dissipate energy and impede the progress of the Armenian Revolution.

II *Methods*. The party expected to accomplish its objectives:

1. By uniting all patriotic Armenians who believe in the same ideal;

2. By giving central directions to their followers;

3. By organizing the Armenian people and requesting them, without coercion, to contribute to the organization;

4. By disseminating revolutionary ideas through literature and oral propaganda, by proper education, by the cultivation of regular and continual relationships, and by setting up the noble character of their party leaders as good examples;

5. By inculcating in the people the spirit of self-defense—training them in the use of arms and military discipline, supplying them with arms and money, and organizing guerrilla forces;

6. By preparing the people for a general movement, especially when the external circumstances—the disposition

of the foreign powers and the neighboring races—seem to favor the Armenian cause; and,

7. By avoiding demonstrations, the use of terror, and the death penalty except under exceptional circumstance, and eliminating untimely agitations.

III *Organization*. The party was divided into active and auxiliary members. Active members were those who paid dues and complied with the rules and regulations of the party. Auxiliary members were those who gave moral and financial support, but were not obligated to comply with party rules and regulations. Fifteen per cent of the dues of the active members in Turkish Armenia was to be allotted to the Central Body and another fifteen per cent was to be given to the District Committees. Forty per cent of the proceeds from active members abroad was to be allocated to the Central Body.

IV-V *The Central Body*. This was composed of representatives from each District. It directed and supervised the revolutionary work of the organization. The District was composed of groups or cells made up of active members. A Special Committee composed of representatives of the various groups or cells in the District directed local revolutionary activities. The Special Committee might coöperate with revolutionary bodies outside of the party with the permission of the Central Body. Each District had its special bylaws which served the demands of the locality and were in accord with the *Program*.

VI *Organ*. Under this heading the *Program* states that the journal *Armenia* is to disseminate the ideas of the organization. The party was to help the journal both morally and financially, but its editor had no responsibility in the executive and financial activities of the Armenakan Party.

VII *Revision of the Program*. This could be secured by a majority vote of the representatives in the District Special Committees.[36]

The *Program* did not specifically state where the revolutionary activity of the Armenakans was to take place. It is not clearly stated whether the party's objectives were limited to Turkish Armenia or were to encompass all the political divisions of Armenia in Turkey, Russia, and Persia. Since the work of the party was primarily in Turkish Armenia, and more specifically in the province of Van, it might be assumed that the activity of the organization was first concerned with Turkish Armenia.

The Armenakans emphasized the preparation for a revolution some time in the future. They believed that much preliminary work had to be accomplished for this future revolution and that an immediate revolution was not desirable. Cultural, political, and military education was an essential part of the preparation. This educational program had already been laid down by Portugalian in his schools in Van. Particular attention had been given to military training,[37] a field unfamiliar to the native Armenians. Instruction in the use of arms and military tactics had been given in the Normal School by a certain Major Kamsaragan,[38] an Armenian, who was the Russian Acting Vice-Consul in Van.[39] It was continued secretly by Armenakan leaders as part of their program of self-defense and guerrilla warfare.

PARTY ACTIVITY

In preparation for the revolution, the Armenakan Party began to organize branches in the province of Van, the center of operations. Branches were also started in Moush, Bitlis, Trebizond, and Constantinople. There were other Armenakan organizations in Persia, in Russian Transcaucasia, and in the United States.[40] Outside of Turkey the Persian branch was the most important. In this neighboring country the party had groups in Tabriz and in the district of Salmast, in which the villages of Haftvan and

Mahlam were the leading centers.[41] However, the Armenakans were destined to remain active primarily in the
Turkish province of Van, their place of origin where
Mekertitch Terlemezian, commonly known by the alternative surname Avetisian, was the most important leader.[42]

One of the primary concerns of the party was to protect
their compatriots from incursions by Kurdish tribesmen.
For this purpose they used arms and munitions obtained
from Turkey and Persia. Most of the military equipment
was procured from Turkish officials through bribery, and
although the transportation of arms from Persia was difficult and hazardous work, some came from that source.
Party leaders were sent to Persia, especially Tabriz and
Salmast, to buy arms and munitions which were sold there
on the open market. Those who smuggled military equipment into Turkey were involved in great risks. They were
obliged to cover long distances before reaching their desti-
nation and were exposed to police inspections en route.

A major event in the party's history was the sanguinary
encounter between three revolutionaries and some Turkish
officials in May 1889. The comrades Karapet Koulaksizian,
Hovhannes Agripasian, and Vardan Goloshian, armed with
rifles and disguised in Kurdish costume, left the village of
Haftvan, in the Salmast district in Persia, for Van, on the
night of May 16, 1889. After nine or ten days of travel by
foot, they passed the Persian frontier into Turkey. As they
proceeded on their journey to Van, they were stopped on
the Bashkaleh road near Van by four *zaptiehs* (Turkish
police) who were accompanying a caravan. The *zaptiehs*
demanded that the three men disarm. When they refused,
the *zaptiehs* fired on them, killing Goloshian immediately.
Agripasian was seriously injured and then murdered after
being brutally tortured. Koulaksizian managed to escape
unharmed.

The incident would have passed without too much alarm
had it not been for the credentials found on the Armenians.

On examining the possessions of the two dead men, the Turkish authorities found three papers that disclosed revolutionary objectives. These were in the form of two letters addressed to Koulaksizian, one from Avetis Patiguian of London and the other from Mekertitch Portugalian in Marseille. The third paper was Koulaksizian's diary, covering the period May 16, 1889, to May 24, 1889.

The event caused concern to the Turkish government, which believed that the men were members of a large revolutionary apparatus. The episode was highly publicized. Accounts of it were printed in newspapers in the capital, including the *Eastern Express, Oriental Advertiser, Saadet,* and *Tarik,* as well as the Armenian papers. In Armenian revolutionary circles Goloshian and Agripasian were considered martyrs and their deaths served to open the door to more bloodshed.[43]

Certain episodes indicate that the Armenakans did not stop at mere defensive action, but also incited trouble and committed terroristic acts.[44] Three of these acts of agitation are documented: (1) Avetisian with three other men made a surprise attack on a Kurdish gathering with the intention of killing the chieftain. They were unsuccessful in their objective, but the raid resulted in the killing of two other Kurds;[45] (2) aggressive action—including assassinations—was taken against Turks and Kurds by the two Kurdish-speaking Armenakans, Tchato and Shero;[46] and (3) the murder of Nouri Effendi, a police agent of Van, on October 16, 1892, is attributed to four Armenian revolutionaries, among whom were Armenakans.[47]

REVOLUTIONARIES AND THE OTTOMAN GOVERNMENT

Armenian revolutionaries were continuously sought by the Turkish police. Members of the Armenakan Party were among those revolutionaries who were interrogated. Their homes were searched; some were arrested, imprisoned, and

banished.[48] In reality the Armenian population as a whole
was ". . . possessed of a minimum capacity for causing any
serious trouble to the Turkish Government." [49] The government had an exaggerated notion regarding the numbers
and strength of the revolutionaries.[50] Officials would often
distort Armenian activities, even those of religious, cultural, or charitable nature, and describe them as "revolutionary" in order to secure personal honors and promo-
tions.[51] The restrictions became so severe in Van that scores
of innocent persons were exposed to government prosecu-
tion and were treated as harshly as if they had been
criminals.[52] These repressive measures by the officials only
increased "the innate sentiment of disaffection to the Turk-
ish-Moslem Government." [53]

The repressive measures of the government were part
of a program that went beyond the stamping-out of revolutionaries. It became apparent that the Porte, as part of
its plan for Islamic revival, had intentions of placing all
Armenians—men, women, and children, both guilty and
innocent—into a single category marked for extinction.
The Porte aimed at the destruction of the whole Christian
nation. In pursuit of this cruel policy, a series of organized
massacres commenced in 1894 and continued through 1895
and 1896. Thousands of unarmed Armenians were the help-
less victims of these brutal crimes. The exact number of
dead cannot be accurately determined, but numbers vary
from conservative figures of about 50,000 to as high as
300,000 persons.[54]

THE DEFENSE OF VAN

Van became the center of conflict in June, 1896.[55] Already the population had been alerted to the intended massacre. Preparations had been made by the Armenian
revolutionaries to defend the city against the government
forces. Armenakans, assisted by members of the Hunchak

and Dashnak organizations[56] and other able-bodied men of Van, rose in defense of their homes and families. For many days there was continuous fighting between the Armenian and Turkish troops. The action on the part of the revolutionaries was instrumental in diverting the strength of the invading forces and saving the inhabitants of the city from wholesale massacre.[57]

This clash in Van during June, 1896, was advantageous to the Turkish officials. The Armenian revolutionaries now came out of hiding and joined together as a fighting team. The Turkish government was able to plan its military and political tactics in such a way that the Armenian revolutionaries were driven toward the east, and the few survivors were forced to enter Persian territory. The retreat left the Van region, for a time, without organized leadership.

Although the 1896 defense of Van was the most significant organized operation of the Armenakans in the nineteenth century, they had by that time become a secondary party. Mekertitch Portugalian, who had encouraged resistance in the early period, now rebuked the Armenakans as well as other revolutionaries for their imprudence.[58]

As narrated in the preceding pages, the Armenakan Party had played its role in furthering the cause of freedom through revolution. This first political party had continued previous underground revolutionary activities in Turkish Armenia. It also represented an outgrowth of the uprisings and secret societies that had appeared first at Zeitun in 1860–1862, and later, in the 'seventies and 'eighties, in the provinces of Erzerum and Van. The Armenakans were influenced by the nationalistic fervor of the times and were more immediately inspired by the educator Mekertitch Portugalian. This same schoolmaster also indirectly influenced the founding of another political party, the Hunchakian Revolutionary Party, which we shall next describe.

V

The Hunchakian Revolutionary Party, 1887–1896

The Hunchakian Revolutionary Party[1] was the first socialist party in Turkey and Persia. All its founders and theorists were Marxists.[2] It was formed by seven Russian Armenian students who had left Russia to continue their higher education in universities in Western Europe. They were young persons, in their twenties, and were from well-to-do bourgeois families who were financially supporting them. In the course of this chapter these individuals, where necessary, will be more fully identified. None of them ever lived under the Turkish flag, yet they were personally concerned with the living conditions of their ethnic brothers in Turkish Armenia. For the purpose of furthering revolutionary activity in Turkish Armenia, the seven young Armenians formed what was later to be called the Hunchakian Revolutionary Party in Geneva, Switzerland, in August, 1887.

PRELIMINARIES TO THE FOUNDING

The immediate motivation for the establishment of the Hunchakian Revolutionary Party had been the influence of the journal *Armenia,* published in Marseille by Mekertitch Portugalian. The Armenian students in Montpellier, Paris, and Geneva, who later became Hunchak leaders, had read in the pages of Portugalian's journal a proposal for a large organization that should contribute to the success of the revolutionary movement in Armenia. They had expected Portugalian to assume the leadership in such an enterprise, but they waited in vain for action. Instead, Portugalian continually postponed setting the exact time and place for a convention which should create the new organization.[3] While this procrastination continued, Armenian students in Western Europe were coming into closer contact with one another and were soon to take definite steps toward the formation of a new political revolutionary organization.

In the summer of 1886 Avetis Nazarbekian (known also as Avetis Nazarbek and sometimes called Lerents), who had written some of the strongest revolutionary articles in the journal *Armenia,* traveled from Paris to Geneva. With him was his fiancée, Mariam Vardanian (Maro). Both Avetis and Maro were dynamic personalities in their twenties. Avetis, a strikingly handsome young man with the look of a poet, was a master of dialectics. His uncle, Melikazarian, one of the wealthiest Armenian capitalists of Tiflis (in Russian Transcaucasia), was financing his education.[4] Maro was a vivacious and intelligent woman with a fiery disposition. After her graduation from the Tiflis Gymnasium she had gone to study in St. Petersburg, where she had become a member of a secret Russian revolutionary band. Because of political difficulties Maro had fled to Paris, where she had met Nazarbekian.[5] Both were concentrating on the social sciences, from which they gained broader knowledge of the economic and political theories of the day. They were both very much in favor of the proposed convention for the formation of an Armenian revolutionary organization, and their enthusiasm made an indelible impression on four Russian Armenian students, Gabriel Kafian (Shemavon) and Ruben Khan-Azat, both specializing in agriculture; Nicoli Matinian,[6] and Mekertitch Manutcharian, all of whom were then in Geneva.

The constant subject of conversation among these students was the conditions in Turkish Armenia and the necessity for a revolutionary organization such as had been proposed in many of the articles in the *Armenia*.[7] At this time (the summer of 1886), Avetis Nazarbekian sent a letter to Portugalian in which he suggested that, since the question of holding a convention had been postponed, donations should be sent to Portugalian for a future revolutionary organization of which Portugalian should be the temporary treasurer. Portugalian refused the offer, saying that he had already founded an organization, the bylaws of which would be published in a short time.[8]

When the students realized that they would not get the coöperation of Portugalian in forming the new revolutionary organization, they decided to act alone. Gabriel Kafian went to Montpellier to enlist the interest of Armenians there. On his return to Geneva he brought with him four Armenian students who seemed to be in harmony with his ideas. The students were Mattheos Shahazizian, who had written many revolutionary articles in the *Armenia*, Gevorg Gharadjian, Christopher Ohanian, and Poghos Afrikian. After a few months three of the students, Shahazizian, Afrikian, and Manutcharian, broke off relations with the rest of the group. By the late summer of 1886 only six Armenian students remained in the Geneva group: Avetis Nazarbekian and Mariam Vardanian from Paris, Gevorg Gharadjian and Christopher Ohanian from Montpellier, and Ruben Khan-Azat and Gabriel Kafian from Geneva.[9]

These six students, who had made Geneva their headquarters, published and distributed a pamphlet by Nazarbekian entitled *Armenian Eating Chameleon (Hayaker Kamelion)*. In the pamphlet these students severed their relations with Portugalian, the editor of the *Armenia*. Meanwhile, Portugalian published the bylaws of his newly founded organization, the Armenian Patriotic Union. The purpose of this Union was to send Armenian youth to Europe, where they were to be educated and were to return thereafter to improve Turkish Armenia. Portugalian's newly-formed organization had nothing to do with the armed revolution that had been advocated by many Armenians in the pages of *Armenia*.[10]

Portugalian's former students in Van had responded to the journal *Armenia* by forming the Armenakan Party, which was operating on a small scale in the province of Van (see chapter iv). In contrast to the Armenakan Party, the six Armenian students whose headquarters was in Geneva had in mind designs for a large, powerful, active revolutionary party that would encompass the whole territory of Turkish Armenia and would have branches in the Armenian communities abroad. Dissatisfied with Portugalian's failure to give forceful leadership, the young students in Geneva decided, in 1886, to publish their own paper in opposition to *Armenia*. They began to raise funds for the journal by holding a "Caucasian Evening" at which they presented a drama and dance performance and had a buffet dinner. This social affair was attended by many students, faculty members, and friends, and proved to be financially profitable. The students then wrote to the Mekhitharist Monastery in Vienna for a font of Armenian type.[11] In the meantime they printed circulars and distributed them. Many were mailed to Armenians who were potential adherents of the revolutionary party, but this campaign had no success. They also drew up a program for the new revolutionary party.

THE PROGRAM

In the latter part of 1886 the six Geneva students chose a committee of three, consisting of Mariam Vardanian, Avetis Nazarbekian, and Gevorg Gharadjian, to draft the plan for the future organization.[12] The plan, which later became the program of the Hunchakian Revolutionary Party, may be summarized as follows:

I. The ideological impact of the times led them to a new view of society. They could now penetrate into current world conditions and see the inequalities that existed everywhere. The vast majority of the people were being oppressed and exploited by a small minority, who by virtue of their privileged positions were able to control and rule the impoverished masses.

To achieve full and real freedom for this large majority, it was imperative to establish a new order based on humanitarian and socialistic principles. The present state of affairs had to be destroyed by means of a revolution. Then, on the ashes of the old society, a new one might be built, based upon "economic truths" and "socialistic justice."

II. The immediate objective of the party was the political and national independence of Turkish Armenia. The conditions of the Armenians in Asiatic Turkey were described and the need to concentrate Hunchak activities in this area was explained. Here was set forth also the exploitation of the Armenians by the government, the aristocracy, and the capitalists through high taxes, land seizure, and the deprivation of the fruits of labor. Besides these injustices, the people were shorn of their political rights and were forced to remain silent in their position as slaves of their parasitic overlords. They were not free to worship as they pleased and lived forever in fear of marauding tribesmen. In order to save the Armenians from this slavery, the Hunchaks proposed to direct them on the road to socialism and to work toward their immediate objective, the freedom of Turkish Armenia.

After the immediate objective had been realized, certain political and economic aims were to be put into operation. The political aims were:

1. A perpetual popular Legislative Assembly elected in free elections by universal and direct suffrage. The voters were to have full powers in regard to all national administrative questions.

   a. The peoples' representatives were to be elected from all ranks of society.

   b. The seat of the Legislative Assembly was to be in one of the important cities of Armenia.

2. Extensive provincial autonomy.

3. Extensive communal autonomy.

   a. Concerning points two and three—the people were to have the authority to elect all public administrators.

4. Every individual, without distinction of position or wealth, was to have the right to hold office.

5. Complete freedom of press, speech, conscience, assembly, organizations, and electoral agitation.

6. The person and home of every individual was to be inviolable.

7. Universal military service.

The economic aims of the new party were to be determined after careful investigation into the needs and desires of the people. Two economic objectives were described in the program. These were the establishmnt of a progressive system of taxation above a certain income bracket and a system of universal compulsory education.

III. The Hunchak program advocated revolution as the only means of reaching the immediate objective. The arena of revolutionary activity was designated as Turkish Armenia. The Hunchaks said that the existing social organization in Turkish Armenia could be changed by violence against the Turkish government and described the following methods: Propaganda, Agitation, Terror, Organization, and Peasant and Worker Activities.

Propaganda was to be directed to the people to educate them toward two goals. The party was to explain to them the basic reasons and the proper time for revolution against the government, thereby indoctrinating them with the basic idea of revolution. This goal, however, was not sufficient in itself. The people had to have a knowledge of the social order that was to be established *after* the successful revolution.

Agitation and *Terror* were needed to "elevate the spirit of the people." Demonstrations against the government, refusal to pay taxes, demands for reforms, and hatred of the aristocracy were part of the party's agitation campaign. The people were also to be incited against their enemies and were to "profit" from the retaliatory actions of these same enemies.

Terror was to be used as a method of protecting the people and winning their confidence in the Hunchak program. The party aimed at terrorizing the Ottoman government, thus contributing toward lowering the prestige of that regime and working toward its complete disintegration. The government itself was not to be the only focus of terroristic tactics. The Hunchaks wanted to annihilate the most dangerous of the Armenian and Turkish individuals who were then working for the government, as well as to destroy all spies and informers. To assist them in carrying out all of these terroristic acts, the party was to organize an exclusive branch, specifically devoted to performing acts of terrorism.

The *Organization* of the party was to be a centralized system directed by a central executive committee. The Hunchaks believed that the revolution could not be won by the participation of the party organization alone. They considered it absolutely essential to win the active support of the peasants and workers. There were to be two large revolutionary groups, one of peasants and the other of workers. Besides these separate groups, there would be guerrilla bands, composed of both peasants and workers, who would become fighting units during the anticipated revolution. The role of the peasants and workers was not to end after the victory, for the Hunchaks saw in these two groups the very basis of the society that was to be thereafter established. The peasants and workers were to protect the gains and interests of the people, and were to take the reins of government and rule according to democratic principles. The plan giving the details of these governing principles was to be published at a later date.

IV. The most opportune time to institute the general rebellion for carrying out the immediate objective was when Turkey was engaged in a war. The Hunchaks were ready to fight not only the Ottoman regime, but any other power that wished to dominate Turkish Armenia.

The non-Armenians of Turkish Armenia were not overlooked. The party declared that in order to better the condition of the non-Armenians, it was necessary to get the sympathy of other minorities, such as the Assyrians and Kurds, for the revolutionary cause. These groups were to help bring about a revolution against the Turkish government when circumstances should be favorable.

V. This final part of the program pointed out that the greatest number of Armenians lived in Turkish Armenia, and that the area also comprised the largest part of historic Armenia. Here the majority of the Armenian people were living under impossible conditions imposed by their Ottoman rulers, as the Great Powers had recognized when they sanctioned reform in Turkish Armenia in Article LXI of the Treaty of Berlin.

These considerations led the Hunchaks to demand that

all revolutionary forces devote themselves to winning the independence of Turkish Armenia. Again, the party cautioned its followers against the selfish interests of other powers in regard to this region, and predicted that, after the fall of the already bankrupt Ottoman regime, the European Powers would systematically carve up the empire, including Turkish Armenia, for themselves. The Hunchaks therefore warned against allowing Turkish Armenia merely to pass from the hands of one oppressive overlord to another. Here they again restated their "immediate objective"—the political independence of Turkish Armenia.

The program envisaged a continuation of the fighting after the establishment of an independent Turkish Armenia. The revolution would then be extended into the Russian and Persian dominated areas of Armenia, with the purpose of establishing a politically independent Armenian federative democratic republic composed of Turkish, Russian, and Persian Armenia. The independent country would then lead the Armenians in the homeland and abroad toward the Hunchak "future objective"—a socialistic society for all humanity.

In a short note inserted at the end of the program, the Hunchaks reaffirmed the need for a government based on democratic principles, which they considered an absolute necessity for the progress of all humanity. Progress, it added, was impossible under the Turkish regime, or in any other autocratic state—even in a government ruled by an Armenian nobility or by Armenian autocrats. The sole guarantee for Armenian progress was a free people's government in an independent Armenia.[13]

Two predominant objectives were revealed in the program. The immediate objective was the independence of Turkish Armenia; the future objective was Socialism. These two objectives were complementary. Both liberation and the building of socialism were to be striven for at the same time. The breadth of the political and ideological objectives of the Hunchaks is noteworthy. They were the only Armenian political party in the nineteenth century whose program unambiguously demanded an independent and unified Armenian Republic, and beyond this, a socialistic order for all the peoples of the world.

The program of the Hunchakian Revolutionary Party was both socialistic and nationalistic. The first part proclaimed the Marxian class struggle and predicted the triumph of the exploited classes through revolution. It called for "economic truths," which, although not described in detail, can be attributed to Marxian influences. Hunchak adherence to Marxian dialectical materialism is later defined in the pages of its party organ and other official publications.

The plan as a whole reflected the influence of Russian revolutionary thought. The "methods" outlined in part three very nearly duplicated those put forth in the Russian *Narodnaya Volya (People's Will)*, and strikingly coincided with it in regard to propaganda, agitation, and terror. Also following *Narodnaya Volya*, the organization was based on a centralized system of administration. The proposed use of guerrilla bands, however, was probably a result of Greek and Bulgarian revolutionary influence.

It is not surprising that these students were so strongly influenced by the Russian *Narodniki*. All of them were either born in Russia or educated there, and all were well acquainted with Russian revolutionary ideology.[14] Mariam Vardanian (Maro), a member of the committee that wrote the plans for the revolutionary organization, had worked with the Russian revolutionaries in St. Petersburg and, according to the late Mushegh Seropian, hers was the ruling intellect of the group.[15]

The Geneva students also associated and were on good terms with the Russian Social Democrats G. V. Plekhanov and Vera Zasulich, who were then in Geneva.[16] Both had been former members of the secret Russian revolutionary societies *Zemlya i Volya* (Land and Freedom) and *Cherny Peredyel* (Black-Earth Distribution), and at the time of the founding of the Hunchakian Revolutionary Party, Plekhanov was known as the leading Russian exponent of Marxism.

Nationalism is evident throughout the program. The immediate objective itself—the independence of Turkish Armenia—shows the patriotism of the young founders. Part two is almost entirely devoted to a sympathetic description of the Armenians in Asiatic Turkey. Nowhere in the program is there any sign of conflict between national aspirations and universal socialism. For the Hunchaks, nationalism and socialism were mutually compatible and could be harmoniously developed together.

Although the Hunchaks were strong nationalists, this did not prevent them from concerning themselves with the condition of the non-Armenians in Armenia. Yet, while Assyrians and Kurds are specifically referred to in their program, there is no mention of the Turkish people. This is a conspicuous omission. But it should be noted that the party, from its early days, made a distinction between the Turkish government and the Turkish people.[17] The party did not necessarily identify the Turkish people with their corrupt administrator, and worked with Turk as well as with Greek, Assyrian, Druz, Kurd, and Turkoman revolutionists.[18]

The students unanimously accepted the plan that had been drawn up by their committee. The name of the new revolutionary organization had not as yet been chosen. In the sequel, it was named after its party organ, the *Hunchak* (or *Hentchak*), the Armenian word for bell. The name was reminiscent of the journal *Kolokol* (Bell) published by Alexander Herzen, a contributor to the ideology of the Russian social revolutionaries.

THE FOUNDING AND ACTIVITIES, 1887–1890

The party of the Hunchaks, founded in Geneva in August, 1887,[19] did not have an official name until 1890, when it became known as the Hunchakian Revolutionary Party. The seven official founders were Avetis Nazarbekian, Mariam Vardanian (Maro), Gevorg Gharadjian, Ruben Khan-Azat, Christopher Ohanian, Gabriel Kafian, and Levon Stepanian.[20]

When at last the Armenian type arrived in Geneva, the students began at once to learn how to set it up and to prepare the paper. Nazarbekian and Gharadjian, who were the best equipped in the Armenian language, were appointed to write the articles for the first issue. These were read orally to the rest of the students to obtain their approval. When Gharadjian's article was rejected he was so angered that he broke off relations with the others of the group.[21] Nazarbekian's articles were accepted and published in the first issue of the *Hunchak (Bell)*. The paper first appeared in Geneva in November, 1887, three months after the party was formed.

The first editorial of the *Hunchak* appealed to its readers to join the party and spread revolutionary activity. Although the ideology of the party was socialistic, help from the capitalist European Powers was to be accepted if any was forthcoming. The first editorial read in part:[22]

The accomplishment of the freedom of Armenia from Turkey cannot be realized from the outside alone, but it can succeed from within. If we fold our hands and wait for European intervention, the Armenian people will sink into unbearable misfortune. It is true that there may be created such political upheavals that a particular European government might find it profitable to bring forth the Armenian Question and might, in a direct or indirect manner, demand its just solution. Just as in the past, such possible circumstances make it necessary for us to prepare for such an occasion from which to benefit. However, we must add that the present policy and diplomacy of the European Powers is like a windmill—it turns in this direction of the wind today, while tomorrow, according to the pleasures of the same wind, it may turn in the opposite direction.

The publication of the *Hunchak* was accomplished in complete secrecy. Three false addresses were given so that no one would know the paper was being published in Geneva. All correspondence and gifts went to three addresses, in Paris, Montpellier, and Geneva. The students were particularly careful about copies of the paper that were sent to Turkey and Russia, since they could not gain legal entry there. Such copies were printed on thin paper, wrapped in packages, and posted at intervals from Paris, Geneva, and Leipzig.[23]

The students published their program for the first time in the October–November 1888 issue of the *Hunchak,* and also in a separate pamphlet.[24] The implementation of the Hunchak program encountered strong resistance from various intransigent religious, nationalistic, and social groups in the Ottoman Empire.

To get the sympathy and coöperation of the Moslem masses, the Hunchaks distributed among them propaganda literature in the Turkish language,[25] but considering the profound differences that existed between the Moslems and Christians, the Hunchak efforts were bound to encounter great opposition. The Pan-Islamic movement, which had been fostered by Sultan Abdul Hamid II, had greatly deepened the cleavage between the followers of the two faiths. This new Islamic movement stressed the superiority of Islam and had as its object the unifying of all the Moslems under the Ottoman Caliph—Sultan Abdul Hamid II.

The socialistic ideas of the Hunchaks were disapproved by some important Armenian groups as well, especially by the Russian Armenian bourgeoisie. At first the latter extended some help to the Hunchaks in their revolutionary activity, but at no time were they willing to accept socialistic doctrines. The initial coöperation came to an abrupt end, and the wealthy Russian Armenian bourgeoisie, as a whole, decided to resist the spread of Hunchak influence. The well-to-do Armenians in Turkey also found it to their advantage to condemn Hunchak ideas and activity.[26] Despite any such ideological enemies however, the Hunchaks were still determined to launch their program in Turkish Armenia.

The Hunchaks quite naturally chose Constantinople for the center of their organization and activity in Turkey. Within seven months they enlisted seven hundred members in the capital. Most of the members came from the educated class; they were mainly persons who held positions in foreign consulates and maritime companies.[27] The Hunchaks sent out leaders from Geneva and Constantinople to numerous towns and villages in Turkey to organize the Armenians. The places in Asiatic Turkey to which these leaders went included Bafra, Marsovan, Amasia, Tokat, Yozgat, Akin, Arabkir, and Trebizond.[28] It was not long before hundreds of young Armenians in Turkey, Russia, and Persia rallied to the Hunchak banner. The Hunchaks also attracted supporters in Europe and the United States. In 1890 the union of the separate groups resulted in the adoption of the party's official name, the Hunchakian Revolutionary Party.[29]

The party translated the *Communist Manifesto* into Armenian and published Marxist writings in the pages of the *Hunchak,* but these had no important effect upon the Armenians. Many party members were not socialists by persuasion, but rather joined the Hunchaks because of their immediate objective of winning the freedom of Turkish Armenia. The Hunchaks, in fact, did not insist that those who joined them should adopt socialistic principles.

This fact cannot be over-emphasized, for it will account for much of the future strife within the ranks of the party.

THE DEMONSTRATION OF KUM KAPU

The Hunchakian Revolutionary Party revealed its power for the first time in Constantinople on Sunday, July 15, 1890, when it organized the Demonstration of Kum Kapu. The purpose of the demonstration was ". . . to awaken the maltreated Armenians and to make the Sublime Porte fully aware of the miseries of the Armenians."[30] The demonstration started in the Armenian Cathedral in the Armenian Quarter of Kum Kapu. Here Patriarch Khoren Ashegian was addressing a large congregation gathered for the Vartavar (Transfiguration of our Lord) services. In the cathedral, Haruthiun Tjankulian, a party member, read a Hunchak protest directed to the Sultan which advocated Armenian reforms. Afterward, he went to the Patriarchate and smashed the Turkish coat of arms.[31] Although the Armenian Patriarch protested, he was forced by the Hunchaks to join them in presenting the protest to the Sultan. Hardly had the procession toward Yildiz Palace started when it was blocked by Turkish soldiers, and a riot ensued in which a number of people were killed and wounded.[32] Tjankulian, who was considered the Hunchak hero of the demonstration, was arrested and sentenced to life imprisonment. The Porte ignored the reforms urged by the Hunchaks, and the European Powers did not support them. Instead, a number of Hunchak leaders, as well as other demonstrators, were killed, wounded, and imprisoned. The casualties were not confined to Armenians alone, for a Turkish gendarme and a soldier were also killed during the riot.[33] Although the Demonstration of Kum Kapu was obviously unsuccessful, it did have an importance, for it ". . . appears to be the first occasion since the conquest of Constantinople by the Turks on which Christians dared resist soldiers in Stamboul." [34]

The Hunchaks believed that the Demonstration of Kum Kapu, though in some degree a failure, had nonetheless served to arouse the European Powers in regard to the Armenian Question. The *Hunchak*[35] wrote that England and Russia were vitally concerned with the whole Eastern Question, but could not agree between themselves about it. England wished to control Crete, and Russia was desirous of adding Turkish Armenia to its own territory.[36] The Hunchaks opposed Russian territorial aims and insisted on a completely independent Armenia. They would reject any European proposals that were contrary to that supreme objective, and declared themselves ready to shed their "last drop of blood" for the cause.[37]

These party declarations were bold statements, which, when analyzed, bring up the following questions. How much blood was to be sacrificed for the revolution and who were to die for the cause—only a few Hunchak revolutionaries or numerous Armenian inhabitants of the interior provinces? What would be the value of an independent country whose people had been nearly wiped out in the revolutionary process? The opponents of the Hunchaks were not willing to see a large part of their nation destroyed in order that the Hunchaks might attain a dubious political goal.

But the Hunchaks were not to be deterred. They continued to organize demonstrations and insurrections in towns and villages inhabited by Armenians. In 1891 they joined the Oriental Federation, which was composed of Macedonian, Albanian, Cretan, and Greek revolutionaries,[38] hoping to synchronize their efforts. Hunchak revolutionary activities were markedly evident in 1892, and even more so in 1893. The Hunchaks made the most of Turkish oppression by spreading various alarming reports through their publications, including exaggerations of Turkish atrocities. Hunchak revolutionaries posted placards on public buildings and walls of houses in the regions of Marsovan, Yozgat, Amasia, Chorum, Tokat, Angora, Sivas, and Diarbekiar.[39] These placards were in Turkish and were addressed to Moslems everywhere, including India, encouraging them to rebel against oppression. By such methods the Hunchaks hoped to arouse the Turkish people against their government.[40]

On January 5, 1893, the placards were posted in Marsovan on the premises of Anatolia College, which was administered by the American Missionary Board. This act aroused the Turkish government against the missionaries.[41] The Reverend Edwin Bliss has written that Professors Thoumaian and Kayayan, who were members of the faculty, were accused, though without proof, of having something to do with the placards, and they were arrested and imprisoned. Although the Turkish authorities may not have had definite evidence against Professor Thoumaian, we know from the Hunchak Aderbed (Sarkis Mubaihadjian) that Thoumaian was carefully watched by the government and that, as early as 1891, he and other Hunchaks were consulting with one another and planning revolution against the state.

In 1893 the Turkish government arrested and hanged many revolutionaries as well as other prominent Armenian intellectuals, merchants, and clergymen, especially in the region of Marsovan and Yozgat. In the same year the famous Hunchak hero and revolutionary pioneer, Zhirayr Poyadjian, brother of Murat (Hambardsum Poyadjian), was also hanged by the Turkish government in Yozgat. Also in 1893 Damadian, another Hunchak leader, was arrested on the road between Moush and Sassun.[42]

THE SASSUN REBELLION

In the region of Sassun (located in the province of Bitlis), a revolutionary named Damadian, the Hunchaks, and others had been exciting hostilities between the Kurds and the Armenians;[43] and in August, 1894, an actual rebellion broke out. The Sassun Rebellion represented one of the major efforts of the Hunchakian Revolutionary Party against the Turkish government and the Kurds.

In the region of Sassun the Armenians had been paying tribute (*hafir*) to the Kurds to assure themselves of Kurdish protection and assistance. The size of the annual tribute was assessed according to the resources of the Armenians. Any refusal to pay elicited prompt and violent Kurdish reprisals; yet, somehow, the two peoples got along without actual fighting until about 1890–1891. There were two primary reasons why hostilities should flare up at that time: (1) the establishment of a solidarity among the Kurdish tribes through religious propaganda of the sheiks; and (2) agitation among the Armenians, which had been started by such men as Damadian and later continued by the Hunchak Murat (Hambardsum Poyadjian). The rebellion began when the Kurds, secretly encouraged by the Turkish government, attacked and plundered the Armenian village of Talori.

In the spring of 1894 the Hunchak leader Murat had arrived in the region of Sassun. He too, like Damadian, encouraged the Armenians to refuse to pay the *hafir* and to free themselves from what he called a system of bondage. Murat and a band of followers started minor acts of aggression against the Kurds, who countered with attacks against the Armenians. The government interpreted the Armenian activities in Sassun as a rebellion against the state and sent troops to quell it.[44]

Under Murat's leadership the Armenians resisted the far superior Turkish forces for more than a month; but the Turks finally succeeded in capturing Murat and a number of his men[45] and in subduing the Armenians. This latest Armenian uprising and the Turkish reprisals had aroused Great Britain, France, and Russia, who sent a

Commission of Inquiry to Sassun to investigate the situation. The Commission found that the sole crimes of which the Armenians were guilty were that they (1) had sheltered Murat and his band; (2) had indulged in a few isolated acts of brigandage; and (3) had resisted the government troops under conditions that were not entirely clear.[46] The Commission concluded that the thorough Turkish devastation of the region was far in excess of what the punishment for the revolt should have been. It formally stated its belief that the misery to which the Armenians were reduced could not be justified.[47]

The Hunchaks considered the Sassun Rebellion a great victory for their party as well as for the Armenian cause. They believed that because of their revolutionary activities, particularly in Sassun, the European Powers at last had recognized the crying need for reforms in Armenia. On May 11, 1895, indeed, Great Britain, France, and Russia sent a memorandum to Sultan Abdul Hamid II urging reforms in the six Turkish Armenian provinces.[48]

The *Memorandum*[49] included a *Project of Reforms for the Eastern Provinces of Asia Minor*.[50] Instead of signing and enforcing this program, Sultan Abdul Hamid procrastinated as usual. In the meantime the persecution of the Armenians continued, especially in the Armenian provinces.

THE DEMONSTRATION OF BAB ALI

In a protest against the Sultan's refusal to decree reforms, the Hunchaks staged the Demonstration of Bab Ali in Constantinople on September 18/30, 1895. The demonstration was accompanied by much bloodshed. At this time the Hunchaks decided to present their own petition—which they called their "Protest-Demand"—to the Sultan. For a better understanding of this demonstration we should first

examine the organization of the Hunchakian Revolutionary Party in Constantinople.

In the Turkish capital there were two separate Hunchak
committees. One was the Board of Directors; the other was
the Executive Committee. The Board gave instructions for
nearly all of the revolutionary activity in Turkey, with the
knowledge and approval of the General Headquarters at
Geneva. The Executive Committee of Constantinople directed the organizational work according to the instructions
of the Board of Directors. The members of the Board of
Directors and the Executive Committee did not know one
another, but there was complete coöperation between them.
This coöperation was achieved by having one man, called
the Representative of the Two Committees, who acted as
the intermediary between the two groups.[51]

The Executive Committee, after receiving the order
from the Board of Directors to organize the Demonstration
of Bab Ali, chose three men to supervise the project. The
leader was Karo Sahakian (Heverhili Karon).[52] Patriarch
Mattheos Ismirlian, hearing rumors of a demonstration,
called Karo and asked if the rumors were true. If there was
to be a demonstration, the Patriarch insisted that it should
be a peaceful one. Karo also wished a peaceful demonstration, but some members of the Committee did not agree;
the matter was left to the Board of Directors, who decided
that it should be peaceful.[53]

Months of secret preparations ended on September
16/28, 1895. On that day the Hunchaks presented the following letter, written in French, to the foreign embassies
and to the Turkish government:[54]

Your Excellency,

The Armenians of Constantinople have decided to make
shortly a demonstration, of a strictly peaceful character, in
order to give expression to their wishes with regard to the

reforms to be introduced in the Armenian provinces. As it is not intended that this demonstration shall be in any way aggressive the intervention of the police and military for the purpose of preventing it may have regrettable consequences, for which we disclaim beforehand all responsibility.

Organizing Committee
(Seal of the Hintchak Society)[55]

The demonstration took place on Monday, September 18, 1895, two days after the foreign embassies were informed. The Turkish government had itself taken security measures; soldiers were posted on the streets around administrative buildings, and the police in Constantinople were alerted for possible action. It was almost noon on Monday when the Hunchak leaders entered the Armenian Patriarchate, from which they were to lead thousands of demonstrators to the palace of the Sultan.[56]

The Hunchak Karo, the head of the demonstration, was to present the petition to the Sultan on behalf both of the Armenians of Constantinople and of the six Armenian provinces. The petition, written by the Hunchak Board of Directors, complained against (1) the systematic massacre of the Armenians by the Turkish government, (2) the unjust arrest and the cruel punishments of prisoners, (3) the Kurdish injustices, (4) the corruption of tax collectors, and (5) the massacre at Sassun. It demanded: (1) equality before the law; freedom of the press; freedom of speech; and freedom of assembly; (2) that all persons under arrest be given the right of *habeas corpus,* and that the Armenians be granted permission to bear arms if the Kurds could not be disarmed; (3) a new political delineation of the six Armenian provinces; (4) a European governor for the six Armenian provinces; and (5) financial and land reforms.[57]

In their petition the Hunchaks expressed the principle of "egalitarianism" by asking that the rights demanded for themselves also be given such other Ottoman subjects as were without such rights. They warned that if the situation continued as it was the Ottoman Empire itself would suffer.[58]

Karo Sahakian and some of the demonstrators, after reaching the Gates of Bab Ali, were denied entrance by the officer in charge, and Karo was seized by the *zaptiehs* (Turkish police). Severe fighting and violence broke out at once. In the meantime Karo was brought before a Turkish official, who, after receiving the petition, had him imprisoned. On that Monday, and for several days ensuing, hundreds of demonstrators were imprisoned. The prisons became crowded with wounded men, and scores of dead bodies were collected from the streets of Constantinople.[59]

The rioting and bloodshed in Constantinople alarmed the Turkish government and disturbed Europe. The Ottoman Council of Ministers assembled to discuss the situation, while some of the leading European papers gave much attention to the rioting in Constantinople. The London *Times* on October 1, 1895, described "the affair" as one of "a most grave character." It went on to say that "the rioters, who were armed, offered a most stubborn resistance," and that "the Armenians, on being arrested, were thrown to the ground, disarmed, beaten, and then bound." [60]

Even before the Demonstration of Bab Ali, the Europeans were of course aware of the Armenian Question, as it was generally referred to at the time. During the years 1894-1895, hundreds of books, pamphlets, and articles relating to the Armenian atrocities were disseminated in Europe (especially in England) and in the United States. British public opinion, in particular, favored a peaceful and friendly solution of the Armenian Question. In any event, the Powers were now made to realize the seriousness of the situation and they (England, France, and Russia, supported by Germany, Austria, and Italy) demanded that the Sultan introduce the Armenian Reform Program of May 11, 1895.[61]

The pressure of the European governments induced Sultan Abdul Hamid to sign the Armenian Reform Program on October 17, 1895, about a month after the bloody demonstration. The Hunchakian Revolutionary Party considered this a great victory, and their party organ, the *Hunchak,* carried the following:

A telegram received today, the 18th, communicates the news that at last the Sultan, by signing an official *irade,* has accepted the recently revised Armenian Reform Program presented to him by the three Great Powers in May.

Thus, at last, we have forced our ferocious executioner to recognize the rights of the Armenian people, to listen to their voice, and to bow before their aspirations and moral strength.

Thus, at last, today all the Armenians and the whole world are witnesses to the Party's great victory, which we won by the expenditure of so much blood and zeal.

Thus, this work of ours has been great and triumphant.[62]

Unfortunately, the Hunchaks and the Armenians in general were too optimistic. The signing of the Armenian Reform Program by Abdul Hamid did not bring peace to the Armenians in Turkey. Like so many of the Sultanic *irades* (decrees), this one, too, became a dead letter, and the persecution of the Armenians continued.

THE ZEITUN REBELLION

Previous to the signing of the Reform Program, Zeitun had once again become the center of Armenian protest against the Ottoman regime. Since the Zeitun Rebellion of 1862 the inhabitants of Zeitun never ceased criticizing the central government. Their resentment was heightened in 1878, when, following another rebellion, the Turks built a fortress at the entrance of the town. On October 12, 1895, the Zeitunlis rebelled once again—this time under the guidance of the Hunchakian Revolutionary Party. The six Hunchak leaders in Zeitun—Aghassi, Apah, Heratchia, Neshan, Meleh, and Karapet—hoped that the uprising of Armenians there would be quickly followed by Armenians throughout Cilicia.[63]

Before the insurrection gained momentum, Turkish forces attacked Alabash, an Armenian village near Zeitun.[64] This was the beginning of fighting that was to involve Zeitun as well as the numerous nearby villages. After four months of fierce fighting the Zeitun Rebellion ended on February 1, 1896,[65] following the intervention of the European Powers. After laborious negotiations the peace terms formulated by the six European consuls of Aleppo were accepted by the Porte. These peace terms, as summarized by the French ambassador to Constantinople, were as follows:

Surrender of all war arms; a general armistice; expulsion from the territory of the Empire of five foreign revolutionary committee members [all Hunchaks]; abandonment by the Porte of all arrears of taxes; promise of reduction of land taxes; and application of reforms contained in the general act.[66]

However, these peace terms, like the Armenian Reform Program, soon became non-effective.

The most active era of the Hunchakian Revolutionary Party ended in 1896. The primary purpose of the party's activities since 1887 had been to bring about European intervention with the Porte in favor of freeing Turkish Armenia. But, as it turned out, the Hunchaks had little success in securing European support.

The result of the Demonstration of Kum Kapu (1890) was the sacrifice of many Armenian lives without either persuading Turkey to carry out the promised reforms or convincing the European Powers that they should force

Turkey to do so. The rebellion precipitated by the Hunchaks at Sassun (1894), which cost the lives of thousands of Armenians, succeeded in bringing a Commission of Inquiry to Sassun, and compelled the European Powers to present the Armenian Reform Program to the Sultan on May 11, 1895. But history showed that the program of reforms proposed by the European Powers was not worth these thousands of human lives. Although the immediate result of the Demonstration of Bab Ali (September 18, 1895) had been the signing of the Reform Program by Sultan Hamid, the bloody demonstration in the long run was of little value because the Program was never enforced. Even the military victory of the Hunchaks in the Zeitun Rebellion of October, 1895–February, 1896, when the Turks suffered heavier casualties than did the Zeitunlis, was hollow, since the Turks could afford heavy sacrifices of men, and no amelioration of conditions followed.

The Hunchaks relied in vain on the European Powers to use coercive measures against the Sultan for the purpose of making him put into effect the Armenian Reform Program which he had signed in October, 1895. The activities of the Hunchaks had only helped to enrage Sultan Abdul Hamid II, who already hated the Armenians and feared that they, like the Balkan countries, would obtain their freedom.

It was evident that the Sultan had decided to settle the Armenian Question in his own way—by the massacres of 1894 and 1895, culminating in that of 1896. Thus, the year 1896 brought one of the blackest pages in the history of the Armenian people, as well as a near deathblow to the Hunchakian Revolutionary Party.

SPLIT IN THE PARTY

In 1896 there was much dissension among the members of the Hunchakian Revolutionary Party. The two primary causes for this disunity were socialism and differences concerning tactics. Many of the members of the party believed that the European Powers had abandoned the Armenian Question because of the socialist doctrine of the Hunchaks. These members insisted that the socialist doctrine be eliminated from the party's program and that the party should work solely for the political independence of Armenia.[67]

The dissenters also blamed Nazarbekian, the editor of the *Hunchak,* for their party failures. They criticized him for writing editorials that advocated insurrections and incited fighting wherever there were Armenian revolutionaries. They likewise accused him of writing indiscreet editorials that gave the Turkish officials much information that was detrimental to the revolutionary cause.[68]

The party soon fell into two factions. One was the pro-Nazarbekian faction, which was in accord with the existing program of the Hunchakian Revolutionary Party; the other was the anti-Nazarbekian faction, which desired the elimination of socialism from the party program and called for changes in tactics and administration.

In contrast to conflicts in European socialist organizations of the day, the rift in the Hunchaks was not based on variations in socialist ideology. The anti-Nazarbekian faction wished to eliminate socialism completely from the program, leaving no room for compromise within a socialistic framework. The August 1896 convention of the anti-Nazarbekians firmly excluded socialism from their own program, saying that it was not necessary for the freedom of Turkish Armenia; at the same time they decided to work in absolute secrecy. Two years later (1898), at a meeting in Alexandria, Egypt, they reasserted their London decisions of 1896 and named their organization the Reformed Hunchakian Party.[69]

The anti-Nazarbekians demanded that a meeting be held to elect a new Central Committee, but this demand was refused by Nazarbekian and his wife Maro, both of whom were on the Central Committee.[70] The pro-Nazarbekians accused their adversaries of trying to hold a meeting before that of the Second General Congress of the Hunchaks, which was to take place in September of that same year (1896).[71] The anti-Nazarbekians, whose request for a meeting was refused, decided not to wait for the convocation of the General Congress, but held a convention of their faction in London, in August, 1896. The inter-party conflict of the Hunchaks at London in 1896 took place in the shadow of the Fourth Congress of the Second International, held July 27–31, 1896.[72] It is not known whether there was any direct connection between the Hunchak clash and the Socialist International Congress at London.[73]

The Hunchakian Revolutionary Party, now no longer including the anti-Nazarbekian faction, held its Second General Congress in London during September, 1896. In that year the party decided to abandon its old policy of public demonstrations, but its organ, the *Hunchak,* persisted in maintaining socialist doctrines.[74] Many pamphlets, mostly translations from Marxist ideology, continued to be printed,[75] and the party continued the publication of *Aptak (Slap),* a satirical journal on political and national affairs, which was first published in Athens during the year 1894.[76]

The 1896 rift among the Hunchaks markedly weakened the party. Still another political party, later known as the Armenian Revolutionary Federation or Dashnaktsuthiun, which had been established on Russian soil in 1890, became a prominent revolutionary organization. The Hunchakian Revolutionary Party had been invited to join the Dashnaktsuthiun in 1890 and had temporarily merged with the new federation, but this association endured for less than a year. After certain disruptions, which will be described in chapter vii, the Hunchaks completely separated from the newly formed party and continued as a separate organization. They continued to form Hunchak branches in cities and towns in Turkish, Russian, and Persian Armenia and in communities among the Armenians of the Diaspora, as far off as the United States. These branches remained in existence even after 1896, when the most active period of the Hunchakian Revolutionary Party came to an end.

While the Hunchaks were launching their vigorous campaign in Turkish Armenia, the Dashnaktsuthiun was establishing a firm foothold among the Armenians in Russia and was beginning to make itself felt in Turkish Armenia. Previous to the establishment of this new political party in 1890, revolutionary circles had already existed among the Armenians in Russia during the 'sixties, 'seventies, and 'eighties. We shall next consider these early organizations in Russia, which were devoted to aiding and if possible liberating the downtrodden Armenians under Turkish rule.

VI

Revolutionary Activities among the Armenians of Russia, 1868–1890

The Armenian revolutionary groups and societies that were established on Russian soil during the nineteenth century comprised an important part of the Armenian Revolutionary Movement. Russian Armenians, especially the intellectuals, had for some time been aware of the plight of their compatriots on the Turkish side of the frontier. Among the leading Armenian revolutionary propagandists were a number of writers who lived under the Tsar. Among them were Khatchatur Abovian, Mikael Nalbandian, Kamar Katiba (Rafael Patkanian), and Raffi (Hakob Melik-Hakobian), whose activities have been described in chapter ii.

Khatchatur Abovian had exemplified the fighting spirit of the new age during the first half of the nineteenth century. Ardent patriots and revolutionists followed in his path during the succeeding decades. Mikael Nalbandian helped to expand the Armenian Revolutionary Movement and connect it with that of Russia. Kamar Katiba and

Raffi used the pen to embolden their people to throw off their chains. As early as 1854, Katiba had helped found a literary society in Moscow with patriotic objectives. Raffi, a Persian Armenian, lived for many years in Tiflis and wrote historical novels that encouraged a people's uprising for a new and better Armenia.

REVOLUTIONARY GROUPS IN RUSSIA DURING THE 'SIXTIES AND 'SEVENTIES

The Turkish Armenians were befriended not only by individuals residing in Russia but also by organized groups. In the 'sixties and 'seventies two societies were formed which concerned themselves with the situation in the provinces of Turkey. One of them was called the Goodwill Society (Barenepatak Enkeruthiun), and the other, the Devotion to the Fatherland Bureau (Kontora Hairenaits Siro).

The Goodwill Society was formed in Alexandropol, Russian Armenia in 1868.[1] It pretended to be a group engaged in cultural, educational, and philanthropic pursuits, but this disguise was assumed so that it might receive the legal approval of the Tsarist government. In reality, its principal aim was political in nature; for it was dedicated to freeing Armenia from foreign domination. The primary aim of the Society was opposition to the Ottoman regime. Although it concentrated its own efforts in the province of Van, it advocated the organization of revolutionary resistance throughout Turkish Armenia.

The original membership of the Goodwill Society comprised forty-three teachers, students, artisans, and merchants. The society's constitution laid down the purpose, rules, and regulations, of the society. It defined the qualifications and duties of the membership, which was fixed at a maximum of fifty persons; the process for expelling unworthy members; the procedure for meetings and special committees; the collection of dues. There were also articles dealing with the reading of books and other literature, organizing public assemblies, and collecting money. Besides the constitution, there was also a special record book called *Parki Tak (Crown of Glory)*, which listed the names and contributions of the members.[2]

The founder and director of the Goodwill Society was Arsen Kritian, a twenty-four-year-old Alexandropol teacher. He had had experience in the book trade and had published numerous patriotic poems and articles in journals of the period. Kritian had also made translations from Russian works into the Armenian language.[3]

Another active member of the society was Petros Haikazuni, also a teacher and journalist. On behalf of the society, he went to the province of Van as an observer and appealed to the people to stand up and fight for national liberation.[4]

As a group these men worked in distributing patriotic propaganda, organizing meetings, collecting money for buying arms, and forming a fraternal bond with the Turkish Armenians. Their investigations in Ottoman territory, especially in the province of Van, indicate that they were in contact with revolutionary groups in that area. It is even possible that the society's propaganda campaign in Van may have been helpful in encouraging the inhabitants of that province to form the Union of Salvation in 1872. The Union sent representatives to Russian Armenia, and it is most probable that they were in close contact with the members of the Goodwill Society. Both organizations were interested in arming the population of Van; however, there was a significant difference between the two—the Armenians of Van desired to organize for self-defense, while those in Alexandropol advocated a revolution in Turkey which would completely detach the Armenian provinces from Ottoman rule.

The Goodwill Society became less active after 1871, but continued to function until April, 1875, at which time the political aspect of the society was exposed to the Russian officials. Zolotovsky, the chief of the Erivan gendarmes, began arresting the members, and after a year of investigations and deliberations, a verdict was rendered in May, 1876. Arsen Kritian was imprisoned for one and a half years and the group was rebuked for forming such a society without government approval.[5]

The devotion to the Fatherland Bureau (Kontora Hairenaits Siro) was founded in the village of Medz Gharakilisa in the province of Alexandropol on June 20, 1874. It, too, appeared to be a society devoted to "activities beneficial to the nation," [6] but its real objectives were political, and similar to those of the Goodwill Society.

The society was composed of young men who met three times a week to read, study, and discuss such Armenian subjects as were not displeasing to the Russian government. The director of the group was Gevorg Khosroviants, a vineyard farmer living in the village. The office of secretary was held by Hambardsum Palasanian, who had been an interpreter in the cities of Kars and Alexandropol. Other members included three Medz Gharakilisa residents: Baghdasar Tchariktchiants, a saddle maker; and the Lazariants brothers—Aleksander, a salt and cotton merchant, and Mekertitch, a shoemaker.[7]

Suspecting that the real motives of the society were political rather than cultural, the Russian officials arrested some of its members in April, 1875. The gendarmes found several poems that had political connotations, referring to Turkish Armenia and the need for the people to fight to reëstablish Armenian independence. After one and a half years of imprisonment the members of the society were released on life probation.[8]

Too little is known of the accomplishments of the Devotion to the Fatherland Bureau during its short existence of less than a year for us to evaluate the effectiveness of the group.

THE ARMENIAN QUESTION AND
THE RUSSIAN ARMENIANS

It should be noted that the penalties for the political offenses of both of the above organizations were very mild. This leniency can probably be attributed to the fact that both organizations were primarily concerned with the political aspect of life in Turkish Armenia, and not life in Russia. Both societies strove for revolution against the Sultan, an eventuality that would have been to the advantage of the Tsarist government.

It was profitable for the Russians to win the favor of the Armenians, who occupied important areas on the Russo-Turkish frontier. The Russo-Turkish War (1877–1878) was already pending when the decisions for the offenses were made, in 1876. The opening of hostilities between the two countries and the subsequent Russian victory increased world interest in Turkey's Christian provinces. No longer was interest in the Armenian situation confined principally to nationalists. The Treaties of San Stefano and Berlin had brought the Armenian Question into the sphere of international politics.

The political and diplomatic ferment was translated into patriotic feeling among the Armenians. A great nationalistic fervor was felt, especially among the youth who lived outside of the Turkish provinces. Patriarch Varzhabedian and Khirimian Hairig spurred the younger generation to interest themselves in the homeland in Turkish Armenia. The "Depi Yerkir" or "To the Fatherland" movement came into being, reminiscent of the "To the People" (v Narod) movement in Russia. People were encouraged to go to the Turkish provinces, where they might contribute their energies for the benefit of the nation. Politically minded Armenians in Russia had heretofore concentrated their efforts on bettering conditions there. Many had been members of Russian organizations such as the *Zemly i Volya*

(Land and Freedom) and the Narodnaya Volya (People's Will), but the 'eighties brought about a change of direction for a number of these people. Becoming more nationalistic, more conscious of the political situation in Turkish Armenia, they began to relegate the problems of Russia to a secondary place and concentrated upon alleviating the plight of the Armenians in Asiatic Turkey. This change of viewpoint was evident among the youth of Transcaucasia, St. Petersburg, and Moscow.

REVOLUTIONARY GROUPS IN TRANSCAUCASIA

The various nationalities in Transcaucasia worked together in Russian revolutionary organizations during the early 'eighties. The committee of *Narodnaya Volya* in Tiflis was composed of three Georgians and the three Armenians, Grigor Ter Grigorian, Abraham Dastakian, and Tamara Adamian. The power of nationalism soon separated the Armenians from the committee. Under the leadership of Dastakian, they formed their own circle in 1881 or 1882. Its work was to be completely devoted to the ". . . undefended claims of the unfortunate Armenian people." [9] The circle soon attracted other active participants,[10] and by 1883 it had assumed the leadership of various informal groups in the city of Tiflis.

Under the sponsorship of the Dastakian circle, general meetings of these groups were called. At the sessions, lectures were presented, which were mainly concerned with national history and culture. The members of the Dastakian circle also took active measures in regard to the Armenian Question. Grigor Aghababian and Shirvanzade (Aleksander Movsesian) assisted them in publishing by collotype a few issues of a secret paper called *Munetik* (*Crier*).[11] The circle also published another secret paper called *Hairenaser Dzain* (*Patriotic Voice*).[12] Both of the publications discussed the Armenian Question and called upon patriots, young and old, to save Turkish Armenia. This area was to be rescued first, but the situation in Russia was not overlooked. The *Munetik* advocated armed resistance against Russian oppression, while the *Hairenaser Dzain* attempted to stir up resistance of nonviolent character.[13] Other papers, which were produced by lithograph, were also circulated. The titles of articles appearing in them were often familiar quotations from the writings of Nalbandian, Kamar Katiba, and Raffi, and thus had a patriotic appeal for the readers.[14]

The sending of observers from Russia "to the Fatherland" in Turkish Armenia was another of the circle's political projects. Two members, Aleksander Petrosian (Sandal) and Tigran Pirumian, were sent to Turkish Armenia in 1883, where they studied the country in order to lay the groundwork for insurrection. Two other Russian Armenians, Haik Melik-Dadayan and Tavakalian (who later became a priest and was known as the revolutionist Zakki), made observations in the same area in 1883. However, it is not known exactly which group they represented at the time.[15]

The Dastakian circle decreased in strength in the fall of 1883. At that time, Dastakian, Nersessian, Tamara Adamian, and Simeon and Srapion Ter Grigorian left Tiflis to continue their education in St. Petersburg and Moscow.[16] They served to strengthen the Armenian revolutionary groups already in existence in the two Russian cities. Other revolutionary pioneers remained in Transcaucasia and carried on united efforts for the national cause during the 'eighties. They served in many groups in Tiflis and in its villages, Erivan, Baku, and Karabagh.[17]

TIFLIS REVOLUTIONARIES

Refugees and émigrés from Turkey, as well as local intellectuals and students, were particularly active in political undertakings in Transcaucasia. A group of Turkish Armenian laborers from Moush formed their own society in Tiflis. The members, many of whom had had no opportunity for education, were taught fundamental school subjects. At the same time, they were imbued with ideas of rebellion. The laborers were being prepared for actual participation in revolutionary work. They were taught the use of arms and practiced with weapons on holidays outside the city. Gabriel Mirzoyan, with the assistance of Aleksander Simonian (Santro) and Ghazakhetsi Meghak, directed the group until 1884.[18] The leadership was then continued by Christopher Mikaelian, a member of the Narodnaya Volya, who later became one of the founders of the Armenian Revolutionary Federation or Dashnaktsuthiun.

ERIVAN REVOLUTIONARIES

A secret society, the name of which is not now ascertainable, was operating in Erivan during the early 'eighties. It too was dedicated to freeing Turkish Armenia through revolution. For this purpose money was collected and arms were bought for the people across the border. Field workers were also sent there. Two of these were Tavakalian (Zakki) and Darlageaztsi Ter-Grigor. The society remained in existence for only a few years. V. Yeghiazarian, T. Vardanian, T. Mehirian, and other members were arrested and exiled by the Russian government.[19]

KARABAGH REVOLUTIONARIES

The district of Karabagh was another center of revolutionary efforts. Emancipative measures were not unfamiliar to the area. During the seventeenth and eighteenth centuries it had been the home of such pioneers of the liberation movement as Israel Ori and David Beg. In the eighteen-eighties the town of Shushi in Karabagh had an active group of nationalists. These were members of the secret society called "Uzh" ("Strength"),[20] which attempted to aid the national cause by means of money and arms. The society served increasingly to familiarize its members with Armenian subjects. Books banned by the government were secretly read and the study of Armenian history, language, and culture was encouraged.

REVOLUTIONARY GROUPS IN ST. PETERSBURG AND MOSCOW

As the revolutionary movement among the Armenians of Transcaucasia continued to become more widespread, those nationals studying in far-off St. Petersburg and Moscow were communicating with each other to serve the homeland. In the past the institutions of both these Russian cities had attracted young Armenians. Here they came into closer contact with Russian thought and culture and socialistic trends. Many of them became assimilated into Russian life and lost interest in their own people. Others, more patriotic and devoted to their native institutions, assisted in the awakening and emancipation of their people.

Moscow's Lazarian Institute, with its educational facilities and press, played an important role in making Moscow an intellectual center for the Armenians of Russia. From Moscow, Stepanos Nazariants' journal *Hiusissapile* (*Aurora Borealis*) in the 'fifties and 'sixties had striven for intellectual awakening among the Armenians. Students in Moscow and St. Petersburg were encouraged to form close associations devoted to national problems. Many of them became the armed fighters and propagandists of the 'eighties and 'nineties who went "to the Fatherland" (Turkish Armenia), and others became founders and leaders of Armenian political parties.

The St. Petersburg Armenian students during the 'eighties had their own circle, which was particularly conscious of the political events in Turkish Armenia and in the Balkans. The sacrifices of the Balkan peoples, which led to their political independence from the Ottoman Empire, were looked upon with great admiration by these students, who wished to encourage their own people in this direction. The students printed and distributed brochures on the Greek and Bulgarian revolutions, depicting such heroes as Marko Botzares and Vasil Levski.[21] Their publications, which numbered as many as fifteen, included *Bulgar Avazakapet* (*Chief of the Bulgarian Brigands*), *Dantcho, Azrayil,* and *Sarkavag* (*Deacon*). Thousands of these brochures were scattered throughout the provinces inhabited by the Armenians of Turkey in hopes of rousing them to emulate the Balkan example.[22]

The Armenian students of Moscow were also greatly influenced by the events in the Balkans. The successful independence movements of other Ottoman subjects encouraged them to start revolutionary publications even before the St. Petersburg circle did so. The Moscow students had formed an organization called the "Union of Patriots" ("Hairenaserneri Miuthiun") in the spring of 1882,[23] which was dedicated to the welfare of their people under Ottoman rule.

At the first meeting the founders outlined the methods to be used for freeing their compatriots in Turkish Armenia. They considered it necessary to use illegal means in reaching their objective since no legal processes were available to them: revolution, after the Balkan example, seemed to them to be the most expedient road to freedom. They decided to form branches of their society in other communities and to introduce their ideas to others by means of circulars. The participation of Armenian nationalists all over the world was needed, but special attention was to be given to organizing the youth of Transcaucasia. The above decisions were reached by the four persons present at the first meeting: Nerses Abelian, Margar Artenian, Mikael Zalian, and Davit Nersessian. A fifth student, Karapet Ter Khatchaturian, soon joined the group and together they started to put their program into operation.[24]

The Union of Patriots, in a pamphlet produced by collotype, presented the objectives of their organizations. This pamphlet was brought to Transcaucasia by Davit Nersessian in the summer of 1882.[25] The objectives, methods, and ideology of the society were given in fuller detail a few years later in the pages of their organ, the *Herald of Freedom (Azatuthian Avetaber)*.

The *Herald of Freedom* first appeared in 1884. It was the result of a group project which included former members of the Dastakian circle of Tiflis: Abraham Dastakian, Davit Nercessian, Simeon and Srapion Ter Grigorian, and Tamara Adamian. These students had conferred with members of the Union of Patriots in Moscow on New Year's Day, 1884.[26] Together, they had begun publishing the new secret revolutionary journal, which was under the sponsorship of the Union.

The *Herald of Freedom* showed the influence of both European and Russian revolutionary thought and socialistic ideas. In order to free Turkish Armenia, the society wished to use the same methods advocated by the *Narodnaya Volya*—propaganda, agitation, organized bands, and terror.[27] Their organ declared that the Turkish government was the greatest oppressor of the Armenian people. It trampled upon the human rights of the people it ruled, deprived them of the gains from their hard toil, and hindered their progress. The Union called upon dedicated men to join them in sacrificing their very lives in the fight "to exterminate that infected governmental organization. . . ." [28]

Political independence alone was not considered a sufficient fulfillment of the society's objectives. The society believed that "The cornerstone of peoples' freedom is their economic independence," [29] and that land, natural resources, and the means of production rightfully belonged to the workers. A new government was needed in which the community should be the sole owner of all property, since it was the only producer and consumer. The community and the individual were to be equally concerned with each other, thereby arriving at a "social accord." [30] Other people inhabiting Turkish Armenia deserved equal consideration. Mutual respect and understanding and equal political and social advantages were advocated for the maintenance of a "firm solidarity among the peoples living in Armenia. . . ." [31]

The *Herald of Freedom* was at first produced by collotype, but was later published on the society's private printing press. This was the first printed journal under the sponsorship of an organized secret Russian Armenian revolutionary society. This press even preceded by one year Portugalian's *Armenia,* founded at Marseille in 1885.

In contrast to the *Armenia,* the Moscow publication had added socialistic ideology to its exhortation for the freedom of Turkish Armenia. The *Herald of Freedom* advocated both individual freedom and group solidarity, showing the influence of the theories of the Russian revolutionary Peter Lavrov. The journal wrote of the economic inequalities of society and stressed the need for public ownership of all sources of production. Portugalian showed little consciousness of such social and economic problems. He did not advocate socialistic ideas and did not have a definite program of methods to be used by revolutionists.

In comparison to the *Armenia,* the *Herald of Freedom* was of short duration. Only a few issued were ever published. The paper was discontinued, and its sponsor, the Union of Patriots, was forced to disband when the Russian government discovered their existence.[32] The members of the Moscow society dispersed in 1886 and went to other areas.[33]

THE ARMENIANS AND THE RUSSIAN GOVERNMENT

Meanwhile, the Armenians of Transcaucasia had been feeling the effects of Tsarist oppression, which was specifically directed at them. There had been a steady anti-Armenian campaign by the government, commencing in the early 'eighties.[34] A concerted effort was made to eliminate Armenians from appointments to civil and military positions. They were even restricted in their opportunities to participate in purely peaceful cultural activity.[35]

Restrictions were made more pronounced by the *ukaz* of 1884, which resulted in the closing of all Armenian parochial schools in 1885.[36] This "infamous document" [37] did not pass without protest from certain members of the community. Christopher Mikaelian, who later became a founder of the Armenian Revolutionary Federation, and another student, Gabriel Mirzoyan, printed and distributed anti-Tsarist pamphlets protesting the closing of the schools. The people were urged to resist the unfair encroachment by the regime. At that time, however, little resistance was shown by the population as a whole.[38]

The anti-Armenian campaign carried on by the Russian government in the 'eighties served to drive those with nationalistic inclinations away from Russian circles. Persecution, as among other stateless people, made the Armenians more conscious of their identity. The lukewarm members of the society were left by the wayside to be assimilated into other cultures; the stronger members became more vehement in their attachment to their cultural heritage and national identity.

Separatism from Russian circles also occurred among the Georgians, who, for a short time, had formed a Georgian federation of Transcaucasia.[39] They published a pamphlet in which they invited the other peoples of Trancaucasia to join them in working toward political independence from

Russian despotism and in forming a new system based on federative principles.[40] The Georgian proposal for unified action between the two nations was not a new idea in the history of the Armenian liberation movement. During the eighteenth century Joseph Emin had advocated that King Heraclius I of Georgia sponsor the Armenian bid for independence. The same proposal was made by Movses Bagramian of Madras in his *Exhortation*, published in 1772. The Georgian proposal for federative unity in the eighteen-eighties, like the proposals presented in the eighteenth century, was to remain dormant. The Armenian secret societies of Transcaucasia did not accept the Georgian invitation, and united federative efforts between the two peoples were not to come to fruition until the twentieth century.

The Russian Armenians of the nineteenth century continued their revolutionary pursuits without coördinating their activities with Georgian nationalists. An attempt was made in 1887 by Christopher Mikaelian and Stepan Zorian to publish a secret journal in Tiflis. Although the press of the *Herald of Freedom* was at their disposal, the attempt failed because the cost of operations was prohibitive.[41]

The chief desire of the secret groups in Transcaucasia was to aid the Turkish Armenians, but these groups had no organized program for action.[42] The first step toward a coördinated effort was the founding of the Young Armenia Society (Yeritassard Hayastan), which later gave rise to the Armenian Revolutionary Federation.

THE ACTIVITIES OF THE YOUNG ARMENIA SOCIETY, 1889–1890

The Young Armenia Society was organized in Tiflis under the leadership of Christopher Mikaelian during the winter of 1889.[43] The society was soon referred to as the "Iuzhnye Nomera" ("Southern Pension"), after the name of the pension in which meetings were held. The main objective of the organization was to send men across the border into Turkey for punitive actions against the Kurds. By such encounters, it was believed that the Armenians would attract the attention of the European Powers and that the latter would be encouraged to enforce the reforms specified in Article LXI of the Treaty of Berlin. Other work undertaken by the organization included coördinating the activity of various other groups; sending observers across the border into Turkish territory to collect information about the condition of the people and the possibilities of uprising; preparing men in Russian Transcaucasia for possible future armed combat on Turkish soil; and smuggling arms into Turkey through the Persian frontier.[44]

The members of the Young Armenia Society included many young Armenian men and women, a number of whom were students.[45] The nucleus of the organization was the Droshak (Flag, or Banner) group. This inner group was established at Tiflis, but soon had branches in other cities and villages in Russia, Turkey, and Persia. Okoyan, for example, was dispatched to Turkey where he organized a committee in Erzerum.[46] During the summer of 1890 M. Shatirian went to Alexandropol, to the villages of the Shirak area, and to Kars, where he formed other Droshak committees.[47] Tabriz became the center of the group in Persia, where also Tigran Stepanian, who had received scientific training in Moscow, established a small arms factory. From Tabriz weapons were smuggled into Van.[48] These Droshak branches in Russia, Turkey, and Persia later became incorporated into the new political party, the Armenian Revolutionary Federation, or Dashnaktsuthiun, to be described in chapter vii.

During its short existence (1889–1890) the Young Armenia Society was quite active. It commissioned Martiros Margarian and Hovsep Arghuthian to make investigations in Turkish Armenia.[49] Indeed, there was a great deal of interest in these Asiatic provinces of Turkey, and other Russian Armenians were making similar investigations. Some went "to the Fatherland" (Turkish Armenia) individually, while others represented a group of Armenian students in Moscow. The Young Armenia Society actively coöperated with the St. Petersburg students, whose leader, Sarkis Googoonian, was preparing an expedition into Turkish Armenia;[50] but many other groups formed between 1889 and 1890 and remained unattached to the Young Armenia Society.

There was an influx of students from Moscow and St. Petersburg into Transcaucasia who started their own circles. Armenakan observers and agitators were also continually crossing the Russo-Turkish frontier and bringing new information from the Van region. The Hunchaks had sent Khan-Azat to Tiflis in 1890 for the purpose of forming another branch of the party, but his first attempt to join other revolutionaries under the Hunchak banner was unsuccessful.[51] Meanwhile, the *Armenia* and the *Hunchak* were being read and were introducing new concepts.

The urgent need for a more comprehensive program than that laid down by the Young Armenia Society was made manifest in 1890 by two major events in Turkey: the local disturbance at Erzerum on June 20,[52] and the Hunchak Demonstration of Kum Kapu in Constantinople on July 15. These events made many of those living in Russian territory believe that an organized revolution in Turkey was close at hand. Revolutionaries under Tsarist rule wished to help accelerate that movement in Turkey, but their efforts were not unified.

The events in Turkey during June and July, 1890, gave impetus to many revolutionaries to form a new political organization. A secret committee started making plans that would help consolidate the numerous existing groups into one powerful federation. Grigor Ardzruni, editor of the

Mushak and a prominent member of the community, was asked to take the lead in forming the new organization. He was even offered the sum of 100,000 rubles[53] by a Tiflis merchant, Arakel Dzaturian, if he would establish headquarters in a foreign country from where he could head the political organization. Ardzruni refused, preferring to remain in Tiflis and continue the publication of the *Mushak*.[54] But there were other Armenians living in Russia who came forward to take the lead in forming the new political organization.

A BRIEF EVALUATION, 1868–1890

The time was overdue for a union of all Armenian revolutionary groups in Russia to join together under one banner. As described in this chapter, from 1868 to 1890 there had been many circles, societies, and organizations, primarily among the students and the intelligentsia, which were interested in freeing the Armenians of Asiatic Turkey. The period can be divided into two general parts: 1868 to the Russo-Turkish War (1877–1878); and the postwar period, between 1878 and 1890.

Prior to the Russo-Turkish War there had been at least two organizations directly interested in promoting rebellion in Turkish Armenia. These had been the Goodwill Society (1868–1875) and the Devotion to the Fatherland Bureau (1874–1875). In the sparse material available, there is no detailed account of the particular ideology of these two societies, nor is there any information concerning their link with revolutionaries other than those of Armenian origin.

The Russo-Turkish War and the international agreements that followed it (the Treaty of San Stefano, the Cyprus Convention, and the Treaty of Berlin) aroused further interest in the Armenian Question. This intensified interest was also reflected among the Armenians in Russia.

Their nationalistic tendencies, already notable in individuals, became more evident as expressed in groups in the period 1878–1890. Patriotic feeling gained still more momentum in the 'eighties and was aided by an Armenian reaction to the anti-Armenian Russification campaign carried on by the Tsarist government.

In the period following the Russo-Turkish War we saw among the Russian Armenians a rapid growth of revolutionary organizations, which concentrated their efforts on the political affairs of Turkish Armenia. All the groups wanted a change of administration in that area and advocated rebellion as a means of achieving it. The Armenians in Russia were generally optimistic in regard to the possibility of liberating the Armenians on the other side of the frontier.

The successful revolutions in Greece and Bulgaria helped to convince Russian Armenian revolutionaries that the Armenians could also be liberated from the Ottoman Empire. They saw in the Balkans the beneficial results of revolution and urged in their writings that the Armenians use the same methods to achieve immediate independence.

During the 'eighties many of the Armenians drew away from Russian circles and formed their own ethnic groups. Many of the intelligentsia and young students who had been working for reforms in Russia through secret Russian societies (*Zemlya i Volya, Narodnaya Volya,* and *Chernyi Peredel*) started forming groups that became primarily concerned with Armenian politics. The influence and ideas obtained by Armenians who worked in Russian revolutionary circles were also transferred into Armenian affairs.

The strength of Russian revolutionary theories greatly contributed to making Armenians more eager for revolutionary action. This ideological influence was conspicuous among the Armenian revolutionary organizations formed after the Russo-Turkish War. Nearly all these Armenian organizations in Russia were led by persons who were members or close associates of the Russian Narodniks. They included followers of the sociological theories of Mikailovsky and Lavrov as well as members and adherents of Russian revolutionary societies, particularly the Narodnaya Volya.

The Russian Armenian revolutionary societies, both in the pre- and the post-Russo-Turkish-War period (1868–1890), contributed to the Armenian Revolutionary Movement. All encouraged more nationalistic feeling, advocated rebellion in Turkish Armenia, and brought about a closer bond between Russian and Turkish Armenians. Some of the societies, especially the Union of Patriots (1882–1886), circulated socialistic literature, the purpose of which was to make the Armenians more conscious of socioeconomic problems. In the period 1868–1890, attempts were made to smuggle arms and munitions into Turkish Armenia, and observers and agitators were sent there. The societies of this period failed, however, to accomplish their objective of freeing Turkish Armenia. At this stage of the movement there was not sufficient contact between the many groups scattered over the various regions in Russia. The groups were small, and they had come into existence simultaneously. By 1890 there was a great need to unite all of the various and sundry groups and establish a firm program for aiding the Turkish Armenian cause.

The desire for a united revolutionary front was the culmination of a long tradition of personal concern on the part of the Russian Armenians for their exploited brothers on the Turkish side of the border. The men who were to become part of this new united front were the spiritual descendents of Abovian, Nalbandian, Kamar Katiba, and Raffi, as well as of the Russian Armenian patriotic groups of the 'sixties, 'seventies, and 'eighties. They opened the decade of the 'nineties by laying the foundation of a new political party, the Armenian Revolutionary Federation, or Dashnaktsuthiun.

VII

The Armenian Revolutionary Federation or Dashnaktsuthiun, 1890–1896

The Armenian Revolutionary Federation, first known as the "Federation of Armenian Revolutionaries" and commonly referred to as the "Dashnaktsuthiun" ("Federation"),[1] was the result of a merger of various Armenian groups, primarily in Russia, into a single political party. Those chiefly instrumental in bringing about this political unification during the summer of 1890 were the triumvirate Christopher Mikaelian (1859–1905), Stepan Zorian (Rostom, or Kotot) (1867–1919), and Simon Zavarian (1866–1913).[2]

THE FOUNDING OF THE PARTY

There are no records regarding the preliminary negotiations and discussions that led to the founding of the Dashnaktsuthiun at Tiflis (in Russian Transcaucasia) in the summer of 1890. Minutes of their discussions and negotiations or the names of the participants representing different groups at the conclave are not available. Only one document that dates back to this initial meeting is preserved—the *Manifesto* of the party. The exact day on which the Dashnaktsuthiun was established is not known and writers cannot even agree on the month of the year.[3]

Before the federation could be formed, a common formula had to be devised which would be acceptable to several groups whose members held sharply different opinions in regard to Armenian affairs. Some were interested merely in promoting peaceful Armenian educational and cultural activities; others of more revolutionary tendency differed both in regard to the geographical area in which they wished to operate and in their political philosophies.

The nonsocialist nationalist revolutionaries concentrated on the development of the liberation movement in Turkish Armenia. These included persons who were in sympathy with the Armenakan Party and others, mainly Armenian students from St. Petersburg, who had as their spokesman the wealthy Russian Armenian Kostantin Khatisian. The latter group were referred to as "Northerners,"[4] after the name of their headquarters, the Tiflis pension "Severnye Nomera" ("Northern Pension").

The socialist revolutionaries, although differing in ideology, were primarily influenced by Russian political thought, especially the sociological theories of Lavrov and Mikailovsky. Many of them held membership in secret Russian revolutionary societies, such as the Narodnaya Volya.

The Armenian socialist revolutionaries, on the other hand, can be divided into two general categories: those who wished to work in coöperation with Russian and Georgian revolutionists toward the overthrow of the Tsarist regime; and those who, like the above-mentioned nonsocialist nationalists, wished to concentrate their efforts on freeing Turkish Armenia. Socialists of both categories drew their support mainly from the Armenian students of Moscow; in

Tiflis they assembled at the pension "Iuzhnye Nomera" ("Southern Pension"), from which name they became known as the "Southerners." [5] Also to be numbered among the socialist revolutionaries who were concerned with Turkish Armenia were the members and adherents of the pro-Marxist Hunchakian Revolutionary Party.

Many sessions were held at Tiflis before the delegates were able to adjust their differences and arrive at a compromise. According to Khan-Azat, there were five major issues confronting the delegates:[6] (1) socialism as an objective; (2) the name of the new paty; (3) the location of the party headquarters; (4) the party's official journal; (5) the Googoonian Expedition.

SOCIALISM AS AN OBJECTIVE

The acceptance of socialism as one of the objectives of the new party was among the demands made by the Hunchakian Revolutionary Party through their Tiflis representative, Khan-Azat. The Hunchaks feared that their party would be falling under the domination of the bourgeoisie if they joined a federation that did not uphold the socialist cause. On the other hand, the word "socialism" was repugnant to many of the delegates at Tiflis, and it was difficult to compromise.

Christopher Mikaelian and Simon Zavarian, two leaders, were able to bring about an accord between the Marxist Hunchaks and the antisocialist representatives. Both these men were active members of the Narodnaya Volya, and their sincerity in regard to the socialist cause was not doubted by the Hunchak Khan-Azat. Also, they were personal friends of the Hunchak delegate and had assured him that their leadership in the new organization would maintain the furtherance of the proletarian movement. Mikaelian and Zavarian worked with great tact so as not to alienate those delegates opposed to socialism. They were careful to employ phraseology that recognized proletarian objectives without actually using the word "socialism." The opposition was won over by disguising socialist ideology in the Dashnak *Manifesto,* which states merely that the object of the party was "the economic and political freedom of Turkish Armenia. . . ." [7]

Khan-Azat agreed to accept this statement as evidence that socialism had been accepted as part of the program. However, the central headquarters of the Hunchakian Revolutionary Party at Geneva demanded more concrete assurances on the socialist issue. For this reason they dispatched to Tiflis another plenipotentiary, Hakob Meghavorian, with specific instructions. Meghavorian arrived in Tiflis while the conferences were in progress and started negotiations with the leaders. An agreement was reached between the Hunchakian Revolutionary Party and the other delegates, and a compact was signed by the two Hunchak representatives. [8] In accordance with this compact the Hunchaks agreed to dissolve their party and become an integral part of the Dashnaktsuthiun. However, the dissolution of the Hunchakian Revolutionary Party did not actually take place. As will be described later, the Hunchaks quickly separated from the new party and continued to function as a separate organization.

THE NAME OF THE PARTY AND ITS HEADQUARTERS

When the Hunchakian Revolutionary Party first agreed to enter the proposed federation, it became necessary to find a name acceptable to the pro-Marxist as well as to the other groups. The most appropriate and descriptive name agreed upon by the delegates was the "Federation of Armenian Revolutionaries" ("Hai Heghapokhakanneri Dashnaktsuthiun"), commonly called the "Dashnaktsuthiun" ("Federation"). The headquarters of the new party was to be in Trebizond. This city was suggested by Khan-Azat as a compromise between Geneva, the Hunchak center, and Tiflis—the home of most of the Dashnaks. Although Trebizond was selected, it is evident that the functioning center was Tiflis, the residence of most of the leaders of the new party.

The Central Committee or Bureau, which was the chief administrative force, was composed of five men, most of whom continued to stay in the Georgian capital. The five elected to the executive position were Christopher Mikaelian, Simon Zavarian, Abraham Dastakian, H. Loris-Melikian, and Levon Sarkisian. They controlled the centralized system of administration adopted by the conclave of 1890.[9]

THE PARTY'S OFFICIAL JOURNALS

The delegates agreed to have two journals, the *Hunchak* (*Bell*) and the *Droshak* (*Flag*, or *Banner*). The former was to be edited in Geneva by Avetis Nazarbekian and Christopher Mikaelian and was to appear once a month as the "scientific organ" of the Dashnaktsuthiun. The other and newer journal, the *Droshak* (or *Droschak*) a name derived from the former secret Russian Armenian group, was to be published in Tiflis. It was to appear at least once a week as the "rebellion-promoting organ" of the paty. The editorial board was to be selected at a later date.[10]

THE GOOGOONIAN EXPEDITION

While the Tiflis conference was taking place the people of the Caucasus were encouraged by the military preparations being made by Sarkis Googoonian, a former St. Petersburg student. Strengthened in his determination by the Kum Kapu and Erzerum disturbances, Googoonian had left his studies to come to Transcaucasia for the purpose of working for the liberation of the Armenians of Asiatic Turkey. For many months he had been recruiting a fighting force that would cross into Turkish territory, divide into guerrilla units, and produce a state of chaos. He believed that such agitation would forcibly remind the European Powers of the promised reforms for Armenia.

Googoonian's plans for the invasion of Turkish Armenia drew the attention of the Tiflis delegates, who were naturally concerned with such activities. They wished to have the expedition under their direction and therefore sent a courier to Googoonian informing him of the formation of the Dashnaktsuthiun. He was advised to enter Turkey with his men without further delay, since the Russian government might soon discover his plans and issue a warrant for his arrest. The courier returned with the news that Googoonian did not wish to recognize the new political party and was not yet ready to move his men across the frontier.[11] Googoonian's expedition to Turkish Armenia, which will be described later, took place in September, 1890, after the delegates at Tiflis had completed their final sessions.

THE *Manifesto*

The decisions reached at Tiflis during the summer of 1890 were declared in the *Manifesto* of the new organization. This document announced the entrance of the Armenian Question into a new era. Turkish Armenia was no longer to be the slave of the "confiscatory policy of the thievish rulers." Under the banner of the Federation of Armenian Revolutionaries the Party had declared a "people's war against the Turkish government," which aimed at the political and economic freedom of Turkish Armenia. No longer would they beg Europe for assistance, for such reliance had proved to be useless. The Dashnaks declared that there was a limit to patience and that barbarism in Armenia could no longer be endured. The Armenian had "resolved to defend his rights, his property, his honor and family with his own hands," and was now demanding the freedom of Turkish Armenia. The document called for all true patriots to join forces with the new organization and ended with the words, "Let us unite, Armenians, and carry on fearlessly the sacred task of securing national freedom!" [12]

The *Manifesto* was written in a forceful style with much emotional appeal. However, when the document is scrutinized, the need for clarification and elaboration is apparent. What was the Dashnak definition of the word "freedom," and what was meant by a "people's war" against the government? The phrase "the economic and political freedom of Turkish Armenia" had been written into the *Manifesto* as a substitute for the word "socialism." The statement was not interpreted as reflecting socialist objectives by the nonsocialist delegates, of course, and confusion and further difficulties became inevitable. Other questions suggest themselves: Had the Dashnaks completely dismissed Europe as a source of assistance? How was the Armenian going to defend himself solely "with his own hands"? If this could be done, how and where were Armenians to get enough financial support and military equipment to overcome successfully the powerful forces of the Ottoman government?

The leaders of the Dashnaktsuthiun certainly stated patriotic objectives, but had not devised a program to implement these objectives. Unity was called for, but how could there be unity if there were no immediate plans to put into effect? Within a short space of two years, this indecision and vagueness became a major cause of disillusionment for many revolutionaires.

THE CONSEQUENCES OF THE GOOGOONIAN EXPEDITION

Before strong discontent began to be felt, the attention of the revolutionaries of Transcaucasia was absorbed in the events surrounding the plans of Sarkis Googoonian.[13] Following the initial conference at Tiflis, the party decided that the Googoonian Expedition was no longer advisable, since Googoonian had procrastinated too long. The party then made continued attempts to influence Googoonian to change his ill-advised plan to enter Turkish territory. They first sent Kostantin Khatisian, and later Zavarian and Hovsep Arghuthian, to Kars to confer with the expedition leader and continued their pleas by letters and telegrams. All their efforts were in vain.

The Googoonian Expedition started on its "Divine Mission" to Turkish Armenia on September 23, 1890, with a force numbering 125 persons, some on horses and others on foot.[14] They were given a triumphant farewell by a large group of Armenians of Transcaucasia who for months had known of the preparations. The men started their journey toward the Fatherland with great hopes, singing:[15]

Let Armenian maidens cry for us
Let Armenian braves with arms in hand join with us. . . .

The expeditionary force bore on their shoulders the letters *M. H.,* symbolizing Mayr Hayastan ("Mother Armenia") or Miuthiun Hairenaserneri ("Union of Patriots") and carried a flag sewn by the young Armenian women of Kars. One side of the flag had the initials *M. H.* and five stars surrounding the number *61* (symbolizing five of the Armenian provinces and Article LXI of the Treaty of Berlin); and the other side bore the slogan of the times, "Vrezh! Vrezh!" ("Revenge! Revenge!") and a skull.[16]

The high hopes of the expeditionary force were soon shattered, under the trying circumstances of the three-day journey that followed. At the outset the group lost its direction, wasting much time and valuable supplies. More difficulties were encountered when they became involved in skirmishes with Russian border guards and Kurdish tribesmen, who now sought revenge for the cold-blooded killing of some of their people by members of the expedition.[17] Before reaching Turkish territory the exhausted, hungry, and thirsty men of Googoonian's dwindling force were attacked by Russian Cossacks, captured, and then placed under arrest.

For nearly two years they remained in Russian prisons while long investigations and court trials took place. Finally, they were found guilty of conspiring against the Tsarist government in a plot that aimed at forming a United Armenia, which was to include territory under the Russian flag. As evidence of such alleged plans the court interpreted the letters *M. H.* as the initials for the words Miatsial Hayastan ("United Armenia") instead of Mayr Hayastan ("Mother Armenia") or Miuthiun Hairenaserneri ("Union of Patriots"). The twenty-six convicted men were given severe sentences and were sent to prison in Siberia.[18]

The Googoonian Expedition of 1890 was obviously a failure. The European Powers were not aroused to the miserable suffering of the Armenians in Asiatic Turkey, and Article LXI of the Treaty of Berlin was still far from being implemented. Many lives were lost; much money (collected by public appeal) had been spent; and relations with the Kurds had been needlessly strained.

Although the whole scheme might be interpreted as ending in a fiasco, the Googoonian Expedition had a great effect on the Armenians,[19] especially those of Russian Transcaucasia. Bloodshed became a more commonly acknowledged form of patriotic sacrifice, and such men as these were idealized as heroes.[20] For the nation as a whole the venture served as the first major revolutionary enterprise emanating from Russian Armenia and directed at Asiatic Turkey. Varandian, the Dashnak historian, states that this event helped create a stronger spirit of national unity among the Armenians in Turkey, Russia, and Persia.[21] Henry Howard, the British diplomatic representative to St. Petersburg, expressed a similar opinion. In a letter to Salisbury he wrote: "The solidarity shown in this case between the Russian and Turkish Armenians, as regards their patriotic aspirations, seems to me of importance." [22]

The Googoonian Expedition was another display of the romantic spirit of the age. It was evidence in action of that same emotionalism that was reflected in the works of the nineteenth-century Armenian literary renascence. To die for the Fatherland, to shed blood, to seek freedom, were considered necessary for the accomplishment of the "Divine Mission" of the revolutionary. Such romanticism in action had already been shown by the Hunchaks in 1890 in their Demonstration of Kum Kapu. The period produced many men who, like Raffi's Khente (The Fool), dreamed of a new era for their country and made plans for its quick realization. In the early 'nineties a scheme was devised for capturing the whole city of Constantinople by simultaneous coups, which would result in the occupation of all the minarets of the capital.[23] Another plan called for the manufacture of bombs for the use of the future invaders and liberators of the Armenian provinces of Asiatic Turkey. But all such plans came to nought.

The year 1892 [24] marked a low ebb in the optimism of the patriot. This disillusionment, for a time, penetrated the ranks of the Dashnaktsuthiun and came close to putting an end to the young party. When the party was established in the summer of 1890, there was widespread feeling among the people of Transcaucasia that the crumbling of the Ottoman Empire was imminent. Decaying from within and greedily watched by the Great Powers, the Empire needed only a spark to start a revolution that would overthrow the regime. Armenian revolutionaries thought they could serve as such a spark, and the Googoonian Expedition was a sad example of their ambitious ventures. Months passed and nothing happened to force the European Powers to exert their authority on Turkey, in accordance with the international agreement at Berlin, so as to relieve Armenia's suffering. Instead, Armenian revolutionaries were encountering even sterner repressive measures both in Turkey and in Russia.

THE TURKISH AND RUSSIAN GOVERNMENTS IN REGARD TO THE ARMENIAN QUESTION

In 1891 Abdul Hamid had formed the Hamidiye, a new fighting force bearing his name. The troops were comprised solely of Kurdish tribesmen and organized into regiments modeled after the Russian Cossacks. In the capital they served as Hamid's personal bodyguard and in the provinces they allegedly acted as a frontier corps. The Hamidiye served more than just the military needs of the Sultan. It strengthened his Pan-Islamic policy and also provided a method of separating the Moslem Kurds from possible coöperation with the discontented Armenians. The separation of the two nationalities was not a normal development, for less than three decades earlier both Armenians and Kurds had fought as brothers in Van (1862) against Ottoman misgovernment.

The Sultan's newly formed regiments were allowed to act without restraint in the provinces, where they deliberately raided Armenian villages, ruined crops, and massacred the inhabitants.[25] Hamidiye regiments did not stop at destroying the means of livelihood of the Christians: their marauding also caused much economic damage to peaceful Turkish, Arab,[26] and Kurdish[27] inhabitants. These regiments were a formidable force in counteracting Armenian revolutionary activities, and of course these were regular soldiers operating in the provinces against mere partisan bands.

Across the border, in Russian Armenia, a change of governmental policy had occurred in regard to the Armenian Question and Russo-Turkish relations. Beginning in 1890, approximately, there was a conspicuous rapprochement between Russia and Turkey.[28] The Pan-Slavism displayed during the Bulgarian crisis of the 'seventies was now unpopular in Tsarist diplomatic and political circles. Russia was now not so interested in the suffering Christians under Ottoman rule, and the Armenian situation ceased to receive close diplomatic attention by the Russian government. In less than two decades the treatment of the Armenians within the Tsarist realm had passed from a policy of favoritism to one of persecution.

The political trials of the Goodwill Society (Barenepatak Enkeruthiun) and the Devotion to the Fatherland Bureau (Kontora Haireniats Siro) during the late 'seventies had ended in leniency toward the guilty defendants. This treatment contrasted sharply with the harsh punishment meted out to the participants of the Googoonian Expedition in the early 'nineties, who, like their brothers before them, had directed their energies against the Sultan. Already in the eighteen-eighties an anti-Armenian campaign which was part of a Russifying program had begun. The nationalistic aspirations of the Armenian people and the rise of the political parties were not palatable to the Tsar. He feared that an autonomous or independent Armenia might deprive him of Russian Armenia, a small part of his domain.

Russia's interest in the Near East as a whole began to wane with the start of construction on the Siberian Railroad in 1891. Constantinople and the Straits faded into the background for a time as the ambitions of St. Petersburg were directed toward expansion in the Far East and the Pacific.[29] The rapprochement with Turkey aided in ensuring the integrity of the weakened Ottoman Empire against possible European dismemberment at a time when Russia was pursuing her expansionist policy in the Far East. The change of Russian attitude toward the Ottoman Empire was a blow to the Armenian revolutionary, whose people faced near extermination in Turkey and Russification in Russia. The newly formed Dashnaktsuthiun was hard hit by the changed international scene, and to the unfavorable external pressures were added internal dissensions that created severe disruption within the party.

PARTY CONFLICTS

The Hunchakian Revolutionary Party had agreed in 1890, according to the compact signed at Tiflis, to cease operating as a separate organization and become an integral part of the Federation of Armenian Revolutionaries. Indeed, within six months after the agreement, many Hunchak branches on Russian territory became part of the newly formed Federation or Dashnaktsuthiun. But contrary to what had been expected, the union did not bring about a stronger and more harmonious fighting front.

Former Hunchaks soon became exceedingly dissatisfied with the manner in which they were treated by the Dashnak members. They sent bitter complaints to the central office at Geneva, asserting that they were not being treated as equals and were even being insulted and discriminated against by members of the new party. These letters were presented to Khan-Azat when he arrived at the Hunchak headquarters in Geneva early in the year 1891. His fellow comrades at Geneva also were greatly dissatisfied with the compact with the Dashnaks. They believed that the union of the two groups had not been brought about in good faith on the part of the non-Hunchak delegates at Tiflis. There was also evidence that the new organization was led, not by the socialists Mikaelian and Zavarian, but by the antisocialist, anti-Nazarbekian group in the Central Bureau at Tiflis.[30]

Avetis Nazarbekian accused the Dashnaks of being extremely slow in executing their plans. He had been told to stop publishing the *Hunchak* because the new Dashnak organ, the *Droshak,* was to be issued. Yet six months had elapsed and not even the first issue of the *Droshak* had appeared. The Hunchak editor was also extremely critical of a recent Dashnak circular called *Droshaki Trutsik Tert* (*Circular of the Droshak*).[31]

The Geneva headquarters discussed at length the many objections to the recent union and decided to nullify the compact with the Dashnaks and continue the Hunchakian Revolutionary Party as a separate organization.

The Central Committee of the Hunchakian Revolutionary Party issued official notices, which were published on May 18, 1891, and June 5, 1891, declaring that the Hunchakian Revolutionary Party had no connection with the Dashnaktsuthiun.[32] The Central Committee at Geneva also sent out notices and letters concerning the Hunchak decision.[33] The Hunchak Central Committee also informed the Central Bureau of the Dashnaktsuthiun, operating from Tiflis, but the latter did not acknowledge the communication.[34] The secession of the Hunchaks from the Dashnaktsuthiun weakened the ranks of the latter and in the long run precipitated conflicts between the two parties which were extremely damaging to the success of the Armenian Revolutionary Movement.

While the Hunchaks were announcing their severance from the party, the Dashnaks in Transcaucasia were occupied with another disruptive move. Some members believed that the Central Bureau was not working vigorously enough for the successful operation of the party. A group of those disaffected members broke away from the party in the latter part of October, 1890,[35] and formed a new organization called the "Fraktsia"[36] under the leadership of the nonsocialist Kostantin Khatisian.[37] Khatisian went to the Balkans, where he began manufacturing bombs for revolutionary purposes in Turkish Armenia. His plans were unsuccessful chiefly because of Bulgarian governmental restrictions and confiscations.[38] He returned to Transcaucasia at the end of the year 1891,[39] and shortly after, the Fraktsia came to an end.[40]

The Fraktsia was not the only group in Transcaucasia which splintered the revolutionary movement. An organization called the "Committee for the Freedom of the Turkish Armenians" ("Tadjkahayots Azatuthian Varchuthiun") had been established in Tiflis in the latter part of 1890. Made up of conservative elements, the Committee was led by one Haruthiun Tchagerian, who represented himself as one of the barons of Zeitun.[41] The purpose of the organization was to aid the revolutionary movement of the Turkish Armenians by assisting them with arms and provisions. An *Official Announcement* for the freedom of Turkish Armenia was issued by this Committee, requesting funds for their cause, and on November 15, 1890, Tchagerian made a similar announcement to nationalists in Rumania and Bulgaria.[42] Toward the beginning of 1892 the Dashnaktsuthiun was nearly in a state of collapse, under the heavy burden of external and internal troubles. The Central Bureau was bombarded with criticism by members and by the general public, who had expected great strides by this time toward the salvation of Turkish Armenia. The Russian Armenians were losing faith in the revolutionary movement and a general reaction set in against it.[43]

A set program to direct the activities of the organization was obviously lacking. The 1890 *Manifesto* spoke only in general terms; it did not present a concrete plan or constitution for carrying out the objectives of the Dashnaktsuthiun. Early in 1891 the Dashnaks had published *Droshaki Trutsik Tert, No. 1* and *No. 2*,[44] and in May had finally begun to issue their organ, the *Droshak*.[45] But these party publications did not fulfill the need for a detailed program.

THE FIRST GENERAL CONGRESS

In April, 1892, a group of Dashnaks in the city of Tabiz (Persia), realizing the need for drastic changes, advocated the convocation of another general meeting in a circular entitled *Invitation to the First General Congress of Armenian Revolutionaries.*[46] This circular explained the reasons for their action, outlined the order of business, and stressed the need for elaborating the following points: (1) The revolutionary objective of the Dashnaks, (2) the form of organization to be followed, (3) the methods and tactics to be used by the party.[47]

The circular was greeted with approval by party members. The result was the First General Congress of the Federation of Armenian Revolutionaries. The conclave took place in Tiflis (in Russian Transcaucasia) in the summer of 1892, some two years after the founding of the party. As with the 1890 meeting, no documents are known to be extant containing a report of the deliberations or the names of the delegates in attendance. The only significant document resulting from the meeting was the *Program of the Armenian Revolutionary Federation*. This document was to serve as the constitution of the Party, which now, with the removal of the Hunchaks, was called the "Armenian Revolutionary Federation" ("Hai Heghapokhakan Dashnaktsuthiun") instead of the "Federation of Armenian Revolutionaries" ("Hai Heghapokhakanneri Dashnaktsuthiun). This important document was printed both in the pages of the *Droshak*[48] and in a separate pamphlet.[49]

THE PROGRAM OF THE ARMENIAN REVOLUTIONARY FEDERATION

The *Program* begins with a lengthy introduction containing socialistic principles. It predicts the ultimate victory of the exploited working class or proletariat over the exploiting and oppressive ruling class, which is described as physically and morally degenerate. The latter is referred to as the "bourgeoisie" or "capitalist-usurer" class, which, in coöperation with government officials, the clergy, and the nobility, ". . . with iron claws, drains the blood of the working people." The conditions of the Armenian people of Turkey are described and their position is compared with that of the helots under Spartan rule. Consideration is also given to the position of other peoples, such as the Arabs, Kurds, Turks, and Yezidis who wished to have, like their fellow Armenians, a government that would work for the betterment of the majority.

Following this introduction, the *Program* states that the purpose of the Dashnaktsuthiun is ". . . to bring about the political and economic freedom of Turkish Armenia by means of rebellion and by making the following demands at present:" [50]

1. The future democratic government of free Armenia, serving the interests of the general public, shall of course be established by the vote of all adults, based on the principle of a free and nondiscriminated electorate. In order to truly protect these rights, the principle of free election must be extended more and more from the central government to the peasant of the remotest province.

2. The strictest provisions for the security of life and labor.

3. Equality of all nationalities and creeds before the law.

4. Freedom of speech, press, and assembly.

5. Give land to those who have none and guarantee the tiller the opportunity to benefit from the land.

6. The amount of all taxes should be decided according to the ability to pay and according to communal principles, which for centuries have been deeply rooted in our people.

7. Eliminate all forced and unpaid labor, such as the *gor* and *begar, angaria, olam, etc.* [These terms describe various forms of forced labor and tribute to the government and powerful land owners.]

8. Eliminate the military exemption tax and establish conscription according to the locality and needs of the time.

9. Assist in every manner the intellectual progress of the people. Make education compulsory.

10. Assist the industrial progress of the people by giving them modern methods of production based on the principle of

communal enterprise, and assist them in the methods of increasing exports.

11. Assist in strengthening the communal principles of the peasants and artisans, by advancing those communal establishments and methods which have appeared on the soil of Armenia as a result of local and historic influences. Broaden the area of such communal establishments, from the quarter to the village, to the province, and then to the whole country; in that way, at the same time, safeguard each member of society from the disasters of nature and the mishaps of everyday life.

The methods to be used by revolutionary bands organized by the party were the following:

1. To propagandize for the principles of the Dashnaktsuthiun and its objectives, based upon an understanding of, and sympathy with, the revolutionary work.

2. To organize fighting bands, to work with them in regard to the above-mentioned problems, and to prepare them for activity.

3. To use every means, by word and deed, to elevate the revolutionary activity and spirit of the people.

4. To use every means to arm the people.

5. To organize revolutionary committees and establish strong ties among them.

6. To investigate the country and people and supply constant information to the central organ of the Dashnaktsuthiun.

7. To organize financial districts.

8. To stimulate fighting and to terrorize government officials, informers, traitors, usurers, and every kind of exploiter.

9. To protect the peaceful people and the inhabitants against attacks by brigands.

10. To establish communications for the transportation of men and arms.

11. To expose government establishments to looting and destruction.

The last major section of the *Program* was devoted to the organization of the party. It declared that the principle of decentralization was essential to the satisfactory working of the various branches of the party. Each of the branches, some of which worked in units on a district basis, had the privilege of making its own decisions. This independence, however, was not extended to individual members. These were to work jointly with the central committee of the nearest district. There were two Central Executive Committees or Bureaus working in conjunction with each other. The Bureaus were to receive requests, reports of important activities, and surplus money from the various branches. The *Program* provided for the establishment of a central treasury, and also an official organ, the *Droshak*, for the circulation of all information deemed pertinent by the Bureaus. Besides the *Droshak*, the party allowed, under special conditions, the publication of pamphlets by local branches.[51]

The political plank in the *Program* of the Armenian Revolutionary Federation or Dashnaktsuthiun differed somewhat from that of the Hunchakian Revolutionary Party. The Hunchaks had stated clearly that they wanted a politically independent country, composed of Turkish Armenia, Russian Armenia, and Persian Armenia. The Dashnak *Program* of 1892 did not even mention the word independence. It affirmed the need for reforms in Asiatic Turkey, but said nothing of complete separation from the Ottoman Empire. The Armenakan *Program*, like that of the Dashnaks, did not specifically speak of an independent country, but stated that the party wished to have the Armenian people "rule over themselves." The Armenakans were vague as to what precisely was to be their area of operation; yet it might be assumed that they were concerned principally with Turkish Armenia. All three party programs, however, stated that revolutionary methods would be necessary for the relief of the suffering of the Armenians under Ottoman rule.

The political objectives of the Dashnaks were made

clearer in the first *Droshak* editorial, which stated that the demands of the party were approximately the same as those in Patriarch Nerses Varzhabedian's *Program*,[52] presented at the Congress of Berlin (1878) by the Armenian delegation. This *Program* had called for reforms and the appointment of an Armenian governor-general over the Armenian provinces.[53]

The demands of the Dashnaktsuthiun were further elaborated upon by the three founders—Christopher Mikaelian, Rostom (Stepan Zorian), and Simon Zavarian—in a series of articles which appeared in the *Droshak* under the title of "Ayb U Ben" (A and B).[54] They stressed the fact that political independence was not synonymous with freedom. In their opinion the freedom desired by the Armenian people was neither political freedom, national independence, nor an Armenian government in the place of the Turkish one. What was wanted was freedom that embodied political and economic reforms and provided conditions for peace and progress. The Dashnak objective of winning reforms for the Turkish Armenian provinces within the Ottoman political framework remained unaltered for nearly three decades.[55]

Ideologically the Dashnak *Program* advocated socialistic principles. The Dashnaks, like the Hunchaks, spoke of the exploited and exploiter classes of society and of the need to do away with bourgeois capitalist-usurers. The Dashnaks concentrated their efforts on socializing Turkish Armenia, while the Hunchaks wanted socialism not only for their people in Turkish Armenia but also for those in Russian Armenia and Persian Armenia. The Hunchaks stressed the need for preparing their people mentally for the future socialistic order and firmly advocated a world revolution that would establish a socialist order for all humanity. The Armenakan Party, in contrast to both the Dashnaktsuthiun and the Hunchakian Revolutionary Party, was not socialistic and consistently refused to endorse any socialist platform. The Dashnaktsuthiun clarified and elaborated upon its socialist platform at the Fourth General Congress in 1907.[56] Thereafter, the Dashnaktsuthiun became the most important socialist Ottoman organization attached to the Second International.[57]

The *Program* of 1892 officially sanctioned terrorism as a method of activity and in this respect coincided with the tactics of the Hunchaks. But the program of the Armenakans did not advocate terroristic methods (although this policy was ignored by certain individual members). The Dashnaktsuthiun had used terroristic methods even before 1892. A notable case was the murder in Erzerum of Khatchatur Kerektsian, a former leader of the Protectors of the Fatherland (Pashtpan Haireniats) in 1881–1882. The murder was later considered a regrettable incident by the Central Committee or Bureau,[58] but terrorism was nevertheless included in the party program.

The organization of the Dashnaks differed considerably from that of the Hunchakian Revolutionary Party. The Dashnaks had followed the policy of centralized administration during the first two years of its history. The same principle of organization was used by the Narodnaya Volya, and by most European revolutionary societies, as well as by the Hunchaks. There had been debates on administrative organization at the 1890 founders' meeting, and the same issue arose again at the First General Congress.

After giving due consideration to the geographical distribution of the Armenian people, the Dashnak delegates at Tiflis in 1892 decided to decentralize their organization. Although the *Program* provided for such administration, in practice the two Dashnak Central Committees or Bureaus had certain centralized powers which increased during the following decades.[59]

The Dashnak *Program* made a clear distinction between "peaceful Moslem Turks" and the "corrupt Ottoman government," against whom Dashnak efforts were directed.

The Hunchaks had also pursued a similar policy. Both parties actively supported these Turkish organizations which supposedly advocated reforms for the country. This cooperation with Turkish groups culminated in an agreement in 1907 between the Dashnaks and the *Ittihad ve Terakki* (Committee of Union and Progress) and the secret agreement between the Hunchaks and the *Hurriyet ve Itilaf* (Freedom and Unity) in 1912.[60] The Armenakan program differed radically from that of the Dashnaks and Hunchaks in respect to Armenian coöperation with foreign elements. The Armenakans emphatically declared that they did not wish to work with any non-Armenian groups to promote their own objectives. Thus, the Armenakans completely omitted mention of possible assistance from liberal Turkish elements. However, it must be recognized that, although there were expressions of a democratic attitude toward the Moslem Turkish and Kurdish people in Dashnak and Hunchak official publications, individual members of both parties (as well as members of the Armenakan Party) often failed to put such principles into practice.

On the whole, there was no radical difference between the Dashnak *Program* of 1892 and the aims and activities of the Hunchaks. The underlying cause of disagreement between them can be attributed more to petty jealousies and personal feuds than to differences of socialist ideology, administrative organization, or geographical boundaries for revolutionary activity. It was unfortunate for patriots that the two major parties were unable to come to any permanent accord; and that their relations with one another often resulted in conflicts and rivalries, which in turn were harmful to the very objectives they were pursuing.

Unification would have been a strengthening force, but, in spite of the Hunchak withdrawal from the Armenian Revolutionary Federation in 1891, the Dashnaks were able to survive. The external and internal crisis had been partially overcome with the help of the First General Congress and the agreements set forth in the *Program* of 1892. The Dashnaktsuthiun was now prepared to pursue a more vigorous program of action.

DASHNAK ACTIVITIES

By 1892 branches of the party had already been formed in many cities in Turkish Armenia, Russian Armenia, Persia, Transcaucasia, in the Black Sea ports of Trebizond and Odessa, and in the Turkish capital. Persian soil became a Mecca for revolutionaries, who, in contrast to the situation less than a century before, were now allowed freedom in the Moslem land of the Shah, whereas they were persecuted in Christian Russia. Persia thus became the launching ground for operations in nearby Turkish Armenia.

The Dashnak centers in Persia were in the northwestern part of the country, particularly in Tabriz, Salmast, and Khoi.[61] Field workers from Transcaucasia crossed the Russo-Persian frontier and, under such guises as teachers, priests, pilgrims, and merchants, organized branches, preached rebellion, and made preparations for entering Ottoman territory. Among the first Dashnak organizers in Persia was Tigran Stepanian, a former member of the Droshak group. He came to Tabriz and there, in 1891, he founded a small arms factory called the Khariskh Zinagordzaran (Central Arms Factory).

The arms factory had branches in various Armenian quarters of the city of Tabriz and served mainly as an assembling plant. Skilled men, who had studied at the Tula arms factory in Russia, worked in the plant. Military equipment was bought by party agents in Tula and obtained from Russian workers in the government armory at Tiflis.[62] The guns and munitions were then stored in arsenals in different cities of Transcaucasia, whence some were carefully transported to the plant in Tabriz. Here the parts were assembled, completed, and stored for use by guerrilla forces.[63] After proper preparations had been made, arms and munitions were transferred from Tabriz to different points on the Turco-Persian frontier.

An important stopping-place for revolutionaries entering Turkey was the Armenian Monastery of Derik,[64] on the Persian side of the frontier. The monastery had for years been in disrepair, but gained special attention in the early nineties because of its strategic military position. Bagrat Vardapet Tavakalian, known as the revolutionist "Zakki," became the Abbot of Derik and encouraged military activity in connection with the sanctuary. During his abbacy, the Monastery of Derik was restored, with the help of both Armenakans and Dashnaks, who used it as a retreat and arsenal.

The strategic importance of the location of the monastery was well known to the local Kurds and the Turkish police. For years the patriots occasionally skirmished with local tribesmen, who resented the presence of others in a primarily Kurdish area. Turkish officials were even more concerned, since the monastery was a source of supply for guerrillas entering the province of Van. As a result of such conflicts, a major clash occurred at Derik on July 21, 1894.[65] A punitive Turkish force, aided by local Kurds, crossed the frontier and attacked the monastery. After encountering stiff resistence from the Armenians, the invading troops were forced to withdraw without accomplishing their mission.

For years revolutionaries entered the Asiatic provinces of Turkey from adjacent regions in Persia and Russia. In Turkish Armenia they secretly organized other small guerrilla forces, formed party branches, and disseminated propaganda.[66]

The Dashnaks did not recruit only among the Armenians. Like the Hunchaks, the Dashnaks tried to enlist the support of other nationalities in the cause. The Kurds were considered a potentially valuable element and special effort was made to win their friendship and coöperation. Organizers were sent to Kurdish areas in Van and Moush, one of the most prominent of these being Yerzenkatsi Keri (Ruben Shishmanian), who worked among the tribesmen at Dersim. The Dashnaks were successful in obtaining the support of a Kurdish resident in Geneva named Abdurahman. The latter wrote articles in Kurdish inviting his countrymen to join the revolutionaries in their fight against the government and to refrain from participating in harmful acts against the Armenians. These articles, written in Arabic characters, were distributed among the Kurds.[67] But the writings of Abdurahman and the activities of political organizers were not enough to effect any kind of harmonious relations between the two peoples.

The Dashnaktsuthiun was more successful in winning the coöperation of the Young Turks and of discontented Christian elements. Worthy of note are the cordial relations that existed between Dashnaks and Balkan Christians. By 1895 an agreement had been established between the Bulgarian-controlled Internal Macedonian Revolutionary Organization (Centralists) led by Boris Sarafov[68] and the Dashnaktsuthiun. The ties between the two parties were so close that in Geneva Dashnaks and Bulgars led by Simon Ratev at times held joint meetings.[69]

Until the year 1896 the party had emphasized the formation of new branches, organizing small guerrilla movements, spreading propaganda, obtaining military equipment, and negotiating with other revolutionary groups. The party had not sponsored any major demonstrations such as those staged by the Hunchakian Revolutionary Party in its early years. The Dashnaks had stood against the large-scale Hunchak-sponsored Demonstration of Bab Ali (September 18, 1895), calling it ill-prepared, premature, and the cause of the massacres that followed.[70] Nonetheless, their own policy rapidly changed in favor of holding large-scale demonstrations as a vehicle for attracting European intervention. Less than one year after the Bab Ali incident, the Dashnaktsuthiun engaged in a similar move in the city of Constantinople.

THE OTTOMAN BANK DEMONSTRATION

The capture of the Imperial Ottoman Bank on August 24, 1896, by a group of revolutionists, together with simultaneous acts of agitation in different parts of the capital, was a major political move devised well in advance by the Dashnaktsuthiun. The threat to the Bank was aimed at arousing the attention of the European Powers, which had national interests in the Turkish institution. The Dashnaks hoped the Europeans would thus be forced to intervene in the chaotic affairs of Turkey and render assistance to the Armenian demands for reforms.

In a surprise attack the entrances of the Ottoman Bank were seized by twenty-six Dashnak revolutionists led by a seventeen-year-old youth, Babken Suni. Having the building and its occupants at their mercy, the invaders communicated their demands to the outside world. These were:

1. The nomination for Armenia of a High Commissioner, of European origin and nationality, elected by the Six Great Powers.

2. The Valis, Mutessarifs, and Kaimakams to be appointed by the High Commissioner and sanctioned by the Sultan.

3. The militia, gendarmerie, and police to be drawn from the native population and to be under the command of European officers.

4. Judicial reforms according to the European system.

5. Absolute freedom of worship, education, and the press.

6. The application of three-quarters of the revenue of the country to local needs.

7. The cancellation of arrears of taxes.

8. Exemption from taxes for five years, and the application

for the five years following of the tax payable to the Sultan's Government to the compensation of losses caused by the recent troubles.

9. The immediate restoration of usurped real property.

10. The free return of Armenian emigrants.

11. A general amnesty for Armenians condemned on political charges.

12. A temporary Commission to be formed by the Representatives of the Great Powers in óne of the principal towns of Armenia, with the function of watching over the execution of the aforementioned Articles.[71]

The Dashnak revolutionists who had seized the Bank threatened to blow it up, with the sacrifice of both themselves and the occupants, if their demands were not met within 48 hours. A special declaration was made to this effect to the foreign ambassadors, who immediately took steps to negotiate with the revolutionists. Maximov, the dragoman of the Russian Embassy, who represented the Powers, succeeded in satisfying the revolutionaries by agreeing to comply with their demands. By this time four of the Dashnaks—including their leader, the youthful Babken Suni—had died. Five had been wounded by the explosion of bombs that had been hurled at outsiders trying to enter the Bank. Since the revolutionists, who had already held the Bank for more than 12 hours, faced eventual starvation, they readily accepted Maximov's offer. Thereupon, they were given safe escort from the Imperial Ottoman Bank through angry mobs to the yacht of Sir Edgar Vincent (later Lord D'Abernon), chief director of the Bank. Seventeen of the Dashnaks were subsequently given passage from Constantinople to Marseille on the French ship *La Gironde*.[72]

Peace did not reign in the capital after the bank demonstration, nor did any reforms ensue. The government had been informed in advance of the Dashnak project, but rather than forestall the revolutionaries, it had secretly prepared a brutal retaliation. On the day of the demonstration mobs of ruffians launched a bloody massacre of the Armenian population. Government soliders, *softas* (theological students), and police officers led Turkish mobs in the slaughter of the Armenians. Christians, regardless of guilt, were singled out and bludgeoned to death; women and children were ruthlessly cut down in the streets; and this reign of terror persisted in the capital for many days, resulting in terrible carnage and destruction. More than 6,000 persons perished in the massacre.[73]

This shocking outrage in Constantinople was witnessed by foreign residents and diplomats, who were moved to a gesture of protest. A Collective Note (August 27, 1896)[74] and a Verbal Note (September 2, 1896)[75] were sent by the Ambassadors of the Great Powers in Constantinople to the Sublime Porte, but no really effective action was taken by the foreign powers to correct the evils perpetrated by the government. The Dashnak demonstration was merely made the pretext for barbarous aggression. The promises made by the Great Powers through their representative Maximov proved to be empty, and the capture of the Imperial Ottoman Bank became the Dashnak equivalent of the Hunchak Demonstration of Bab Ali. Yet the Dashnaks were not overwhelmed by their failure in Constantinople. Up to the year 1896 the guarantees of the Treaty of Berlin (1878) for reforms in Turkish Armenia had remained unfulfilled and the inhabitants of that area had witnessed little, if any, improvement in administration.[76] The revolutionists of all the political parties had endured harsh government action, yet at the end of the Black Year of 1896 the Dashnaktsuthiun could still fervently exclaim:[77]

"Arms! Battle! The victory is ours!"

VIII

Conclusion

The Armenian Revolutionary Movement of the nineteenth century was a single phase in the struggle of the Armenian people for freedom which, extending through more than twenty-five centuries of Armenian history, has produced only relatively brief periods of independence.

After the fall of the last Armenian kingdom in the fourteenth century, several missions, encouraged by certain Catholicoi, were sent to various European nations and the Pope to enlist their support in freeing the Armenians from their Moslem overlords. From the fifteenth to the nineteenth century, patriots of the caliber of Shazi Murat, Israel Ori, David Beg, and Joseph Emin arose and, at great personal sacrifice, attempted to rally the Armenians and to arrange such diplomatic negotiations as might favor Armenian independence.

After the ascent of Peter the Great to the Russian throne, Russia was looked to, more than ever before, as the possible savior of the Armenians. But this hope vanished when a part of Armenian territory came under the Tsar in the beginning of the nineteenth century without the achievement of political autonomy.

In the nineteenth century the struggle for Armenian freedom centered in the six provinces of Turkish Armenia. This, the largest geographical area of Armenia, became the focus of attention for Armenian nationalists, not only in Turkey but also in Russian and in Persian Armenia. Under Ottoman rule the Armenian Christians had been for centuries the victims of arbitrary taxes, looting, forced conversions, and personal violence; and had always been denied the political rights and opportunities granted to Moslems. The Armenians now achieved a degree of national self-consciousness, with the result that they could not passively tolerate these conditions.

The movement for freedom, which since the fourteenth century had been carried on by certain patriotic individuals, encompassed a much larger part of the native Armenian population during the last half of the nineteenth century. A change in attitude toward their servile condition was marked by a spirit of insurgence which had been the culmination of several centuries of indoctrination. The ideological aspirations of the French Revolution fostered new hopes. Young Armenians, inspired by the ideals of *liberté, égalité, fraternité,* and encouraged by the European revolutionary movements of 1830 and 1848, began to spread the doctrine of freedom among their countrymen.

The first Armenian eruption—the earliest major physical manifestation—against the Ottoman regime took place at Zeitun in 1862. This rebellion was symptomatic of more than local discontent—the insurgents had advance contact, for example, with a group of revolutionists who resided in Constantinople—and was the beginning of a national movement for liberation from Ottoman control which was to increase in momentum during the following decades. The Armenian leaders became progressively more concerned with the socioeconomic theories of the day and were destined to connect the revolutionary movement of the Armenians with that of international socialism. Thus the uprisings in Turkish Armenia soon became part of the general movement of the masses which, in Europe and Russia, were pressing for economic, social, and political change.

The Ottoman government rebuffed demands for needed reforms in Turkish Armenia. Those Armenians who could no longer patiently endure their suffering then resorted to "non-legal" methods as a way of salvation. At first these took the form of arming for self-protection; later, aggressive methods were adopted.

Numerous revolutionary organizations took part in the movement aimed at bettering the conditions of the Turkish Armenians. In general, those groups formed on Turkish soil took a rather cautious attitude toward aggressive tactics and were not strongly motivated by any particular socio-economic theories. But the secret Armenian organizations formed in Russia and aimed at aiding the Turkish Armenians, especially after the Russo-Turkish War (1877–1878), were deeply influenced by the political policies and tactics of Russian revolutionists. The climax of such group activities was the formation of secret political parties.

The members of these secret parties considered the freeing from Ottoman rule of the Greeks, Bulgars, Serbs, and Montenegrins a succession of triumphs. They believed that this goal had been accomplished, even with the aid of the Great Powers, only because the Balkan peoples had taken the initiative and had risen in revolt against the Turks. The Armenian revolutionists believed that their people should emulate the Balkan example. The revolutionary parties also relied on the sincerity of the European Powers, which had made commitments for reforms in Turkish Armenia in Article LXI of the Treaty of Berlin.

Although the secret political parties advocated rebellion, all did not agree in details. The founders of the Armenakan

Party—which was the first, originating in Van in 1885—were living under Ottoman rule and were intimately associated with the conditions around them. It is not surprising, therefore, that their program was a cautious one, favoring education, preparation, self-protection, avoidance of terroristic methods. Having less contact with the outside world, the leaders of the Armenakan Party were not versed, as were the leaders of the other parties, in the socioeconomic theories of the day, nor did they advocate socialistic principles. As a party they remained localized and accordingly lacked the broad appeal and the strength of the Hunchakian Revolutionary Party and the Armenian Revolutionary Federation or Dashnaktsuthiun, which arose during the next five years.

Both the Hunchakian Revolutionary Party and the Dashnaktsuthiun were formed outside of the geographical area of Armenia: the former in Geneva, Switzerland, in 1887, and the latter in Tiflis (Russian Transcaucasia), in 1890. Their leaders were Russian Armenians who had never lived in Turkish Armenia for any length of time. Both of these parties advocated a socialist order and used terroristic tactics, modeled after the Russian revolutionary organization Narodnaya Volya. The Hunchaks and Dashnaks recognized the need to combine nationalistic and socialistic principles and their programs were early examples of such an attempt. The Hunchaks believed that freedom could not be obtained without a politically independent country; the Dashnaks advocated Armenian reforms within the framework of the Ottoman Empire. Hunchaks and Dashnaks alike believed their activities would attract the European Powers, who, they were sure, would intervene and aid the Turkish Armenian cause.

The revolutionists' fight against the Ottoman regime took place against incredible odds. They did not have sufficient manpower, matériel, or economic strength to combat the powerful forces of the Sultan, yet in the face of oppression that they found intolerable, they had little alternative except to incite revolt. Unfortunately, the parties were unable to enlist adequate support from the Kurds or from those Turks and other Moslems who were being exploited by corrupt administrators. This inability left the Armenians isolated in a geographical region in which they were the minority population.

Moreover, the Armenians were far from being completely united. The revolutionists themselves were young people captivated by new radical ideas and did not always have the coöperation of the conservative-minded and mature leaders of the older generation. Although the older intelligentsia had been instrumental in propagating the new nationalism and played an important role in the literary and educational enlightenment of the youth, they did not readily join the parties or give direction to them.

Other segments of the Armenian community, especially among the well-to-do, were desirous of reforms, but did not wish to be committed to illegal methods. Most of those who were living comfortably were not willing to donate money and risk their lives and wealth for revolutionary objectives. Certain wealthy bourgeois capitalists actively opposed the revolutionists in the major parties because of their socialist doctrines.

None of the three religious groups—the national Armenian Church, the Armenian Catholic Church, or the Protestant Church—took an official position in regard to the revolutionary political parties. As a whole, clergymen of all denominations were concerned with religious undertakings and were apathetic toward political developments. However, there were individual clerics, especially among those of the national Armenian Church, who were active party members.

In sum, a considerable number of Armenians stood in the way of the revolutionists because of special motives and attitudes—from disapproval of the methods of the parties (as more destructive and dangerous than salutary), from a desire to preserve the status quo, or from a mere lack of concern.

Then too, the parties were further handicapped by a lack of cohesiveness. There was an unwillingness to put aside personal feuds and theoretical problems in the interests of a common revolutionary front. Paradoxically, these same men were ready and willing to sacrifice their very lives to help their suffering nation.

All such weaknesses might probably have been overcome if the revolutionists had received assistance from the European Powers—a vital factor in their program. The idealistic revolutionists were persistently naïve in their evaluation of European politics and diplomacy: they never gave up hope for some kind of assistance, military or otherwise; and after nearly 20 years they continued to hope that Article LXI of the Treaty of Berlin would be enforced— a treaty long forgotten in international politics. The demonstrations and insurrections, which were organized to attract European intervention, were predestined to failure under the existing circumstances, and resulted in the deaths of many defenceless Armenians, since the violent activities of the parties brought reprisals against the Armenian populace. Moreover, the government was extremely well informed about the plans of the revolutionists. Unknown to the party leaders, the secret service files of the Porte contained detailed information on revolutionary leaders inside and outside of Turkey. Nonetheless, for almost twenty years following the Ottoman Bank disaster of 1896, the parties continued to resist corrupt government. Even after the fall of the Ottoman Sultan, the Armenian population experienced sporadic massacres by the ensuing Young Turk constitutional regime of 1908 toward whom the Dashnaktsuthiun had at first shown a conciliatory attitude. Up to and beyond the Balkan War (1912–13), in which Turkey was defeated by an alliance of Greece,

Serbia, Bulgaria, and Montenegro, the Armenian population was in a relatively thriving condition, but in 1915, the Turks brutally massacred Armenian men, women, and children on an unparalleled scale and drove the remaining survivors from Turkish Armenia. The Armenians of Russian Transcaucasia under the leadership of the Dashnaktsuthiun formed the short-lived Armenian Republic at Erivan (May 28, 1918), which was overthrown and became the Armenian Socialist Soviet Republic in 1920. This Russian Armenian area now remains one of the republics of the Union of Socialist Soviet Republics. The attempts of the Armenians to restore their ancestral home were not successful. These people were dispersed to alien lands.

This study has attempted to provide only a modest sketch of the revolutionary activity of the Armenians in the nineteenth century. It does not presume to weigh the results in terms of success and failure. Certainly these patriots met frustration at every turn, but their efforts did help in hastening the disintegration of the corrupt Ottoman regime. It can be said of them without reservation that they worked at restoring the honor of their people and that they believed as passionately as did their fifth-century ancestors who fought at Avarair: "We die as mortals, that we through our death may be placed among those who are immortal."[1]

Notes

(Complete bibliographical information on works cited here in an abbreviated form is given in the Bibliography.)

NOTES TO CHAPTER I (Pp. 1–29)

1. H. F. B. Lynch and F. Oswald, *Map of Armenia and Adjacent Countries* (London, 1901); Artashes Abeghian, *Hayastan yev Dratsi Yerkirnere [Armenia and Neighboring Countries]* (Stuttgart, 1947), see map; Z. Khanzadian, *Rapport sur l'unité geographique de l'Arménie: atlas historique* (Paris, 1920); Arshak Alboyadjian, *Patmakan Hayastani Sahmannere [The Boundaries of Historical Armenia]* (Cairo, 1950); Felix Oswald, *Geology of Armenia* (London, 1906), pp. 11–12; Frédéric Macler, *La nation arménienne: son passé, ses malheurs* (Paris, 1924), pp. 7–18.
2. The Armenians call themselves "Hai."
3. Jacques de Morgan, *History of the Armenian People*, tr. Ernest F. Barry (Boston, n.d.), pp. 43–49; Abeghian, *op. cit.*, map of Armenia.
4. Léonce M. Alishan, *Sissouan ou l'Arméno-Cilicie: géographique et historique* (Venice, 1899), pp. 1–2. The author's first name is also given as Ghevond.
5. H. R. Hall, *The Ancient History of the Near East* (London, reprinted 1952), pp. 458–459.
6. B. Piotrovsky, "Excavations of the Urartian Citadel on the Karmir-Blur," *Papers Presented by the Soviet Delegation at the XXIII International Congress of Orientalists, Iranian, Armenian and Central-Asian Studies* (Moscow: USSR Academy of Sciences, 1954), pp. 172–173.
7. *Ibid.*, pp. 179–182.
8. L. W. King (ed.), *Bronze Reliefs from the Gates of Shalmaneser King of Assyria 860–825 B.C.* (London, 1915), pp. 10–13, 22, 27, Plates 1–12.
9. For a detailed account of Urartian history and culture, see Nicolas Adontz, *Histoire d'Arménie des origines du Xe siècle au VIe (av. J.C.)* (Paris, 1946).
10. A full corpus on Uratian inscriptions has been published. A. H. Sayce deciphered the Uratian cuneiform inscriptions, which he called Vannic inscriptions. His findings were published in the *Journal of the Royal Asiatic Society* in a series of articles from 1882 to 1929. Attempts had previously been made by the Rev. E. Hinks, M. Lenormant, Dr. A. D. Mordtmann, Dr. Louis de Roberts, and Stanislas Guylard.

11. Mardiros A. Ananikian, "Armenian Mythology," *The Mythology of All Races* (Boston, 1925), VII, 11.

12. Herodotus, VII, 73. The late Armenian scholar Arshak Safrastian of London alleged that Herodotus was incorrect when he attributed Phrygian origins to the Armenians and that this erroneous assumption has been repeated by modern writers as fact. According to Safrastian's own researches, no Phrygian migration to Armenia ever took place and the Armenians have been known in history by various names. Their cultural history dates to the Khurrians, who later became known as Urartians and are today called Armenians or Hais.

13. René Grousset, *Histoire de l'Arménie des origines à 1071* (Paris, 1947), pp. 69–73.

14. Sahak Ter-Movsisian, *Patmuthiun Hayots Skizben Mintchev Mer Orere [Armenian History from Its Beginnings to the Present]* (Venice, 1922), I, 147–170.

15. *Ibid.*, p. 228.

16. For information on the Artaxian period consult Strabo and other ancient writers, especially Plutarch, Tacitus, and Pliny. See also Herant K. Armen, *Tigranes the Great, a Biography* (Detroit, 1940).

17. For details see Hakob Manandian, *Feodalisme Hin Hayastanum: Arshakunineri ou Marzputhian Shertjan [Feudalism in Ancient Armenia: Arsacid and Marzpan Period]* (Erivan, 1934). According to Manandian, we do not have definite facts about the rise and early stages of feudalism in Armenia. He says, however, that feudalism had a very extended duration in Armenia and had existed there long before the Artaxian dynasty. The beginnings of the breakdown of the system took place before the second half of the fourteenth century. Feudalism in Armenia followed the same pattern as the feudal society that appeared in Western Europe centuries later.

18. The Armenian Arsacids outlived the Parthian Arsacid branch in Persia, which was succeeded by the Sassanid Dynasty in A.D. 227.

19. Malachia Ormanian, *The Church of Armenia* (London, 1912), p. 10.

20. Ghevond M. Alishan, *Arshaloys Kristoneuthian Hayots [Dawn of Armenian Christianity]* (3d ed; Venice, 1920), pp. 15–60; Edgar J. Goodspeed, *The Twelve* (Philadelphia, 1957), p. 98.

21. Ormanian, *op. cit.*, p. 20.

22. *Ibid.*, p. 58.

23. Y. T-Minasian, *Voskedari Hai Grakanuthiune [The Armenian Literature of the Golden Age]* (Erivan, 1946), pp. 6–7.

24. Y. A. Manadian, *A Brief Survey of the History of Ancient Armenia* (n.p., n.d.), p. 16.

25. Y. T-Minasian, *op. cit.*, pp. 8–9.

26. Yeghishe Tourian, *Patmuthiun Hai Matenagruthian [History of Armenian Literature]* (Jerusalem, 1933), pp. 7–10; Koriun, *Vark Mashtotsi [Life of Mesrop Mashtots* (with a preface by M. Abeghian)] (Cairo, 1954), pp. 5–6, 13.

27. Ormanian, *op. cit.*, p. 22.

28. Both were later canonized by the Armenian Church.

29. Tourian, *op. cit.*, pp. 21-24. Of many of these translations the originals have been lost and they remain only in the Armenian translation; e.g., *Chronicle of Eusebius, Homilies of St. John Chrystostom.*

30. See Elisaeus, Bishop of the Amadunians, *The History of Vartan, and the Battle of the Armenians: Containing An Account of the Religious Wars between the Persians and the Armenians,* translated from the Armenian by C. F. Neumann (n.p., 1830).

31. Sirarpie Der Nersessian, *Armenia and the Byzantine Empire* (Cambridge, Mass., 1945), pp. 7-8, 14-17.

32. *Ibid.*, pp. 8-9.

33. H. Adontz, *Patmakan Usumnasiruthiuner* [*Historical Studies*] (Paris, 1948), pp. 23-24, 51.

34. A. A. Vasiliev, *History of the Byzantine Empire 324-1453* (2d English ed., rev.; Madison, Wisconsin, 1952), p. 314.

35. Y. A. Manandian, *op. cit.*, p. 32.

36. Leo, *Ani* [in Armenian] (Erivan, 1946), pp. 37-40.

37. De Morgan, *op. cit.*, pp. 165-168. These were the kingdoms of Antzevatsik, Rushtunik, Vaspurakan, Sunik, Lori, Taiq, and Kars.

38. *Supra*, pp. 2-3.

39. *Supra*, p. 3.

40. De Morgan, *op. cit.*, pp. 273-274.

41. He died in Paris in 1393 and today his tomb can be seen at St. Denis. For an account of Leo V, see K. J. Basmadjian, *Levon V Lusignan Vertjin Takavor Hayots* [*Leo V Lusignan, the Last King of the Armenians*] (Paris, 1908).

42. This Christian city of New Julfa (Nor Julfa or Nor Tjughah) survives to this day and is still predominantly inhabited by Armenians.

43. H. Kurdian, "Grakhosakan Ser Anthoni Sherli" ["A Book Review of the Biography of Sir Anthony Sherley"], *Hairenik Amsagir* [*Hairenik Monthly*], XIV (September 1936), 174.

44. Amy Apcar (ed.), *Life and Adventures of Emin Joseph Emin 1726-1809 by Joseph Emin* (2d ed.; Calcutta, 1918). See especially "Note on the Five Meliks of Karabagh," pp. 333-360. The five provinces were Gulistan, Chrapiert, Khachin, Varranda, and Thizak.

45. Leo, *Hayots Patmuthiun* [*History of the Armenians*] (Erivan, 1946), III, 187-191.

46. *Ibid.*, pp. 193-197; Alishan, *Hushigh Haireniats Hayots* [*Reflections on the Fatherland of the Armenian People*] (Venice, 1869), I, 524-530.

47. Bedros Kasarjian, "Vov E Shazi Kam Shah Murat" ["Who is Shazi or Shah Murat?"], *Nor Or* [*New Day*], December 23, 1949.

48. H. Missak, *Le Père Ottoman 1644-1676* (Paris, 1903), pp. 1-29.

49. Malachia Ormanian, *Azgapatum* [*The Story of the Nation*] (Jerusalem, 1927), II, 2610-2614.

50. Leo, *Hayots Patmuthiun*, III, 520-589. A detailed history of the life of Israel Ori is given by Aschot Johannissjan, *Israel Ory und die Armenische Befreiungsidee* (Inaugural Dissertation, Munich, 1913).

For an attempted refutation of the story of Israel Ori's emancipatory mission see H. Kurdian, "Israyel Orii Keankin Aratjin Shertjane" ["The Early Years of the Life of Israel Ori"], *Hairenik Amsagir,* XXXIV (January 1956), 70–78; "Israyel Orin Mosgovayi Metj" ["Israel Ori in Moscow"], *ibid.,* (February 1956), 79–80; *Ibid.,* (March 1956), 72–80.

51. Edmund Burke, *The Correspondence of Edmund Burke* (Cambridge, 1958–1961), I, 120–122; II, 359–360.

52. Lazarian became strongly influenced by Emin's ideas and in later years he, along with Bishop Arghutiants, tried to interest the Russian government in the Armenian Question. See Leo, *Hayots Patmuthiun,* III, 826 ff. Lazarian also had connections with the Madras Armenians (see chap. ii of present work), who also became active in the liberation movement.

53. Emin wrote his autobiography: *The Life and Adventures of Joseph Emin, An Armenian; Written in English by Himself.* London, 1792. 640 pp.

54. Noel Buxton and Harold Buxton, *Travel and Politics in Armenia* (London, 1914), p. 209.

55. Ormanian, *Azgapatum* (Constantinople, 1914), III, 3685–3699; H. F. B. Lynch, *Armenia Travel and Studies* (London, 1901), I, 218–219, 233–235; K. J. Basmadjian, *Histoire moderne des arméniens* (Paris, 1917), pp. 59–61; B. A. Borian, *Armenia, mezhdunarodnaia diplomatiia i SSSR [Armenia, International Diplomacy and the SSSR]* (Moscow and Leningrad, 1928), I, 167. The complete title of this document is *Polozhenie ob upravlenii delami armiano-grigorianskoi tserkvi b Rossii [Statutes of Administration for the Affairs of the Armenian Gregorian Church in Russia].*

56. Vahe A. Sarafian, "Turkish Armenian and Expatriate Population Statistics," *The Armenian Review,* IX (Autumn 1956), 119.

57. A. O. Sarkissian, *History of the Armenian Question to 1885* (Urbana, Ill., 1938), 14–16.

58. *Ibid.,* pp. 17–19.

59. John A. R. Marriott, *The Eastern Question* (4th ed.; Oxford, 1951), pp. 250, 311.

60. Edwin Pears, *Life of Abdul Hamid* (New York, 1917), pp. 1–2.

61. Ferdinand Schevill, *The History of the Balkan Peninsula* (New York, 1922), pp. 420–421.

62. C. B. Norman, *Armenia, and the Campaign of 1877* (London, 1878), pp. 200–202, 234–235, 262–263, 293–330, 313; Henry Fanshawe Tozer, *Turkish Armenia and Eastern Asia Minor* (London, 1881), pp. 416–419.

63. Sarukhan, *Haikakan Khendiren yev Azgayin Sahmanadruthiune Thurkiayum (1860–1910) [The Armenian Question and the Armenian National Constitution in Turkey (1860–1910)]* (Tiflis, 1912), pp. 353–361.

64. Great Britain, *State Papers, 1877–1878,* LXIX, 739; M. G. Rolin-Jaequemyns, *Armenia, the Armenians, and the Treaties* (London,

1891), p. 33, in reference to the Treaty of San Stefano states: "To this Treaty belongs the honour and merit of being the first international compact which mentions Armenia."

65. Great Britain, *State Papers, 1877–1878,* LXIX, 766.
66. *Ibid.,* pp. 745–746.
67. Great Britain, *Further Correspondence respecting the Affairs of Turkey.* Parl. Pubs., 1879, Vol. LXXIX (Accounts and Papers), c. 2205, Turkey No. 54 (1878), Inclosure in no. 222. Armenians from the Village of Aagh to Vice-Consul Biliotti, pp. 188–190; Great Britain, *Correspondence respecting the Condition of the Populations in Asia Minor and Syria.* Parl. Pubs., 1879, Vol. LXXX (Accounts and Papers), c. 2432, Turkey No. 10 (1879), no. 8. Major Trotter to the Marquis of Salisbury—(Received February 11, 1879), pp. 12–13.
68. *Ibid.,* Vol. LXXX, no. 1. Captain Trotter, R.E., to the Marquis of Salisbury—(Received December 7), pp. 1–3; Norman, *Armenia and the Campaign of 1877* (London, 1878), p. 263.

NOTES TO CHAPTER II (Pp. 30–66)

1. Malachia Ormanian, *The Church of Armenia* (London, 1912), pp. 150–156. Bertrand Bareilles, in the preface of the French edition of this work, states (p. xviii): "In the essentially democratic constitution of the Armenian Church there is inherently a liberality of thought. . . ."
2. Bedros Kasarjian, *Hai Arakelakan Yekeghetsin yev Ir Vardapetuthiune* [*The Armenian Apostolic Church and its Doctrine*] (Paris, 1945), p. 91.
3. Leo, *Hayots Patmuthiun* (Erivan, 1946), III, 937. Nor Nakhichevan is sometimes called New Nakhichevan.
4. Garegin Zarbhanalian, *Patmuthiun Hayeren Depruthian* [*History of Armenian Literature*] (Venice, 1905), II, 6–11. Minas Nurikhan, *The Life and Times (1660–1750) of the Servant of God Abbot Mechitar,* tr. John McQuillan (Venice, 1915), pp. 44–45; H. J. Sarkiss, "The Armenian Renaissance, 1500–1863," *Journal of Modern History,* IX (December 1937), 438; Kevork A. Sarafian, *History of Education in Armenia* (La Verne, Calif., 1930), pp. 117–128.
5. Garegin Levonian, *Hai Girke yev Tepagruthian Arveste* [*The Armenian Book and the Art of Printing*] (Erivan, 1946), p. 81.
6. Sarafian, *op. cit.,* p. 137.
7. Levonian, *op. cit.,* p. 82.
8. *Ibid.,* p. 82.
9. Nurikhan, *op. cit.,* pp. 153–155.
10. Zarbhanalian, *op. cit.,* II, 320.
11. Mesrop Djanachian, *Patmuthiun Ardi Hai Graganuthian* [*History of Modern Armenian Literature*] (Venice, 1953), p. 9.
12. *Ibid.,* p. 23. This classical Armenian grammar was published in 1730.
13. *Ibid.,* p. 24. This vernacular grammar was published in 1727. Mekhi-

thar also wrote another vernacular grammar in 1726 which remains unpublished.

14. Garegin Zarhbanalian, *Patmuthiun Haikakan Tepagruthian Skezbna-vorutenen Mintch Ar Mez* [*The History of Armenian Printing from Its Beginnings to the Present*] (Venice, 1895), pp. 8–9.

15. *Ibid.*, p. 43. Abgar Tbir's son, Sultanshah, remained in Rome. He was adopted by the Pope and given the name Marcus Antoninus or Marco Antonino. He worked in the Vatican as an Armenian scholar.

16. *Ibid.*, p. 47. In terms of the rapid advancement and distribution of modern scientific inventions, the art of printing was very slow in becoming a popular method of reproduction. Abgar Tbir's press at Constantinople (1567) was also the second press established in Turkey. The first press in the Armenian provinces of Turkey appeared nearly three centuries later, in 1858. The Armenians were the first to establish a press in Persia. This was at New Julfa in the Armenian Monastery of Amenaperkitch. The first book printed on this press was in 1640, nearly two centuries after Gutenberg's invention (1455).

17. Zarhbanalian, *Patmuthiun Haikakan Tepagruthian*, pp. 96–109.

18. *Ibid.*, pp. 253–259.

19. Mesrovb Jacob Seth, *Armenians in India* (Calcutta, 1937), pp. 579–580.

20. Shameer Shameerian is also known as Agha Shameer Soolthanoomian.

21. Leo, *Hayots Patmuthiun*, III, 803–806.

22. Seth, *op. cit.*, p. 596.

23. Leo, *Hayots Patmuthiun*, III, 1024–1032.

24. *Ibid.*, pp. 1034–1037.

25. *Ibid.*, p. 808.

26. "Shahan Tjerpeti Antip Namake Ghukas Katoghikosi" ["The Unpublished Letter of Shahan Tjerpet to Catholicos Ghukas"], *Vem*, I (September-October 1933), p. 139 (complete text, pp. 134–140). Copies of this Armenian letter with a French translation were given to the Danish and Prussian ambassadors in Constantinople. The cleric had requested that the letter be delivered to the Catholics of Etchmiadzin in Russian Armenia. It should be noted that this letter was written in Paris shortly after the death of Catholicos Ghukas.

Jacques Chahan de Cirbied was the Professor of Armenian Language at the School of Living Oriental Languages in Paris. He is the coauthor (with F. Martin) of *Recherches curieuses sur l'histoire ancienne de l'Asie* (Paris, 1806). He is also the coauthor (with Mir-Davoud-Zadour de Melik Schahnazer) of *Détails sur la situation du royaume de Perse* (Paris, 1816). Through the encouragement of his Armenian professor, Chahan de Cirbied, M. Bellaud published *Essai sur la Langue arménienne* (The Imperial Press, Paris, 1812).

27. H. Pasdermadjian, *Histoire de l'Arménie depuis les origines jusqu'au traité de Lausanne* (Paris, 1949), p. 298.

28. Rey, *La Protection diplomatique et consulaire dans les Échelles du*

Levant (Paris, 1899), pp. 349–350; cited by Pasdermadjian, *op. cit.*, p. 298.

29. Pasdermadjian, *op. cit.*, p. 298.
30. Frédéric Macler, *La France et l'Arménie à travers l'art et l'histoire* (Paris, 1917), p. 22.
31. Scholars do not agree concerning the year of Abovian's birth. There are various methods of calculating the date and these result in the following conjectures: 1804–1805, 1805, between 1806 and 1810, and 1809.
32. This volume was written in 1840–1841 and first published in Tiflis in 1858, ten years after Abovian's disappearance.
33. Safrastian, "Armenian Thought and Literature since 1828," *Asiatic Review*, XXVI (April 1930, 332.
34. Simeon Yeremian, *Azgayin Demker Graget Hayer* [*National Figures, Armenian Men of Letters*] (Venice, 1913), III, 265–275.
35. *Ibid.*, pp. 276, 365.
36. Djanachian, *op. cit.*, p. 230.
37. Friedrich Parrot, *Journey to Ararat*, tr. W. D. Cooley (New York, 1846), pp. 125–126.
38. Djanachian, *op cit.*, p. 230.
39. *Ibid.*, p. 232.
40. V. Partizuni, *Khatchatur Abovian, Kyanke yev Steghdzagordzuthiune* [*Khatchatur Abovian, His Life and Work*] (Erivan, 1952), p. 65.
41. Djanachian, *op. cit.*, p. 232.
42. Marietta Shaginyan, "Khachatur Abovian," *Soviet Literature* (Moscow, 1956), No. 1, 140.
43. Leon Arpee, *The Armenian Awakening* (Chicago, 1909), p. 51.
44. Kevork Aslan, *Armenia and the Armenians from the Earliest Times Until the Great War (1914)*, tr. Pierre Crabitès (New York, 1920), p. 121.
45. Arpee, *op. cit.*, p. 58.
46. *Ibid.*, pp. 95–96.
47. *Ibid.*, p. 99.
48. *Ibid.*, p. 132.
49. *Ibid.*, p. 137.
50. *Ibid.*, p. 138.
51. Sarkissian, *History of the Armenian Question to 1885*, p. 117.
52. Sarukhan, *Haikakan Khendiren* . . . p. 5.
53. *Ibid.*, pp. 5–7.
54. *Ibid.*, p. 8.
55. Ormanian, *Azgapatum*, III, 3798.
56. Mikael Varandian, *Haikakan Sharzhman Nakhapatmuthiune* [*Introductory History of the Armenian Movement*] (Geneva, 1912), I, 246; Sarukhan, *op. cit.*, pp. 8–9.
57. Sarukhan, *Ibid.*, p. 10.
58. Varandian, *op. cit.*, I, 247–248.

59. H. Oshagan, *Hai Grakanuthiun* [*Armenian Literature*] (Jerusalem, 1942), pp. 275–276; Y. G. M., *Thiurkahayots Hin Vadjarakanuthiunn yev Vadjarakank 1740–1890* [*Early Trade and Merchants Among the Turkish Armenians 1740–1890*] (Constantinople, 1908), pp. 19–33. Following the independence of Greece from the Ottoman Empire (1832), Armenian merchants had taken the place of Greeks (and also the French) as leaders in Turkish trade. By the mid-nineteenth century, the monopoly of trade between Europe and Turkey was mainly in the hands of Armenian merchants. This economic situation was of vital importance in aiding the educational advancement of Turkish Armenians.

60. Sarafian, *op. cit.*, p. 196.

61. Varandian, *op. cit.*, I, 251–254; see also Archag Tchobanian, *Victor Hugo, Chateaubriand, et Lamartine dans la littérature arménienne* (Paris, 1935), and James Etmekjian, "The French Influence on the Western Armenian Renaissance, 1843–1915" (unpublished Ph.D. dissertation, Brown University, 1958).

62. *Azgayin Sahmanadruthiun Hayots 1860* [*Armenian National Constitution 1860*] (Constantinople, 1860), p. 46. (Pages not numbered beyond p. 43.)

63. *Azgayin Sahmanadruthiun Hayots* [*Armenian National Constitution (of 1863)*] (Constantinople, 1908), p. 10. For the complete text in an English translation see H. F. B. Lynch, *Armenia Travel and Studies* (London, 1901), II, 445–467.

64. Sarukhan, *op. cit.*, p. 11.

65. *Ibid.*, pp. 247–249.

66. *Azgayin Sahmanadruthiun Hayots* [of 1863], pp. 12–13.

67. Leon Arpee, *op. cit.* (Chicago, 1909), p. 193.

68. Leo, *Grigor Ardzruni* [in Armenian] (Tiflis, 1903), II, 70.

69. Pasdermadjian, *op. cit.*, p. 301.

70. Oshagan, *op. cit.*, pp. 274–276.

71. This was not a translation from the fifth-century Armenian version of the Bible, the official version of the Armenian Church.

72. Sarafian, *op. cit.*, pp. 163–192.

73. Michael Chamich, *History of Armenia*, tr. Johannes Avdall (Calcutta, 1827), II, 525–532.

74. M. I. Akhov, *I. Ocherki iz istorii armianskogo "gosudarstva" II. Rossiia i armiane* [*I. Essays on the History of the Armenian "State" II. Russia and the Armenians*] (St. Petersburg, 1902), II, 21–22.

75. Grigoris Galemkearian, *Patmuthiun Hai Lragruthian* [*History of Armenian Journalism*] (Vienna, 1893), p. 46.

76. Sarkissian, *op. cit.*, p. 119.

77. *Ibid.*, pp. 119–120.

78. Galemkearian, *op. cit.*, pp. 167–178.

79. Hairig = father.

80. V. G. Zartarian (ed.), *Hishatakaran Hai Yerevelineru* [*Memorials of Some Notable Armenians*] (Constantinople, 1910), I, 2–4. Khirimian

Hairig was elected to the office of Catholicos of Etchmiadzin on May 5, 1892, but because of interference from the Turkish government he was not consecrated until September 26, 1893.

81. *Ardziv Vaspurakan* 1862–1863, no. 1, cited in Varandian, *Haikakan Sharzhman Nakhapatmuthiune*, I, 311–312.

82. Sarkissian, *op. cit.*, p. 120.

83. The *Mushak* appeared as a weekly from 1872–1876. It became bi-weekly until 1878 and a daily until 1884. Because of losses, it was not published for two years. From 1886 to the death of Ardzruni in 1892 it was published triweekly. The paper was carried on by Aleksander Calantar until his death in 1913. The *Mushak* then continued under Hambartsum Arakelian until 1918, and then under Levon Calantar until 1920, when it ceased.

84. For a full account of the life of Ardzruni, see Leo, *Grigor Ardzruni* (Tiflis, 1901–1904), 3 vols.

85. *Mushak* 1877, no. 35, cited in D. Ananun, *Rusahayeri Hasarakakan Zargatsume 1870–1900* [*The Intellectual Enlightenment of the Armenians in Russia 1870–1900*] (Etchmiadzin, 1922), II, 184–185.

86. The journal was edited by Mattheos Mamurian from 1871 to his death in 1901 and was then continued by his son Hrant until 1909.

87. Sarkissian, *op. cit.*, p. 125.

88. *Ibid.*, pp. 125–126.

89. A. M. Indjikian, *Mikael Nalbandiani Kyanki yev Gordzuneuthian Daregruthiune* [*Diary of the Life and Work of Mikael Nalbandian*] (Erivan, 1954), p. 17.

90. M. Nalbandian, *Andip Yerker* [*Unpublished Works*], ed. and comp. Ashot Hovhannesian (Erivan, 1935), p. 398.

91. *Ibid.*, pp. 106–107.

92. Indjikian, *op. cit.*, p. 214.

93. *Ibid.*, pp. 306–307.

94. This work was written under the name of Simeon Manikian. Other pseudonyms Nalbandian used were Koms Emmanuel and Parokh Kalakian.

95. Mikael Nalbandian, *Yerkeri Liakatar Zhoghovadzoy* [*Complete Works*], II, (Erivan, 1947), 258–259.

96. *Ibid.*, I (Erivan, 1945), pp. 93–95.

97. Alice Stone Blackwell, *Armenian Poems* (Boston, 1917), p. 41.

98. *Ibid.*, p. 40.

99. The founders of this club were K. Kanayan, M. Timurian, and R. Badganian (or Patkanian). The name "Kamar Katiba" was derived from the letters of their names. "Kamar" was formed by inserting the vowel *a* between the initials of their first names: KaMaR; "Katiba" was formed by joining the first two letters of their last names: Ka-Ti-Ba.

100. Kamar-Katiba, *Kamar-Katibai Banasteghtzuthiunke* [*The Poetry of Kamar-Katiba*] (Moscow, 1881), pp. 8–10.

101. Blackwell, *op. cit.*, p. 92.

102. *Ibid.*, p. 90.
103. Kamar Katiba, *op. cit.* (in the poem "Ampamats Massis" ["Clouded Ararat"]), pp. 164–166.
104. G. Khalathian, R. *Patkaniani Entir Yerkasiruthiunnere* [*Selected Works of R. Patkanian*] (1893), p. 279, cited in V. G. Zartarian, *op. cit.*, p. 364.
105. See Raffi, *Ardziv Vaspurakani: Khirimian Hairig* [*The Eagle of Vaspurakan: Khirimian Hairig*] (Tiflis, 1893).
106. Raffi, *Kaitzer* [*Sparks*] (3d ed.; Vienna, 1904), I, 394–396.
107. Aram Babayan (ed.), *Hairenik, Hai Groghnere Haireniki Masin* [*Fatherland, Armenian Writers on the Fatherland*] (Erivan, 1946), pp. 139–140 (excerpt from Raffi's "David Beg").
108. Raffi, *Kaitzer*, I, 397–398.
109. Blackwell, *op. cit.*, pp. 245–246 (from Raffi's poem "The Lake of Van").
110. Raffi, *Khente* [*The Fool*] (3d ed.; Vienna, 1905), pp. 411–432.
111. Babayan. *op. cit.*, p. 137.

NOTES TO CHAPTER III (Pp. 67–89)

1. Zeitun = olive.
2. The population of Zeitun has varied from time to time. Zeituntsi, *Zeituni Antsialen yev Nerkayen* [*Out of Zeitun's Past and Present*] (Vienna, 1900), I, 7, states that there are 1,500 homes in the town of Zeitun which are all inhabited by Armenians. There had been 24 Turkish families, but these left the town in 1896. The author states (as of 1900) that there are 32 villages, and that the total number of inhabitants in the district is 21,500, of whom 18,500 are Armenians. Léonce M. Alishan, *Sissouan* . . . (Venice, 1899), p. 194, gives a table showing the 1878–1880 statistics for each of the villages of Zeitun. A total of 28 villages are listed. The total population is 27,460 Armenians and 8,344 Moslems. For a detailed account of the customs and language of Zeitun see H. H. Allahvertian, *Ulnia Kam Zeitun Lernayin Avan I Kilikia* [*Oulnia or Zeitun, a Mountainous Town in Cilicia*] (Constantinople, 1884).
3. Alishan, *Sissouan*, p. 198; H. S. Eprikian, *Patkerazard Benashkharhik Bararan* [*Illustrated Armenian Geographic Dictionary*] (Venice, 1903–1907), I, 772.
4. Zeituntsi, *op. cit.,* I, 30–32. The complete text of this edict is given there.
5. Authors do not agree as to the exact number of these battles. The numbers range from sixteen to fifty-seven for the years 1780–1895.
6. Avetis Nazarbek, "Zeitun," *Contemporary Review*, LXIX (April 1896), 513–514.
7. *Aspirations et agissements révolutionnaires des comités arméniens avant et après la proclamation de la Constitution ottomane* (Constantinople, 1917), pp. 21–22.

8. Zeituntsi, *op. cit.*, I, 91–92.

9. Stepanos Palasanian, *Hayots Patmuthiun* [*History of the Armenians*] (Constantinople, 1919), pp. 525–526.

10. The London *Times*, February 25, 1862, quotes a report from the Turkish paper, *Djeridei Havadis* to the effect that 252,067 Crim and Nogai Tartars had arrived in Turkey after the Crimean War.

11. Great Britain, *Correspendence respecting the Commission Sent by the Porte to Inquire into the Condition of the Vilayet of Aleppo.* Parl. Pubs., 1880, Vol. LXXX (Accounts and Papers), c. 2468, Turkey No. 1 (1880), Inclosure 3 in no. 83. Lieutenant Chermside to Sir A. H. Layard, pp. 77–82. One of the principal causes of the Zeitun Rebellion of 1878 was also the arbitrary confiscation of Zeitunli lands by the government.

12. Zeituntsi, *op. cit.*, I, 101–103.

13. *Ibid.*, pp. 104–105; Sarukhan, *Haikakan Khendiren* . . . , p. 94. citing V-te de Gaton, *Revue de Constantinople*, livre du 1 Octobre 1876, states that Levon died in Milan in February, 1876, leaving his six children in poverty.

14. Aghassi, *Zeitoun depuis les origines jusqu'a l'insurrection de 1895*, tr. Archag Tchobanian (Paris, 1897), p. 122.

15. *Ibid.*, pp. 123 ff.

16. Zeituntsi, *op. cit.*, I, 112.

17. Eprikian, *op. cit.*, p. 780.

18. Zeituntsi, *op. cit.*, I, 26–27; Aghassi, *op. cit.*, p. 134. There were a number of Turkish families in Zeitun which continually fought on the side of the Armenians against the Ottoman government. These included Lazes (people of Lazistan), who had immigrated to Zeitun from Trebizond in 1547.

19. Aghassi, *op. cit.*, p. 138.

20. Zeituntsi, *op. cit.*, I, 124.

21. *Ibid.*

22. *Ibid.*, pp. 125–126.

23. Leo, *Thiurkahai Heghapokhuthian Gaghaparabanuthiune* [*The Ideology of the Armenian Revolution in Turkey*] (Paris, 1934), I, 10.

24. Sarkissian, *History of the Armenian Question to 1885* (Urbana, Ill., 1938), p. 129.

25. *Ibid.*

26. V. Aghuzumtsian, *Mikael Nalbandiani Sotsial-Tentesagitakan Hayatsknere* [*The Social-Economic Views of Mikael Nalbandian*] (Erivan, 1955), p. 100.

27. Zeituntsi, *op. cit.*, I, 124–125.

28. Giut Aghaniants, *Divan Hayots Patmuthian* [*Archives on Armenian History*], Vol. XIII, *Harstahartuhiunner Tadjkahayastanum (Vaveragrer 1801–1888)* [*Oppression in Turkish Armenia (Documents 1801–1888)*] (Tiflis, 1915), pp. 55–56.

29. For a facsimile of this letter see M. Nalbandian, *Andip Yerker* [*Unpublished Works*] ed. and comp. Ashot Hovhannesian, leaf opposite

p. 136. On pp. 137–142 Nalbandian explains the contents of the letter to the Russian authorities in St. Petersburg. Hovhannesian establishes that the letter was written by Tagvorian in 1862 not by Sevadjian in 1861 as previously stated by Yervand Shahaziz, *Divan Mikael Nalbandiani* [*Archives on Mikael Nalbandian*] (Erivan, 1932), pp. 348–350. Shahaziz quotes the complete text of this letter.

30. Mikael Nalbandian, *Yerkeri Liakatar Zhoghovadzoy* [*Complete Works*] (Erivan, 1949), IV 283–284.

31. M. Nalbandian, *Andip Yerker*, leaf opposite p. 136 and p. 241.

32. *Ibid.*, pp. 228–229, 235, 240, 241.

33. *Ibid.*, pp. 235–239; Nalbandian, *Yerkeri Liakatar Zhoghovadzoy*, II, 302–306, IV, 82–86.

34. *Massis*, Saturday, August 25, 1862, no. 551, cited by A. Fenerdjian, "Azat Vormnadruthiune Hayots Metj" [Freemasonry among the Armenians"], *Hairenik Amsagir* [*Hairenik Monthly*], XXXII (October 1954), 95–97.

35. *Massis*, November 8, 1862, no. 560, cited by Fenerdjian, *op. cit.*, 99–100.

36. *Massis*, August 22, 1864, no. 654, cited by Fenerdjian, *op. cit.*, 97–98.

37. A. Aghuzumtsian, *op. cit.*, p. 101.

38. M. Serobian, *Mer Paikare Hai Azatagruthian Ughiov* [*Our Struggle in the Path of Armenian Liberation*] (Cairo, 1848), p. 114.

39. Albert Vandal, *Les Arméniens et la réforme de la Turque* (Paris, 1897), p. 39.

40. Arshak Alboyadjian, *Minas Tcheraz Ir Kianke yev Gordze Ir 60 Amiah Hobeliani Artiv* [*The Life and Work of Minas Tcheraz on the Occasion of the 60th Anniversary of His Public Career*] (Cairo, 1927), pp. 72–73.

41. Ormanian, *Azgapatum*, III, 4169.

42. *Kilikia* [*Cilicia*] (St. Petersburg, 1894), pp. 331–332. The local leaders were a man named Ter Ghevond and a young woman named Yeghisabet. Both were imprisoned for a time by the Turkish government in the city of Aleppo.

43. Personal interview with Father Bedros Kasarjian, a native of Sis in Cilicia. His aunt was a member of the Ser organization and knew Yeghisabet, one of the local leaders. This religious organization is still in existence, particularly in Armenian communities in the Middle East. Its members, who are called Muhapetdjiner, devote most of their lives to prayer and meditation and are accepted as members of the Armenian Church.

44. Ruben Berberian, "Hai Masonnere yev 'Ser' Othiake Polso Metj" ["The Armenian Masons and the 'Ser' Lodge in Constantinople"], *Hairenik Amsagir* [*Hairenik Monthly*], XV (March 1937), 77.

45. *Ibid.*, 77, 82, 84–85.

46. *Ibid.* (May), 122, 126–127.

47. *Ibid.* (March), 84 (April), 130.

48. *Ibid.* (April), 130–131.

49. Alboyadjian, *op. cit.*, p. 73; Ormanian, *Azgapatum*, III, 4323–4324. Ormanian states that the money was bequeathed for the purpose of establishing a college in Cilicia.
50. Alboyadjian, *op. cit.*, p. 74.
51. *Hiusiss* [*North*], 1863, No. 1., cited by M. G. Nersessian, *Hai Zhogho-vurdi Azatagrakan Paikare Thiurkakan Bernapetuthian Dem* [*The Struggle for Freedom of the Armenian People against Turkish Oppression*] (Erivan, 1955), p. 120.
52. Nalbandian, *Yerkeri Liakatar Zhoghovadzoy*, IV, 283.
53. Berberian, *op. cit.* (May 1937), p. 131. Hakobik Noradounghian was the uncle of the Ottoman government legal advisor, Gabriel Effendi Noradounghian.
54. Aghaniants, *op. cit.*, XIII, 55.
55. Berberian, *loc. cit.*
56. Aghaniants, *op. cit.*, 57, 58.
57. *Ibid.*, 57.
58. Berberian, *loc. cit.*
59. Noted are the poems by Mekertitch Beshiktashlian dedicated to Zeitun. Arshak Tchobanian, *Mekertitch Beshiktashliani Gertvadznern U Djarere* [*The Writings and Speeches of Mekertitch Beshiktashlian*] (Paris, 1904), pp. 120–126. An English translation of Beshiktashlian's poem, *Death of a Youth of Zeitoun*, is found in Alice Stone Blackwell, *Armenian Poems* (Boston, 1917), pp. 66–67.
60. Leo, *Thiurkahai Heghapokhuthian Gaghaparabanuthiune*, I, 31.
61. Nersessian, *op. cit.*, pp. 122–123.
62. Frederick Millingen (Osman-Seify-Bey), *La Turquie sous le règne d'Abdul-Aziz 1862–1867* (Paris, 1868), pp. 168–170.
63. *Ibid.*, p. 168.
64. The territorial boundaries of the province of Erzerum saw numerous alterations. In 1875 it was divided into six separate provinces: Erzerum, Van, Hekkiari, Bitlis, Dersim, Kars, and Tchildir. These provinces in turn went through various territorial and administrative changes.
65. A sanjak is an administrative division of the Ottoman Empire. These divisions, in order of descending size, are usually as follows: *vilayet* (province), *sanjak* or *livas* (department), *caza* (arrondissement), *nahies* (canton), and *karies* or *karyies* (communes). They are administered respectively by a *vali* (governor general), *mutessarif* (governor), *kaimakan* (sub-governor), *mudir*, and *mouktar*. For a description of the above administrative divisions see Vital Cuinot, *La Turquie d'Asie: géographie administrative* (Paris, 1890), I, xiii–xv.
66. Millingen, *op. cit.*, p. 170.
67. *Ibid.*, pp. 173–174.
68. *Ibid.*, pp. 171–175.
69. V. Shahriman, *Haikakan Khentirin Dzacoume* [*The Origin of the Armenian Question*] (Constantinople, 1912), p. 35, cited by Sarkissian, *op. cit.*, p. 38.

70. Millingen, *op. cit.*, p. 192.
71. Great Britain, *The Treatment of the Armenians in the Ottoman Empire 1915-1916* (Miscellaneous No. 31, 1916), p. 614.
72. Frederick Millingen, *Wild Life among the Koords* (London, 1870), p. 156.
73. Our basic information on the Union of Salvation, which was formed to alleviate the plight of the Armenian population, comes from a number of documents in Father Giut Aghaniants, *Divan Hayots Patmuthian* [*Archives on Armenian History*]. See Vol. XIII, 269–278.
74. *Ibid.*, pp. 269–270.
75. *Ibid.*, p. 271.
76. *Ibid.*, pp. 273–275.
77. *Ibid.*, pp. 276–278.
78. For a detailed description of these two organizations see chapter vi of the present work.
79. Great Britain, *State Papers, 1877–1878*, LXIX, 766.
80. H. H. Djankulian, *Hishatakner Haikakan Djeknazhamen* [*Memories from the Armenian Crisis*] (Constantinople, 1913), I, 50–51; Ervant D. Megerditchian, *Krakan-Patmakan Hanrakitaran Vaspurakan Ashkharhi* [*Literary-Historic Encyclopedic of the World of Van*], MS.
81. Great Britain, *Despatch from Her Majesty's Ambassador at Constantinople Forwarding a Copy of the Identic Note Addressed to the Porte on the 11th June, 1880*. Parl. Pubs., 1880, Vol. LXXXI (Accounts and Papers), c. 2611, Turkey No. 9 (1880), pp. 1–3.
82. Great Britain, *Further Correspondence respecting the Condition of the Populations in Asia Minor and Syria*. Parl. Pubs., 1880, Vol. LXXXII (Accounts and Papers), c. 2712, Turkey No. 23 (1880), Inclosure 1 in no. 154. Collective Note addressed to the Porte, pp. 275–282. This Collective Note was presented to the Sublime Porte on September 11, 1880.
83. *Ibid.*, 1881, Vol. C (Accounts and Papers), c. 2986, Turkey No. 6 (1881), no. 148. Earl Granville to Her Majesty's Embassies at Paris, Berlin, Vienna, St. Petersburg, and Rome, p. 290.
84. The name of the administrative-geographical area Erzerum appears in Armenian as "Karin" or "Garin." This area is situated in a large geographic area known to Armenians as "Bardser Haik" or "Upper Armenia," one of the fifteen provinces of the ancient historical region of Armenia Major. In D. Ananun, *op. cit.*, II, 205, the 1881–1882 Erzerum organization is called "Gaghtni Enkeruthiun Bardser Hayots" ["Secret Society of the Armenians of Upper Armenia"]. This name is also given to the Erzerum organization by G. Giuzalian, in his *Hai Kaghakakan Metki Zargatsume yev H.H. Dashnaktsuthiune* [*The Enlightenment of the Armenian Political Mind and the A.R. Federation*] (Paris, 1927), p. 117. Giuzalian differs from Ananun in regard to the date of the organization, which he gives as at the end of the 'seventies. A similar name to that given by Ananun and Giuzalian is given by S. Vratzian, "H.H. Dashnaktsuthian Dzenunde yev Him-

nadirnere" ["The Origin and Founders of the A.R. Federation"], *Hushapatum H.H. Dashnaktsuthian 1890–1950 [Historical Collection of the A.R. Federation]*, published by the H.H.D. Buro [*Bureau of the Armenian Revolutionary Federation*] (Boston, 1950), p. 71. Vratzian says that a secret organization was founded in Erzerum in 1881 and was called "Pashtpan Haireniats Gaghtni Enkeruthiun Bardser Hayots" ["Protectors of the Fatherland Secret Society of the Armenians of Upper Armenia"]. Seropian, *Mer Paikare*, p. 181, says that the revolutionary organization Gaghtni Miuthiun Bardser Hayots [Secret Union of the Armenians of Upper Armenia] was formed at Erzerum in 1870. Nersessian, *op. cit.*, p. 182 n. declares that in Erzerum there was a cultural-educational organization called "Bardser Haiki Enkeruthiun" ["Society of Upper Armenia"]. Nersessian does not give a date for this organization. He discusses the 1881–1882 Erzerum secret revolutionary society under the name "Pashtpan Haireniats" ["Protectors of the Fatherland"]. In the article "Entatsk Sharzhman Hai Heghapokhuthian" ["The Course of the Armenian Revolutionary Movement"], by Dz. H. in *Aravot [Morning]*, a journal published in the Caucasus, no. 29, October 24, 1907, and condensed by Shah-Baze for Teodik, *Amenun Daretsoytse [Everybody's Yearbook]* (Constantinople, 1911), V, 171, a secret organization at Erzerum, 1882–1883, is called "Zinakir Enkeruthiun" ["Society of the Bearers of Arms"]. Since some date references are also different from that of the Pashtpan Haireniats [Protectors of the Fatherland] (1881–1882), there is a possibility that sometimes the writer is referring to another secret revolutionary organization which may have existed in Erzerum just prior to 1881.

85. H. M. Nishkian, *Aratjin Kaidzere Etj Me Karno Zartonken [The First Sparks—A Page from the Awakening in Erzerum]* (Boston, 1930). This work gives the most detailed account of the formation and activity of The Protectors of the Fatherland and is probably the only primary source available on the subject. Nishkian was an advisor to the central committee; his brother was one of the founders of the society.

86. *Ibid.*, p. 118.

87. Leo, *Thiurkahai Heghapokhuthian Gaghaparabanuthiune*, I, 139.

88. Seropian, *Mer Paikare*, p. 183.

89. *Ibid.*

90. Nersessian, *op. cit.*, p. 182.

91. Nishkian, *op. cit.*, pp. 9, 115–117, 121.

92. *Ibid.*, p. 117.

93. *Ibid.*, pp. 117–118.

94. *Ibid.*, pp. 118–119.

95. *Ibid.*, pp. 119–124.

96. *Ibid.*, p. 128.

97. The London *Times*, January 3, 1883.

98. *Ibid.*, January 10, 1883.

99. *Ibid.*, January 3, 1883; January 10, 1883.

100. *Ibid.*, January 12, 1883.
101. *Ibid.*, June 8, 1883.
102. Ormanian, *Azgapatum*, III, 4466. See also his *Khohk yev Khosk* [*Thoughts and Talks*] (Jerusalem, 1929), pp. 118–123.
103. The London *Times*, June 23, 1884.
104. Ormanian, *Azgapatum*, III, 4467.
105. Karapet Nishkian escaped arrest and left for the United States on September 1, 1883. His brother H. M. Nishkian joined him in 1888. Karapet died in Fresno, California, in June, 1916, and his brother died there in 1932.
106. Nishkian, *op. cit.*, p. 145.
107. Ananun, *op. cit.*, II, 205.
108. Ormanian, *Azgapatum*, III, 4467.

NOTES TO CHAPTER IV (Pp. 90–103)

1. Var.: Armenagan.
2. Gabriel Lazian, *Demker Hai Azatagrakan Sharzhumen* [*Personalities from the Armenian Liberation Movement*] (Cairo, 1949), p. 1; G. Doumergue, *L'Armenie les massacres et la question d'Orient* (2d ed.; Paris, n.d.), 155; Haïr Andon (Ervant D. Megerditchian), "Megurditch Portaukalian," *Vasbouragan* (edited by Ervant D. Megerditchian and published monthly in Boston), II (March, 1941), 2–3.
3. *Tip U Tar* [*Type and Letters*] (Constantinople, 1912), p. 158.
4. Lazian, *op. cit.*, p. 2.
5. *Ibid.*
6. *Tip U Tar*, pp. 158–159; Lazian, *op. cit.*, pp. 2–3.
7. Lazian, *op. cit.*, p. 3.
8. *Ibid.*, p. 4.
9. Mikael Varandian, *H.H. Dashnaktsuthian Patmuthiun* [*History of the A.R. Federation*] (Paris, 1932), I, 28–29; Mikael Varandian, *Haikakan Sharzhman Nakhapatmuthiune* [*Introductory History of the Armenian Movement*] (Geneva, 1914), II, 269–271; Lazian, *op. cit.*, p. 4.
10. Lazian, *op. cit.*, pp. 3–4.
11. Varandian, *Nakhapatmuthiune*, II, 271; Garnik Giuzalian, "M. Portugalian (Mi Etj Heghapokhakan Patmuthiunits)" ["M. Portugalian (A page from the Revolutionary History)"], *Vem*, XVI (July-October 1936), 8.
12. A. Alboyadjian, *Minas Tcheraz*, p. 90.
13. Hambardsum Yeramian, *Hus015ardsan* [*Memoria*] (Alexandria, Egypt, 1929), I, 32–35, 80–83; Varandian, *Nakhapatmuthiune*, II, 272; Artak Darbinian, *Hai Azatagrakan Sharzhman Oreren (Husher 1890 en 1940)* [*From the Days of the Armenian Liberation Movement (Memoirs from 1890 to 1940)*] (Paris, 1947), pp. 114–117; Great Britain, *Correspondence respecting the Condition of the Populations in Asiatic*

Turkey 1888–89. Parl. Pubs., 1889, Vol. LXXXVII (Accounts and Papers), c. 5723, Turkey No. 1 (1889), Inclosure 3 in no. 85. Vice-Consul Devey to Consul Chermside—Van, April 13, 1889, pp. 71–74.

In Van there were two political groups, mainly concerned with domestic issues. These groups arose during the period of the Crimean War. At that time a dispute occurred concerning the billeting of troops. It was decided that the people should build an army barracks from their own donations so that they would no longer be inconvenienced by the intrusion of troops into their private homes. The funds were collected and the barracks were built. The disputes arising from this activity led to the formation of two opposing political factions: the Boghosians and the Aboghosians. The Boghosians were the reactionary element led by Boghos Vardabet Melikian. The Aboghosians were led by a teacher named Hovhannes, who was called Kolozian by his opponents. The struggle between these two groups went through various aspects during the course of a number of decades. The revolutionary movement, which gathered strength in the 1890's, put an end to the conflict between these factions. They gradually became assimilated within the new revolutionary organizations that had taken the political initiative in the community of Van.

14. Lazian, *op. cit.,* p. 5.
15. *Ibid.;* Varandian, *Nakhapatmuthiune,* II, 272.
16. M. Portugalian, *"Armenia"i Husharar [An Anthology from "Armenia"]* (Marseilles, 1890), p. 4.
17. *Ibid.,* p. 5.
18. *Ibid.,* pp. 4–6; Great Britain, Turkey No. 1 (1889), Inclosure in no. 1. *Appendix to Memorial, Being a Brief Summary of Arrests, Imprisonments, and Banishments Suffered by Individual Armenians for Political Reasons, between the Years 1885 and 1888,* pp. 2–4; *ibid.,* Inclosure 3 in no. 85. Annex 1, *List of Political Prisoners at Van,* p. 75; *ibid.,* Inclosure 3 in no. 85. Annex 2, *List of Armenians Exiled or Punished Summarily,* p. 75.
19. Arpiar Arpiarian, "Hayastan yev G. Bolis" ["Armenia and Constantinople"], *Nor Kiank [New Life],* II (September 1899), 275.
20. Portugalian, *op. cit.,* p. 4.
21. *Ibid.,* p. ii.
22. *Ibid.,* p. 9.
23. *Ibid.,* pp. 45–49.
24. *Ibid.,* p. 75.
25. *Ibid.,* pp. 73–78.
26. *Ibid.,* p. 81.
27. Mushegh Seropian, *Mantchesderi Hai Gaghute [The Armenian Community of Manchester, England]* (Boston, 1911), p. 126; Vicomte des Coursons, *La rébellion arménienne* (Paris, 1895), pp. 39–42. Another name for this organization at London was the "Armenian Society," which was later referred to as the "Anglo-Armenian Association."
28. Portugalian, *op. cit.,* pp. 76 n., 77 n.

29. *Ibid.*, p. 77 n.; Doumergue, *L'Armenie, les massacres et la question d'Orient*, p. 160; Seropian, *Mer Paikare*, p. 184.

30. G. Beozikian (Shikaher), "Khesri Tun" ["House of the Straw Mat"], *Vasbouragan* (edited by Ervant D. Megerditchian and published monthly in Boston), II (April 1941), 2–3; *ibid.*, "Azatakrakan Sharzhumner Vanum" ["Movements for Freedom in Van"], II (September 1941), 2; Personal letters from Mr. Ervant D. Megerditchian.

31. *Armenia* was banned from the Ottoman Empire after the publication of the fourth issue, August 7/19, 1885. Until that date it had four hundred subscribers, three hundred of them in Turkey. The journal was prohibited from entry into Russia on January 20/February 2, 1886.

32. Ruben Khan-Azat, "Hai Heghapokhakani Husherits" ["Memoirs of an Armenian Revolutionary"], *Hairenik Amsagir*, V (June 1927), 68; Great Britain, *Further Correspondence respecting the Condition of the Populations in Asiatic Turkey*. Parl. Pubs., 1892, Vol. XCVI (Accounts and Papers), c. 6632, Turkey No. 1 (1892), no. 63. Vice-Consul Devey to Acting Consul Hampson—(Received at the Foreign Office, August 21), p. 68.

33. Varandian, *Dashnaktsuthian Patmuthiun*, I, 31; Great Britain, *Correspondence respecting the Condition of the Populations in Asiatic Turkey, and the Trial of Moussa Bey*. Parl. Pubs., 1890, Vol. LXXXII (Accounts and Papers), c. 5912, Turkey No. 1 (1890), Inclosure 4 in no. 4. M. Portugalian to M. Koulaksizian, pp. 9–10.

34. Darbinian, *Hai Azatagrakan Sharzhman Oreren*, p. 124.

35. L. Adjemian (ed.), *Husher Armenak Yekariani* [*Memoirs of Armenak Yekarian*] (Cairo, 1947), pp. 81–84. Darbinian, *op. cit.*, pp. 125–128, contains the Armenakan *Program,* but this is not given in its original as in Adjemian. In both the Adjemian and Darbinian texts of the *Program,* the Armenakan is referred to as an "Organization." Other references call it the "Armenakan Party," a name commonly used. Since the Armenakan is a political party, it will be called the "Armenakan Party" throughout this study.

36. Adjemian, *op. cit.*, pp. 81–84.

37. Petros Tonapetian (Vaghinak), *Hayastan yev Hai Zhoghovurde Dareri Mitjov* [*Armenia and the Armenian People through the Centuries*] (Paris, 1949), II, 245.

38. Statement by Mr. Iknadios H. Kazanjian, a native of Van and a former member of the Armenakan Party, personal interview.

39. Great Birtain, *Correspondence respecting the Condition of the Populations in Asia Minor and Syria*. Parl. Pubs., 1880, Vol. LXXX (Accounts and Papers), c. 2537, Turkey No. 4 (1880), no. 26. Major Trotter to the Marquis of Salisbury—(Received September 16), p. 48.

40. Darbinian, *op. cit.*, pp. 124–125.

41. A. Amurian, *H.H. Dashnaktsuthiune Parskastanum 1890–1918* [*The A.R. Federation in Iran 1890–1918*] (Teheran, 1950), p. 14.

42. Other active members included: Hovhannes Agripasian, Aristakes and

Verdenes Akhikian (brothers), Yeghiazar Bambakgizian, H. Barseghian, Grigor Beozikian (Shikaher), Azganaz (also called Avetis) Tchutchian, Arshak and Tigran Tchutchian (brothers), Artak Darbinian, Vardan Goloshian, Yeghiche Gontaktchian, Karapet Koulaksizian, Sayat Hadji, Hovhannes and Shahen Tchortanian (brothers, whose family name was later changed to Hagopian), Ohanes Kankanpanoian, Sano Karapet, Iknadios and Ruben Kazanjian (brothers), Ghevond Khandjian, Garegin Koredzian, Hovhannes Kuloghlian, Tigran Mahelian, Garegin Manukian (known by the surname Bagheshtsian), Murat Muratian (there were two different men with this same name), Voskan Nazar, Mikael Natanian, Tigran Nortuzian, Grigor Odian, Vahan Peneian, Karapet Salakian, H. Servandstian, Hemayeak (also called Mushegh) Tangaradjian, K. Tchapidjian, Grigoris Terlemezian (brother of Mekertitch Terlemezian), Panos Terlemezian (cousin of Mekertitch Terlemezian), Anushavan Ter Mekertitchian, Ter Nersis Kahana (a priest), Y. Voskeritchian, and Armenak Yekarian.

This list was compiled with the assistance of Mr. Iknadios H. Kazanjian, during a personal interview. Mr. Kazanjian, a former Armenakan and active in the party in Van, was personally acquainted with nearly all of these men.

Since individual members of the Armenakan Party, especially before 1896, are not commonly known to writers, it has been considered of value to include the above list in this study.

43. Darbinian, *op. cit.,* p. 123; Adjemian, *op. cit.,* p. 7; Varandian, *Dashnaktsuthian Patmuthiun,* I, 30; Great Britain, Turkey No. 1 (1889), *op. cit.,* Inclosure in no. 95. Extract from the "Eastern Express" of June 25, 1889, pp. 83–84; *ibid.,* no. 102. Sir W. White to the Marquis of Salisbury—(Received July 15), p. 89; Great Britain, Turkey No. 1 (1890), *op. cit.,* no. 4. Sir W. White to the Marquis of Salisbury—(Received August 9), p. 4; *ibid.,* Inclosure 1 in no. 4, Colonel Chermside to Sir W. White, p. 4; *ibid.,* Inclosure 2 in no. 4. Vice-Consul Devey to Colonel Chermside, pp. 4–7; *ibid.,* Inclosure 3 in no. 4. M. Patiguian to M. Koulaksizian, pp. 7–9; *ibid.,* Inclosure 4 in no. 4. M. Portugalian to M. Koulaksizian, pp. 9–10; *ibid.,* Inclosure 5 in no. 4. Extracts from the Diary of M. Koulaksizian, pp. 10–11. For a biography of Goloshian and Agripasian see S. Nervanian, *Heghapokhakanner—Vardan Goloshian, H. Agripasian* [*Revolutionaries, Vardan Goloshian, H. Agripasian*] (Geneva, 1905).

44. Aram-Ruben, *Hai Heghapokhakani Me Hishataknere* [*Memoirs of an Armenian Revolutionary*] (Los Angeles, 1952), II, 268–269.

45. Varandian, *Dashnaktsuthian Patmuthiun,* I, 31.

46. After the death of Tchato, Shero joined the Dashnaks.

47. Great Britain, *Correspondence relating to the Asiatic Provinces of Turkey.* Parl. Pubs., 1896, Vol. XCV (Accounts and Papers), c. 8015, Turkey No. 3 (1896), Inclosure 2 in no. 79. Vice-Consul Devey to Consul Graves, pp. 53–54; *ibid.,* no. 86. Vice-Consul Devey to Acting

Consul Fitzmaurice—(Received at the Foreign Office February 4, 1893), p. 62.

48. Great Britain, Turkey No. 1 (1889), Inclosure in no. 1. *Appendix to Memorial, Being a Brief Summary of Arrests, Imprisonments, and Banishments Suffered by Individual Armenians for Political Reasons, between the Years 1885 and 1888*, pp. 2–3; *ibid.*, Inclosure 3 in no. 85. Vice-Consul Devey to Consul Chermside, pp. 74–75; *ibid.*, Inclosure in no. 4. Appendix to Memorial, pp. 5–6; *ibid.*, Inclosure in no. 96. Mr. Devey to Consul Chermside, pp. 84–85.

49. *Ibid.*, Inclosure 1 in no. 85. Consul Chermside to Sir W. White, p. 71.

50. *Ibid.*, Inclosure 3 in no. 85. Vice-Consul Devey to Consul Chermside, pp. 71–72.

51. *Ibid.*

52. *Ibid.*, Inclosure 2 in no. 68. Vice-Consul Devey to Consul Chermside, pp. 55–56; *ibid.*, Inclosure 3 in no. 68. Memorandum, p. 56; *ibid.*, Inclosure 3 in no. 85. Vice-Consul Devey to Consul Chermside, pp. 71–72.

53. *Ibid.*, Inclosure 1 in no. 85. Consul Chermside to Sir W. White, p. 71.

54. These figures do not include those who died from starvation, exposure, and hardships as a consequence of the massacres. Edwin Munsell Bliss, *Turkey and the Armenian Atrocities* (New York, 1896), pp. 553–554; M. S. Gabriel, *Bleeding Armenia: Its History and Horrors under the Curse of Islam* (New York, 1896), p. 399; Johannes Lepsius, *Deutschland und Armenien 1914–1918* (Potsdam, 1919), p. ix; André-N. Mandelstam, *La Société des nations et les puissances devant le problème arménien* (Paris, 1926), p. 37; Edwin Pears, *Life of Abdul Hamid* (New York, 1917), p. 239; George Horton, *The Blight of Asia* (Indianapolis, 1926), p. 20; Delegation de la Republique arménienne, *L'Arménie et la question arménienne avant, pedant et depuis la guerre* (Paris, 1922), p. 12; Frédéric Macler, *La Nation arménienne: son passé, ses malheurs* (Paris, 1924), p. 45. Bliss declares that on the basis of the statements by the English and French Ambassadors at Constantinople, there were not fewer than 50,000 victims. Gabriel gives the estimate of the Turkish authorities, which is estimated at 80,000. Lepsius claims between 80,000 and 100,000 victims. Pears states that few observers estimate fewer than 100,000 victims. Horton gives a total of 179,570 dead. Macler and the Armenian Delegation declare that 300,000 persons perished. For a description of these Armenian massacres consult the special correspondent of the London *Daily Telegraph*, E. J. Dillon, "Armenia: An Appeal," *Contemporary Review*, LXIX (January 1896), 1–19; J. Rendel Harris and Helen B. Harris, *Letters from the Scenes of the Recent Massacres in Armenia* (London, 1897); Frederick Davis Greene, *Armenian Massacres or the Sword of Mohammed* (New York, 1896); the British Parliamentary Papers; Ministère des affaires étrangères, *Documents diplomatiques, affaires arméniennes, projets de l'empire ottoman 1893–1897* (Paris, 1897).

55. Ministère des affaires étrangères, *op. cit.*, no. 212. M. P. Cambon,

Ambassadeur de la Republique française à Constantinople, à M. Hanotaux, Ministre des affaires étrangères, p. 239; *ibid.*, no. 215. M. P. Cambon, Ambassadeur de la Republique française à Constantinople, à M. Hanotaux, Ministre des affaires étrangères, p. 240.

56. Yeramian, *Hushardsan*, II, 162.

57. Mr. Iknadios H. Kazanjian, personal interview. Mr. Kazanjian, as an Armenakan revolutionary, fought against the Turks during the June 1896 conflicts in Van. Out of hundreds of Armenian revolutionaries who fought at this time, he was one of the few survivors who reached Persian territory.

58. Private correspondence with Mr. Ervant D. Megerditchian, a native of Van and member of the Armenakan Party.

NOTES TO CHAPTER V (Pp. 104–131)

1. In 1890 the organization was officially named the Hunchakian Revolutionary Party. The name was changed in 1905 to Hunchakian Social Democrat Party and then in 1909 to Social Democrat Hunchakian Party, the name it bears to the present day. Hunchakian has been rendered in various spellings: Hunchag, Hentchak, Hentchag, Hintchak, Hintchag.

2. Hagop Turabian, "The Armenian Social Democratic Hentchakist Party," *Ararat*, III (July 1915–June 1916), 451, 456.

3. Ruben Khan-Azat, "Hai Heghapokhakani Husherits" ["Memoirs of an Armenian Revolutionary"], *Hairenik Amsagir*, V (June 1927), 69.

4. Personal interview with the Armenian musicologist Rouben Tigranian, a native of Tiflis. He was personally acquainted with Avetis Nazarbekian as well as his uncle, Melikazarian of Tiflis.

5. Shortly afterward, Avetis Nazarbekian and Mariam Vardanian (Maro) were married. They had two children, a boy, Vatya, and a girl, Byelka. The Nazarbekian family resided in England, but in later years the couple was divorced and Avetis married his cousin. In 1927 Avetis Nazarbekian was in the United States and on the invitation of the Committee of Revolutionary History in Moscow, he went to the Soviet capital, where he was to write a history of the Hunchaks. For a short notice of the Nazarbekians in England in the 1890's see David Garnett, *The Golden Echo* (New York, 1954), pp. 39–40.

6. Nicoli Matinian had to return to Tiflis because of financial difficulties during the first days that Avetis Nazarbekian and Mariam Vardanian came to Geneva.

7. Khan-Azat, *op. cit.*, p. 69.

8. *Ibid.*, p. 71.

9. *Ibid.*, p. 70.

10. *Ibid.*, p. 71.

11. Khan-Azat, *Hairenik Amsagir*, V (July 1927), 53.

12. *Ibid.*, p. 54.

13. *Hunchak*, October-November 1888. *Hunchak* is also spelled *Hentchak*.

14. Leo, *Thiurkahai Heghapokhuthian Gaghaparabanuthiune*, I, 148–152; Avetis Nazarbekian, although born in Tabriz (Persia), was considered a Russian Armenian because he had lived in Russia since his childhood and had been educated there. Khan-Azat, *Hairenik Amsagir*, V (July 1927), 54, states that all the Hunchak founders, including himself, were Russian Armenians.

15. From a personal interview with the late Mushegh Seropian, former Armenian Archbishop of Cilicia, and one of the first members of the Hunchakian Revolutionary Party. He was personally well acquainted with the founders of the party.

16. Khan-Azat, *Hairenik Amsagir*, V (July 1927), 55.

17. Hemayeak Aramiants, *Veratzenundi Erkunke* [*The Pains of Rebirth*] (Constantinople, 1918), pp. 13–14.

18. Aderbed (Sarkis Mubaihadjian), 50 Amyak 1878–1928 Voskya Hobelian Hai Heghapokhuthian [Fiftieth Year, 1878–1928—the Golden Jubilee of the Armenian Revolution], MS dated Leninakan (Soviet Armenia), December 31, 1927.

19. "Soc. Dem. Hunch. Kus. Amer-i Sherdjani" ["Social Democrat Hunchakian Party of America"], *Hunchak Taregirk* [*Hunchak Yearly*] (New York, 1932), p. 25. Hereafter cited as *Hunchak Taregirk*.

20. Levon Stepanian is considered the seventh of the founders of the Hunchakian Revolutionary Party although he was not in Geneva when the plans were drawn up. At that time he was studying in Montpellier and was planning to graduate in the winter of 1887. He had already expressed an ardent desire to join the party. Therefore, the six students in Geneva sent him the plans, which he, too, wholeheartedly accepted. After his graduation he joined his friends in Geneva.

21. Gevorg Gharadjian, who was a dedicated Marxist, went to Montpellier and then to the Caucasus. There he joined the ranks of the Russian Social Democratic Party. He said that when he was among the group the name of the party had not been chosen and that only after the *Hunchak* was published did the Hunchakian Revolutionary Party come into existence.

22. *Hunchak*, November 1887.

23. Khan-Azat, *Hairenik Amsagir*, V (July 1927), 62.

24. *Dzragir Hunchakian Kusaktsuthian* [*Program of the Hunchakian Party*] (2d ed.; London, 1897), Preface; this special pamphlet was an abridged edition of the program. The second edition of the program printed in 1897 was also abridged.

25. *Hunchak Taregirk*, p. 31.

26. Sahakian, "S.D. Hunch. Kusaktsuthian Goyuthian Antsealin yev Nerkayis" ["On the Existence of the S.D. Hunchakian Party in the Past and in the Present"], *Eritassard Hayastan* [*Young Armenia*], 1944.

27. Aderbed, *op. cit.*
28. *Ibid.*
29. Turabian, *op. cit.*, p. 456.
30. *Hobelianakan Tonakataruthiun I Pars S.D. Hunch. Kusaktsuthian 60 Ameaki* [*The Celebration of the 60th Anniversary of the S.D. Hunchakian Party*] (San Francisco, 1948).
31. Aramiants, *Veratzenundi Yerkunke*, p. 13.
32. Seropian, *Mer Paikare*, pp. 189–190; Ormanian, *Azgapatum*, III, 4638–4641.
33. Great Britain, *Correspondence respecting the Condition of the Populations in Asiatic Turkey, and the Proceedings in the Case of Moussa Bey.* Parl. Pubs., 1890–91, Vol. XCVI (Accounts and Papers), c. 6214, Turkey No. 1 (1890–91), no. 86. Sir W. White to the Marquis of Salisbury—(Received August 21), p. 66.
34. *Ibid.*, no. 80. Sir W. White to the Marquis of Salisbury—(Received August 8), pp. 62–63.
35. *Hunchak*, September 7, 1890.
36. *Ibid.*
37. *Ibid.*
38. Khan-Azat, *Hairenik Amsagir*, VI (February 1928), 130–134.
39. Great Britain, *Correspondence . . .* , Turkey No. 3 (1896), *op. cit.*, no. 87. Consul Longworth to Sir Clare Ford—(Received at the Foreign Office, March 3), pp. 62–63.
40. Personal interview with the late Max Balian. Mr. Balian was a student at Anatolia College and was one of the young Hunchaks who secretly posted the placards in the Marzovan region in 1893.
41. Bliss, *Turkey and the Armenian Atrocities*, pp. 336–340.
42. Manoug C. Gismegian, *Patmuthiun Amerikahai Kaghakakan Kusaktsuthiants 1890–1925* [*The History of the Armenian-American Political Parties 1890–1925*] (Fresno, 1930), pp. 56–59.
43. Great Britain, *Correspondence relating to the Asiatic Provinces of Turkey.* Part I *Events at Sassoon, and Commission of Inquiry at Moush.* Parl. Pubs., 1895, Vol. CIX (Accounts and Papers), c. 7894, Turkey No. 1 (1895), Inclosure in no. 23. *Memorandum*, pp. 11–12.
44. Ministère des affaires étrangères, *op. cit.*, no. 86. Annexe à la dépêche de Constantinople du 16 août 1895. Rapport Collectif des Délégues consulaires adjoints à la Commission d'enquête sur l'affaire de Sassoun, pp. 96–111.
45. Gurgen Tahmazian, "Hambardzum Poyadjian (Murat)," *Hisnameak —1887–1937—Sots. Demokrat Hunchakian Kusaktsuthian* [*The Fiftieth Anniversary of the Social Democrat Hunchakian Party, 1887–1937*], published by the Sots. Dem. Hunchakian Kus. Kedr. Vartchuthium [Central Committee of the Social Democrat Hunchakian Party] (Providence, 1938), pp. 114–116. Hereafter cited as *Hisnameak*.
46. Great Britain, Turkey No. 1 (1895) (Part I), Inclosure in no. 252. Report of the Consular Delegates attached to the Commission appointed to inquire into the Events at Sassoun, p. 173.

47. *Ibid.*

48. Great Britain, *Correspondence respecting the Introduction of Reforms in the Armenian Provinces of Asiatic Turkey.* Parl. Pubs., 1896, Vol. XCV (Accounts and Papers), c. 7923, Turkey No. 1 (1896), no. 45. Sir P. Currie to the Earl of Kimberley—(Received May 15), p. 34.

49. *Ibid.,* Inclosure 1 in no. 45. *Memorandum,* pp. 35–45. The major points covered in this *Memorandum* were the following: (i) Eventual reduction of the number of vilayets; (ii) Guarantees in connection with the selection of the Valis; (iii) Amnesty for Armenians condemned or under arrest for political offences; (iv) Return of Armenians who have emigrated or who have been exiled; (v) Final settlement of pending proceedings for crimes and offences against the common law; (vi) Inquiry into the state of the prisons and the conditions of prisoners; (vii) Appointment of a High Commissioner to superintend the execution of the reforms in the provinces; (viii) The creation of a Permanent Commission of Control at Constantinople; (ix) Compensation for losses sustained by the Armenians who suffered in the occurrences at Sassoun and Talori, etc.; (x) Regulations concerning religious conversions; (xi) Maintenance and strict enforcement of the rights and privileges granted to the Armenians; (xii) Condition of the Armenians in the other vilayets of Turkey in Asia.

50. *Ibid.,* Inclosure 2 in no. 45. Scheme of Administrative Reforms to be introduced in the Eastern Provinces of Asia Minor; the existing Vilayets of Erzeroum, Bitlis, Van, Sivas, Mamouret-ul-Aziz, Diarbekir, pp. 46–64. This scheme of reforms consisted of a project of administrative, financial, and judicial reforms, which was drawn up in accordance with the existing laws of the Ottoman Empire.

51. Gegham Vardian, "Pap Alii Tsoytse" ["The Demonstration of Bab Ali"], *Hisnameak,* p. 133.

52. Heverhili Karon, "Pap Alii Tsoytse" ["The Demonstration of Bab Ali"], *Hunchak Taregirk,* p. 36.

53. *Ibid.,* pp. 37–38.

54. Vardian, *op. cit.,* pp. 125–126.

55. Great Britain, *Correspondence relative to the Armenian Question, and Reports from Her Majesty's Consular Officers in Asiatic Turkey.* Parl. Pub., 1896, Vol. XCV (Accounts and Papers), c. 7927, Turkey No. 2 (1896), Inclosure 1 in no. 50. The Armenian Revolutionary Committee to Sir P. Currie, p. 32.

56. Vardian, *op. cit.,* p. 126.

57. *Ibid.,* pp. 132–133.

58. Great Britain, Turkey No. 2 (1896), *op. cit.,* Inclosure 2 in no. 50. Petition, pp. 32–35.

59. Karon, *Hunchak Taregirk,* pp. 41–52.

60. The London *Times,* October 3, 1895.

61. William L. Langer, *The Diplomacy of Imperialism 1890–1902* (2d ed.; New York, 1951), pp. 161, 203; A. J. P. Taylor, *The Struggle for the Mastery in Europe 1848–1918* (Oxford, 1954), p. 359; Morris Wee,

"Great Britain and the Armenian Question 1878–1914" (unpublished Ph.D. dissertation, University of Wisconsin, 1938), p. 283.

62. *Hunchak*, October 20, 1895.
63. Nurhan Lusinian, "Zeytuni Tjakatamarte" ["The Battle of Zeitun"], *Hisnameak*, p. 136.
64. Avetis Nazarbek, "Zeitun," *Contemporary Review*, LXIX (April 1896), 516.
65. Zeituntsi, *Zeituni Antsialen yev Nerkayen [Out of Zeitun's Past and Present]* (Paris, 1903), II, 34. For a detailed account see *ibid.*, pp. 1–76, and Aghassi, *op. cit.*, pp. 183–318.
66. Ministère des affaires étrangères, *op. cit.*, no. 184. M. P. Cambon, Ambassadeur de la République française à Constantinople, à M. Berthelot, Ministre des affaires étrangères, p. 214.
67. *Hisnameak*, p. 149.
68. Gismegian, *op. cit.*, p. 53.
69. *Ibid.*, pp. 66–67.
70. *Ibid.*, p. 60.
71. *Hisnameak*, p. 149.
72. *Bulletin périodique du bureau socialiste International*, 4ᵉ année, No. 10, p. 2.
73. The Hunchakian party was a member of the Second International, but the exact date of its entrance is not clear. It is definite that the Hunchaks were members by 1904, since they had a representative at the Sixth Congress at Amsterdam, G. V. Plekhanov, a member of the Russian Social Democrat delegation. They did, however, participate in European socialist activities prior to this date. In 1903 the Hunchaks sent their own representative, S. Kasian, to the German Socialist Party convention in Dresden.
74. The *Hunchak* was published in Geneva from 1887 to 1892. The party moved its headquarters to Athens in 1893 where the *Hunchak* continued publication under Nazarbekian's editorship. In 1894 the party headquarters moved from Athens to London where, under the editorship of Nazarbekian, the *Hunchak* November 20, 1894 issue appeared. The Reformed Hunchakian Party also started publishing a paper called *Hunchak* as its party organ. A court fight between Nazarbekian and the Reformed Hunchakian Party resulted in a victory for Nazarbekian. Three issues of the Reformed Hunchakian Party paper were published without a name. These nameless issues were later called *Mart [Battle]*. In 1898 the *Nor Kiank [New Life]*, another official organ of the Reformed Hunchakian Party, began to be published in London. The old *Hunchak* continued to be published in London until 1904, when it was moved to Paris. It was published in Paris until 1914.
75. Aderbed, *op. cit.* For a list of pamphlets published by the party to 1894 see the *Hunchak*, June 10, 1894.
76. Mihran M. Seferian, *Hunchakian Mathian [Hunchakian Book]*, 4th pamphlet (Beirut, 1954), pp. 93, 98. At Athens during 1894 the party

also published a scientific monthly, *Gaghapar* [*Opinion*], which was devoted to socialist theory. Official party newspapers and periodicals to 1954 totaled 107 publications in forty-one different cities.

NOTES TO CHAPTER VI (Pp. 132–150)

1. M. G. Nersessian, *Hai Zhoghovurdi Azatagrakan Paikare Thiurkakan Bernapetuthian Dem* [*The Struggle for Freedom of the Armenian People against Turkish Oppression*], p. 142.
2. *Ibid.*, pp. 142–143.
3. *Ibid.*, pp. 144–146.
4. Other leading members of the Goodwill Society were the following Alexandropol students and teachers: Haruthiun Ohantjanian, Melik Tchmeshiants, Aleksander Afrikian, Gevorg Ghasabian, Ohantjan Goroian, Karapet Ohantjanian, and Senekerim Lalayan.
5. Nersessian, *op. cit.*, pp. 146–147.
6. *Ibid.*, p. 171.
7. *Ibid.*, p. 173.
8. *Ibid.*, p. 174.
9. C. Mikaelian, "Bekorner Im Husherits" ["Fragments from My Memoirs"], *Hairenik Amsagir*, II (August 1924), 56–57.
10. These included the brothers Simeon and Srapion Ter Grigorian, Aleksander Petrosian (Sandal), Davit Nersessian, Aresdages Tokhmakhian and Tigran Pirumian.
11. Mikaelian, *op. cit.*, p. 57.
12. Gevorg Ghazarian, "Intchpes Dzenund Arav H.H. Dashnaktsuthiune" ["How the A.R. Federation Was Established"], *Hairenik Amsagir*, IV (November 1925), 10–11.
13. *Ibid.*, p. 11.
14. Mikaelian, *op. cit.*, p. 57.
15. *Ibid.*
16. *Ibid.*, p. 58.
17. *Ibid.*, p. 62; S. Zavarian, "Hishoghuthiunner Utsunakan Tevakannerits" ["Memories from the Eighties"], *Hairenik Batsarik Tiv 2* [*Hairenik*, special issue no. 2] (Boston, 1914), pp. 5–9.
18. Mikaelian, *op. cit.*, p. 58.
19. Vratzian, "H.H. Dashnaktstuhian Dzenunde yev Himnadirnere," *Hushapatum H.H. Dashnaktsuthian 1890–1950*, p. 72.
20. *Ibid.*, pp. 72–73; Varandian, *Dashnaktsuthian Patmuthiun*, I, 54.
21. Varandian, *ibid.*, p. 56.
22. A. Aharonian, *Christopher Mikaelian* [in Armenian] (Boston, 1926), p. 80; Aramayis (Ter Danielian), "Sarkis Googoonian," *Divan H.H. Dashnaktsuthian* [*Archives of the A.R. Federation*], published by the H.H.D. Amerikayi Kedr. Komite [Central Committee of the American Branch of the Armenian Revolutionary Federation] (Boston, 1938), II, 9.

23. Mik. Zalian, "Hairenaserneri Miuthiune" ["The Union of Patriots"], *Vem*, I (September-October), 113–114; C. Mikaelian, *op. cit.*, p. 58, states that the name of this organization was "Miuthium Haireniats" ("Patriotic Union").

24. Zalian, *op. cit.*, p. 114.

25. *Ibid.*

26. Mikaelian, *op. cit.*, pp. 57–58.

27. Ghazarian, *op. cit.*, pp. 11–12.

28. *Azatuthian Avetaber* [*Herald of Freedom*] cited by Varandian, *op. cit.*, I, 50.

29. *Ibid.*, p. 47.

30. *Ibid.*, p. 48.

31. *Ibid.*, p. 47.

32. *Ibid.*, p. 51.

33. Zalian, *op. cit.*, pp. 114–115.

34. Ananun, *Rusahayeri Hasarakakan Zargatsume*, II, 168–170.

35. *Ibid.*, pp. 168–169; Zavarian, *op. cit.*, p. 7.

36. Some of these schools were opened in 1886. For details see Gr. Chalkhushian, *Armianskii vopros i armianskie pogromy v Rossii (Panislamism)* [*The Armenian Question and the Armenian Pogroms in Russia; Pan-Islamism*] (Rostov, 1905), pp. 27–31.

37. H. F. B. Lynch, *Armenia Travels and Studies* (London, 1901) I, 219.

38. Mikaelian, *op. cit.*, p. 59; Zavarian, *op. cit.*, pp. 8–9.

39. Mikaelian, *op. cit.*, p. 60.

40. *Ibid.*

41. *Ibid.*, p. 51.

42. M. Sh. [M. Shatirian], as dictated to N. Hangoyts, "Hayots Hasarakakan Sharzhumneri Patmuthiunits" ["On the General Intellectual Movement of the Armenian People"], *Hairenik Amsagir*, I (March 1923), 31.

43. Mikaelian, *op. cit.*, p. 62.

44. M. Sh., *op. cit.*, p. 27.

45. *Ibid.*, pp. 29–30; Ghazarian, *op. cit.*, p. 19: Vratzian, *loc. cit.*, p. 79. Among the men were Christopher Mikaelian, Hovhannes Usufian, Arshak Tadeosian, Nikol Matinian, Aram Nazaretian, Martiros Shatirian, Tigran Stepanian, Hak. Kotcharian, Hovsep Arghuthian, Tigran Okoyian, Simon Zavarian, and Avetis Sahakian. The society's women members were Natalia and Satenik Matinian (sisters of Nikol Matinian), Ugh. Gheldjian, Anna Sahakian (sister of Avetis Sahakian), Maro Zavarian (sister of Simon Zavarian), Daria Goloshian (sister of Vardan Goloshian, the Armenakan killed in 1889), and Jenev Adamian (sister of Tamara Adamian of the Tiflis Dastakian circle and the Union of Patriots in Moscow).

46. M. Sh., *op. cit.*, pp. 34–35.

47. M. Sh., *op. cit.*, 37–38; (April 1923), 50.

48. M. Sh., *Hairenik Amsagir*, I (March 1923), 38.

49. Mikaelian, *op. cit.*, p. 62.
50. M. Sh., *op. cit.*, pp. 37–38.
51. M. Sh., *op. cit.*, p. 31.
52. Great Britain, Turkey No. 1 (1890–91), *op. cit.*, no. 66. Consul Lloyd to Mr. Fane—(Received at Foreign Office, July 11), pp. 51–53; *ibid.*, no. 106. Sir W. White to the Marquis of Salisbury—(Received October 17), p. 79.
53. Before the First World War the Russian ruble was worth about 51 cents.
54. Mikaelian, *op. cit.*, p. 62.

NOTES TO CHAPTER VII (Pp. 151–178)

1. "Hai Heghapokhakanneri Dashnaktsuthiun" = "Federation of Armenian Revolutionaries" "Hai Heghapokhakan Dashnaktsuthiun" = "Armenian Revolutionary Federation." Members of the Dashnaksuthiun (Federation) are called Dashnaksakans, Dashnaks, Dashnags, Tashnaks, or Tashnags.
2. Mikaelian has written one book, *Heghapokhankani Metkere* [*Thoughts of a Revolutionary*] (3d ed.; Athens, 1931). For biographical material see his "Bekorner Im Husherits" [*"Fragments from My Memoirs"*], *Hairenik Amsagir*, II (August 1924), 54–62, and Aharonian, *Christopher Mikaelian* [in Armenian]. For biographical material on Stepan Zorian (pseudonym, Rostom or Kotot), see Simon Vratzian, *Rosdom, A Biographical Sketch* (Boston, 1950); Aram Altchutjian, "Rostome Bakuyum" ["Rostom in Baku"], *Hairenik Amsagir*, XXXIV (July 1956), 1–12; (August 1956), 41–49; (October 1956), 43–50; (November 1956), 59–66; XXV (January 1957), 77–81; and Yr. Khatanasian, "Rostom (Stepan Zorian)," *ibid.*, XXXIV (December 1956), 109–111. Simon Zavarian's biography has been written by M. Varandian, *Simon Zavarian (Gidzer Ir Kianken)* [*Simon Zavarian (Sketches from His Life)*] (Boston, 1927). For short biographies of the three founders, in English, see Armenian Youth Federation of America: Central Educational Council, *Armenian Youth Federation of America Educational Program 1951–52, Blue Book No. VII* (Boston, 1951–1952), pp. 19–34.
3. Two of the founders, Rostom and Mikaelian, both of whom wrote their memoirs years after the founding meetings, disagree as to the date. The former believes that the organization was founded in July, whereas the latter writes that it was in August. On the basis of certain events that occurred during the year 1890, R. Sevian, in a series of articles in the *Hairenik Amsagir*—"Yerb E Himnevel Dashnaktsuthiune" ["When Was the Dashnaktsuthiun Founded?"], XV (December 1936), 57–66; "H.H. Dashnaktsuthian Skezbnakan Dzragir-Kanonagire" ["The First Program-bylaws of the A.R. Federation"], XV (January 1937), 90–99; "H.H. Dashnaktsuthian Aratjin Kailere

yev Gordzitchner" ["Initial Tasks and Leaders of the A.R. Federation"], XV (April 1937), 59–60—concludes that the Armenian Revolutionary Federation was founded "in 1890 and started work in
September." Simon Vratzian, "Mi Kani Djeshtumner" ["A Few Cor-
rections"], *Vem*, XIV (April-June 1937), 78–82, disputes Sevian's con-
clusions and states that most probably the party was founded in
July and started work in August. A further discussion of this same
viewpoint is given in *Vem*, XXI (January 1938), 112, by an anony-
mous writer (probably Vratzian) in an article entitled "Yerb E
Himnevel H.H. Dashnaktsuthiune" ["When Was the Dashnaktsuthiun
Founded?"].

4. Vratzian, "H.H. Dashnaktsuthian Dzenunde yev Himnadirnere,"
   Hushapatum H.H. Dashnaktsuthian 1890–1950, pp. 80–81.
5. *Ibid.*
6. Khan-Azat, "Hai Heghapokhakani Husherits," *Hairenik Amsagir*
   (June 1927-May 1929). This is the most informative source on the
   meeting. As the representative of the Hunchakian Revolutionary
   Party, he supplies much information not found elsewhere. However,
   his account was written nearly thirty years after this meeting, which
   leaves room for certain inaccuracies and a lack of detailed information.
7. *Ibid.*, VI (December 1927), 118–120.
8. *Ibid.*, VI (January 1928), 120–121. Varandian, the historian of the
   Dashnaktsuthiun, states (*Dashnaktsuthian Patmuthiun*, I, 63) that the
   two Hunchak representatives at the Tiflis conference were Khan-Azat
   and Hemayeak Khushpulian. The latter is not mentioned as the
   other Hunchak representative by Khan-Azat in his "Memoirs." The
   Dashnak writer Sevian, "H.H. Dashnaktsuthian Aratjin Kailere yev
   Gordzitchner," *Hairenik Amsagir*, XV (April 1937), 61, is in agreement
   with Khan-Azat that the other Hunchak representative at Tiflis was
   Hakob Meghavorian.
9. Vratzian, *op. cit.*, pp. 83–85.
10. Khan-Azat, *op. cit.*, VI (December 1927), 122–123.
11. *Ibid.*, p. 123.
12. "H.H. Dashnaktsuthian Manifeste" ["The Manifesto of the Federa-
    tion of Armenian Revolutionaries"], *Divan H.H. Dashnaktsuthian
    [Archives of the A.R. Federation]*, published by the H.H.D. Amerikayi
    Kedr-Komite [Central Committee of the American Branch of the Ar-
    menian Revolutionary Federation], I (Boston, 1934), pp. 88–89. Here-
    after cited as *Divan*. This is the complete text of the *Manifesto*.
13. For a critical analysis of the life and work of Sarkis Googoonian, see
    V. Valadian, "Sarkis Googooniani Arshavanke" ["The Sarkis Goo-
    goonian Expedition"], *Hairenik Amsagir*, XXXV (September 1957),
    1–9; (October 1957), pp. 23–32. The author gives particular attention
    to the relations between Googoonian and Hakob Sarkavag (Deacon
    Hakob), who was very important in the preliminary stages of the
    expedition. Before the expedition got under way, Hakob Sarkavag

was assassinated through the machinations of Googoonian. The latter then became the sole leader of the expeditionary forces which were to invade Turkish Armenia. The life and work of Sarkis Googoonian is also given by Aramayis (Ter Danielian), *Divan H.H. Dashnaktsuthian*, pp. 6–25. The article might be to some degree considered an autobiography, since it is taken from interviews by Aramayis with Googoonian in Baku, 1906–1907.

14. Dzeruni (Stepan Stepanian), "Googoonian Khembi Arshavanke" ["The Expedition of the Googoonian Band"], *Divan*, I, 20.

15. *Ibid.*, p. 21.

16. *Ibid.*

17. *Ibid.*, p. 22.

18. "Googoonian Khembi Ambastanagire" ["The Indictment of the Googoonian Band"], *Divan*, I, 31–86; *Droshak* (June 1912, July-August 1912); A. Amurian, "Husher Googoonian Arshavakhembits Hovsep Movsisiani (Argam Petrosian)" ["Hovsep Movsisian's (Argam Petrosian Memoirs of the Googoonian Expedition"], *Hairenik Amsagir*, XII (February 1934), 79–88; (March), 57–68; (April), 108–122; (May), 128–137; Mayewski, *Les Massacres d'Armenie* (St. Petersburg, 1916), pp. 19–23. A few of the men were able to escape from Siberia. One of these was Yeprem Khan (Yeprem Davitian), who later played an active role in the Persian Revolution of 1905. Googoonian was given the longest term—20 years of hard labor. He was pardoned in 1906 and later joined the anti-Tsarist revolutionary forces. He was again imprisoned, but managed to escape. After being free for a short time, he was captured and placed in a Russian prison where he died in 1913. (*Droshak* is also spelled *Droschak*.)

19. Valadian, *op. cit.* (September 1957), p. 2.

20. M. Sh. [see note 42 to chap. vi], *Hairenik Amsagir*, I (April 1923), 51.

21. Mikael Varandian, *Veradzenvogh Hairenike yev Mer Dere* [*The Rebirth of the Fatherland and Our Role*] (Geneva, 1910), pp. 60–63.

22. Great Britain, Turkey No. 3 (1896), no. 40. Mr. Howard to the Marquess of Salisbury—(Received May 30), p. 21.

23. Khan-Azat, "Hai Heghapokhakani Husherits," *Hairenik Amsagir*, VI, 117–118.

24. Rostom, "Aratjin Kailer" ["First Steps"], *Divan*, I, 89.

25. William L. Langer, *The Diplomacy of Imperialism 1890–1902*, p. 160.

26. Mark Sykes, *Dar-Ul-Islam* (London, 1904), pp. 133–135, 288–289.

27. Arshak Safrastian, *Kurds and Kurdistan* (London, 1948), p. 67.

28. Mason Whiting Tyler, *The European Powers and the Near East, 1875–1908* (Minneapolis, 1925), p. 145.

29. *Ibid.*; Xenia J. Eudin, Pre-Revolutionary Russian Policies in Asia and the Middle East, MS, Hoover Institution, Stanford, California.

30. Khan-Azat, *op. cit.*, VI (February 1928), pp. 124–125.

31. There is not a copy of the *Droshaki Trutsik Tert No. 1* extant, and its exact contents are unknown. It appeared early in the year 1891.

32. *Hunchak,* May 18, 1891, June 5, 1891. These notices stated that the Hunchakian Revolutionary Party was not in union with the Dashnaktsuthiun and that *a union of the two parties had never taken place.* The latter statement does not coincide with historical evidence.
33. Khan-Azat, *op. cit.,* p. 125.
34. *Ibid.,* pp. 125–126.
35. Sevian, "H.H. Dashnaktsuthian Aratjin Kailere yev Gordzitchner," *Hairenik Amsagir,* XV (April 1937), 66.
36. Rostom, *op. cit.,* p. 90.
37. Valadian, *op. cit.* (October 1957), 32.
38. Khan-Azat, *op. cit.,* VI (January 1928), p. 123.
39. Sevian, *op. cit.,* p. 66.
40. Khan-Azat, *op. cit.,* p. 123.
41. Rostom, *loc. cit.;* Sevian, *op. cit.,* pp. 64–65.
42. "Hin Teghter" ["Old Papers"], *Vem,* III (January-February 1934), 115–116. The complete texts of these two announcements are given. The *Official Announcement* has the seal of the Committee for the Freedom of the Turkish Armenians. It is dated 1890 and bears the initials S. H. and A. T., for the names Simon Hakhumian and Aleksander Tarkhanian. The text of the other announcement, dated Tiflis, November 15, 1890, refers to the same Committee and is signed by H. H. Tchagerian.
43. Rostom, *loc. cit.,* p. 90.
44. *Droshaki Trutsik Tert No. 2* [Circular of the *Droshak*] (Vienna, 1891). This special pamphlet was issued as a publication preliminary to the issue of the party organ, the *Droshak.* It states that it was published in Vienna by the " 'Dashnaktsuthian' Azat Teparan" ("Free Press of the Dashnaktsuthiun"), but it was, in fact, published in Tiflis.
45. *Droshak,* May, 1891. The first two issues of the *Droshak* were published in Tiflis, the third issue in Rumania, and all the succeeding ones at Geneva, Switzerland, until September, 1925. *Droshak* publications were interrupted from 1914 to 1925. The October 1925 issue of *Droshak* was printed in Paris and continued there until 1933. The party has issued a total of 179 official newspapers and magazines from 1890 to 1950. The first few issues of the *Droshak* were edited by Rostom (Stepan Zorian).
46. H.H. Dashnaktsuthian Mi Khumb [A Group of Federation of Armenian Revolutionaries], "Hraver Aratjin Endhanur Zhoghovi Hai Heghapokhakannerin" ["Invitation to the First General Congress of Armenian Revolutionaries"], *Divan,* I, 95. Only one copy of this document remains; it is in the archives of the Armenian Revolutionary Federation in Boston, Mass. At the bottom of the circular, in Rostom's handwriting, in Armenian, is written: "Published in Tabriz 1892, April, before a general meeting. Edited by Honan and Okonian."
47. *Ibid.*
48. *Droshak,* August 1894, September 1894.
49. *Hai Heghapokhakan Dashnaktsuthian Dzragir* (Vienna, n.d.). This

document is the first edition of the pamphlet and bears the official seal of the party.

50. The demands listed in this text have been translated as closely to the original Armenian as possible.

51. *Hai Heghapokhakan Dashnaktsuthian Dzragir.*

52. *Droshak,* May 1891.

53. Marcel Léart, *La Question arménienne à la lumière des documents* (Paris, 1913), pp. 28–30; le Vicomte de la Jonquière, Histoire de l'empire ottoman (nov. ed.; Paris, 1914), II, 123–126. Patriarch Nerses Varzhabedian had prepared a "Project of Laws for Turkish Armenia" with a "Memorandum on the Armenian Question" for presentation by the Armenian delegation to the Congress of Berlin (1878).

54. *Droshak,* November 1893, January 1894, March 1894, May 1894. The first two articles were written by Mikaelian and Zavarian as co-authors, and the last two were written by Rostom alone.

55. In 1903 the party extended its revolutionary objectives into Russian Armenian territory where activities were directed against the Tsarist regime. At the Ninth General Congress in 1919, the Dashnak program was broadened to include a politically independent republic comprising all of Turkish and Russian Armenia.

56. H.H. Dashnaktsuthiun [Armenian Revolutionary Federation], *Dzragir* [Program of the Armenian Revolutionary Federation] (Geneva, 1907).

57. Jean Longuet, *Le mouvement socialiste international,* Vol. V of *Encyclopédie socialiste syndicale et coopérative de l'Internationale ouvrière* (Paris, 1913), p. 502.

58. H.H. Dashnaktsuthian Kentron [Central Committee of the Federation of Armenian Revolutionaries], "Haitararuthiun" ["Declaration"], *Divan,* I, 94–95. This is the only document extant issued by the first Central Committee during its two years (1890–1892) as the controlling body of the Dashnaktsuthiun.

59. Their approval was sought in carrying out the Ottoman Bank Demonstration of 1896. The decision of the Ninth General Congress at Erivan in 1919 for the establishment of only one Central Committee or Bureau is evidence of the gradual tendency toward centralization.

60. Sots. Dem Hunchakian Kusaktsuthian Amerikayi Boghokogh Gordz. Marmin [The Executive Committee of the Protesting Faction of the American Branch of the Social Democrat Hunchakian Party in America], *S.D. Hunch. Enkerneru Datastanin* [*The Cause of the Members of the Social Democrat Hunchakian Party*] (Boston, 1920), pp. 82–83; For details of Hunchak history see Louise Nalbandian, "The Origins and Development of Socialism in Armenia: The Social Democrat Hunchakian Party 1887–1949" (unpublished M.A. thesis, Department of History, Stanford University, 1949).

61. Varandian, *Dashnaktsuthian Patmuthiun,* I, 123.

62. Those who had special training in arms were Tigran Stepanian, Galust Aloyan, Katanian, Grigorian, and Samson Tadeuian. Rostom, one of the founding fathers, worked there in 1891.

63. Varandian, *Dashnaktsuthian Patmuthiun*, I, 123–125; A. Amurian, *op. cit.*, pp. 41–42; Khan-Azat, *op. cit.*, VI (January 1928), 122.

64. "Derik" means "little monastery" in the Kurdish language.

65. A. Norian, *Dervagner H.H. Dashnaktsuthian Gordzuneuthiunits [Episodes from the Activities of the A.R. Federation]* (Boston, 1917), p. 112.

66. During the years 1891–1896 the most prominent of Dashnak guerrilla leaders included Arabo (Stepanos Mekhitharian), Peto (Aleksander Petrosian), Abro (Mekertitch Sahakian), Ishkhan (Hovsep Arghuthian), Serop Pasha or Aghbur Serop (Serop Vardanian), Hrayr (Armenak Khazarian), Vardan (Sarkis Mehrapian), Nikol-Duman or Ghara-Duman (Nikoghayos Ter Hovhannesian), and Farhat (Sarkis Ohantjian).

67. Varandian, *Dashnaktsuthian Patmuthiun*, I, 254–255. Varandian states that Abdurahman's articles distributed to the Kurds were written in the pages of the *Droshak* during the years 1895–1896. *Droshak* issues for those years do not reveal such articles. It is possible that special *Droshak* leaflets in Kurdish were released.

68. "Makedonatsi Heghapokhakanneri Namake H. Usufianin" ["The Letter of the Macedonian Revolutionaries to H. Usufian"], *Divan*, I, 214–215.

69. Varandian, *Dashnaktsuthian Patmuthiun*, I, 261.

70. "Trutsik Tert No. 2. H.H. Dashnaktsuthian K. Polis Kedronakan Komitein, 1 Noyemp. 95" ["Circular No. 2 of the Central Committee of the A.R. Federation in Constantinople, November 1, 1895"], *Divan*, I, 226–227.

71. Great Britain, *Correspondence respecting the Disturbances at Constantinople in August 1896.* Parl. Pub., 1897, Vol. CI (Accounts and Papers), c. 8303, Turkey No. 1 (1897), Inclosure 2 in no. 25. The Armenian Revolutionary Committee to the Embassies, pp. 14–15.

72. Ministère des affaires étrangères, *op. cit.*, no. 241, M. de la Boulinière, Chargé d'affaires de France à Constantinople, à M. Hanotaux, Ministre des affaires étrangères, p. 266; *ibid.*, no. 245, M. de la Boulinière, Chargé d'affaires de France à Constantinople, à M. Hanotaux, Ministre des affaires étrangères, p. 268.

73. Great Britain, *Correspondence. . . .* Turkey No. 1 (1897), *op. cit.*, p. 1–52; Ministère des affaires étrangères, *op. cit.*, pp. 264–284, 287–294, 301; *Die Grosse Politik der Europaischen Kabinette, 1871–1914*, XII, nr. 2901, Der Staatssekretar des Auswartigen Amtes Freiherr von Marschall an Kaiser Wilhelm, z.Z. in Barby, August 29, 1896, pp. 21–22; *ibid.*, nr. 2903, Der Boschafter in Konstantinopel Freiherr von Saurma an den Reichskanzler Fursten von Hohenlohe, September 1, 1896, pp. 23–24. In this document it is estimated that 8,000 Armenians perished in the Constantinople massacre; *Divan*, II, 109–112; Armen Garo (Pasdermadjian), *Aprevadz Orer [Memoirs of Past Years]* (Boston, 1948), pp. 101–141; George Washburn, *Fifty Years in Constantinople* (Boston, 1911), pp. 245–249; Dorina L. Neave, *Twenty-Six*

Years on the Bosphorus (London, 1933), pp. 173–195; Sidney Whitman, *Turkish Memories* (London, 1914), pp. 15–24.

74. Ministère des affaires étrangères, *op. cit.*, no. 243. Note collective adressée à la Sublime Porte par les Représentants des Grandes Puissances à Constantinople, p. 267.

75. *Ibid.*, no. 252. Note Verbale collective remise à la Sublime Porte par les Représentants des Grandes Puissances, pp. 271–272.

76. A. W. Ward and G. P. Gooch, *The Cambridge History of British Foreign Policy 1783–1919* (Cambridge, England, 1923), III, 236; R.W. Seton-Watson, *Britain in Europe 1789–1914* (Cambridge, England, 1945), p. 540.

77. *Divan*, II, 293–294.

NOTES TO CHAPTER VIII (Pp. 179–185)

1. Elisaeus, Bishop of the Amadunians, *The History of Vartan, and the Battle of the Armenians: Containing An Account of the Religious Wars between the Persians and the Armenians,* translated from the Armenian by C. F. Neumann (n.p., 1830), p. 20.

Bibliography

(The entries are classified under the headings Documents, Manuscripts
and Unpublished Theses, Encyclopedias and Maps, Newspapers and Periodicals, Books, *and* Articles.)

DOCUMENTS

Aghaniants, Giut. *Divan Hayots Patmuthian* [Archives on Armenian His-
tory]. Vol. XIII: *Harstaharuthiunner Tadjkahaystanum (Vaveragrer
1801–1888)* [Oppression in Turkish Armenia (Documents 1801–1888)].
Tiflis, 1915.
*Aspirations et agissements révolutionnaires des comités arméniens avant
et après la proclamation de la Constitution ottomane.* Constantinople,
1917.·
Azgayin Patriarkaran [National Patriarchate (of the Armenians)]. *Atena-
gruthiunk Azgayin Zhoghovoy* [Records of the National (Armenian)
Assembly]. Constantinople, 1870–1914.
Azgayin Sahmanadruthiun Hayots 1860 [Armenian National Constitution
1860]. Constantinople, 1860.
Azgayin Sahmanadruthiun Hayots [Armenian National Constitution (of
1863)]. Constantinople, 1908.
Delegation de la République Arménienne. *L'Arménie et la question arménienne avant, pendant et depuis la guerre.* Paris, 1922.
Droshaki Trutsik Tert No. 2 [Circular of the Droshak]. Vienna, 1891.
Dzragir Hunchakian Kusaktsuthian [Program of the Hunchakian Party].
2d ed.; London, 1897.
Germany, Auswartiges Amt. *Die Grosse Politik der europaischen Kabi-
nette, 1871–1914.* Ed. by Johannes Lepsius, Albrecht Mendelssohn Bar-
tholdy, and Friedrich Thimme. Berlin, 1922–1927.
Great Britain. Foreign Office. *British and Foreign State Papers.* London,
1812–1900.
———. ———. *The Treatment of the Armenians in the Ottoman Empire
1915–16.* Miscellaneous No. 31, 1916.
———. ———. Historical Section: Peace Handbook No. 62, *Armenia and
Kurdistan,* 1919; *ibid.,* No. 60, *Syria and Palestine.* London, 1920.
———. Parliament. *Sessional Papers. Accounts and Papers.* Turkey. 1877–
1900.
Hai Heghapokhakan Dashnaktsuthian Dzragir [Program of the Armenian

Revolutionary Federation]. Vienna, n.d. This document bears the official seal of the Armenian Revolutionary Federation.

H.H. Dashnaktsuthiun [Armenian Revolutionary Federation]. *Dzragir* [Program of the Armenian Revolutionary Federation]. Geneva, 1907.

H.H.D. Amerikayi Kedr. Komite [Central Committee of the American Branch of the Armenian Revolutionary Federation]. *Divan H.H. Dashnaksuthian* [Archives of the A.R. Federation]. Boston, 1934, 1938. 2 vols.

Mayewski, General. *Les massacres d'Armenie.* St. Petersburg, 1916.

Ministère des affaires étrangères [France]. *Documents diplomatiques, affaires arméniennes projects de reformes dans l'Empire ottoman 1893–1897.* Paris, 1897.

Noradounghian, Gabriel. *Recueil d'Actes internationaux de l'Empire ottoman.* Paris, 1897–1903. 4 vols.

Secrétariat Socialists International. *Sixième congrès socialists international tenu a Amsterdam du 14 au 20 août 1904; Compte-Rendu analytique.* Brussels, 1904.

Turkish Collection in the Hoover Institution and Library on War, Revolution, and Peace, at Stanford University, Stanford, California.

MANUSCRIPTS AND UNPUBLISHED THESES

Aderbed (Mubaihadjian, Sarkis). "50 Amyak 1878–1928 Voskya Hobelian Hai Heghapokhuthian" [Fiftieth year, 1878–1928—the golden jubilee of the Armenian revolution]. MS, dated Leninakan (Soviet Armenia), December 31, 1927.

Cloud, George Hurach. "The Armenian Question from the Congress of Berlin to the Armenian Massacres 1878–1894." Unpublished M.A. thesis. Stanford University, 1923.

Etmekjian, James. "The French Influence on the Western Armenian Renaissance, 1843–1915." Unpublished Ph.D. dissertation. Brown University, 1958.

Eudin, Xenia J. "Pre-Revolutionary Russian Policies in Asia and the Middle East." MS, Hoover Institution, Stanford, California.

Hagopian, J. Michael. "Hyphenated Nationalism: The Spirit of the Revolutionary Movement in Asia Minor, 1896–1910." Unpublished Ph.D. dissertation. Harvard University, 1943.

Megerditchian, Ervant D. "Krakan-Patmakan Hanrakitaran Vaspurakan Ashkharhi" [Literary-historic encyclopedic of the world of Van]. MS, Braintree, Massachusetts, 1958.

Nalbandian, Louise. "The Origins and Development of Socialism in Armenia: The Social Democrat Hunchakian Party 1887–1949." Unpublished M.A. thesis. Stanford University, 1949.

———. "The Religious Wars between the Armenians and Persians during the Reign of Yezdegert II (438–457)." MS, San Francisco, California.

Wee, Morris. "Great Britain and the Armenian Question 1878–1914." Unpublished Ph.D. dissertation. University of Wisconsin, 1938.

ENCYCLOPEDIAS AND MAPS

Abeghian, Artashes. *Hayastan yev Dratsi Yerkirnere* [Armenia and neighboring countries] (Map). Stuttgart, 1947.
Bolshaia sovetskaia entsiklopediia [Great Soviet Encyclopedia]. Moscow, 1927–1947.
Compère-Morel. *Encyclopédie socialiste syndicale et coopérative de l'Internationale ouvrière.* Paris, 1913.
Encyclopedia Britannica. 11th ed.; 1910–1911.
Encyclopedia of Islam. London, 1913.
Encyclopedia of the Social Sciences. New York, 1935.
Lynch, H. F. B., and F. Oswald. *Map of Armenia and Adjacent Countries.* London, 1901.

NEWSPAPERS AND PERIODICALS

Aptak [Slap]. 1894–1897.
Armenia. 1885–1908.
Bulletin periodique du bureau socialiste International. 1909–1911.
Droshak (or *Droschak*) [Flag, or Banner]. 1890–1900.
Hunchak (or *Hentchak*) [Bell]. 1887–1896.
The London *Times.* 1860–1900.
Nor Kiank [New Life]. 1898–1902.
Portugalian, M. *"Armenia" i Husharar* [An anthology from "Armenia"]. Marseilles, 1890. Contains a reprint of the principal sections of the journal *Armenia* for the period 1885–1886, with a preface by its editor, M. Portugalian.

BOOKS

Adjemian, L., ed. *Husher Armenak Yekariani* [Memoirs of Armenak Yekarian]. Cairo, 1947.
Adontz, Nicolas. *Histoire d'Arménie des origines du Xe siècle ou VIe (av. J.C.).* Paris, 1946.
———. *Patmakan Usumnasiruthiunner* [Historical studies]. Paris, 1948.
Aghassi. *Zeitoun depuis les origines jusqu'à l'insurrection de 1895.* Paris, 1897.
Aghuzumtsian, V. *Mikael Nalbandiani Sotsial-Tentesagitakan Hayatsknere* [The social-economic views of Mikael Nalbandian]. Erivan, 1955.
Aharonian, Avetis. *Christopher Mikaelian* [in Armenian]. Boston, 1926.
Akhov, M. I. *I. Ocherki iz istorii armianskoso "gosudarstva"; II. Rossia i armiane* [I. Essays on the history of the Armenian "state"; II. Russia and the Armenians]. St. Petersburg, 1902.
Alboyadjian, Arshak. *Minas Tcheraz Ir Kianke yev Gordze Ir 60 Amiah*

Hobeliani Artiv [The life and work of Minas Tcheraz on the occasion of the 60th anniversary of his public career]. Cairo, 1927.

———. *Patmakan Hayastani Sahmannere* [The boundaries of historical Armenia]. Cairo, 1950.

Alishan, Léonce M. *Hushigk Hayreniats Hayots* [Reflections on the fatherland of the Armenian people]. Venice, 1869. 2 vols.

———. *Sissouan ou l'Arméno-Cilicie: Geographique et historique.* Venice, 1899.

———. *Arshaloys Kristoneuthian Hayots* [Dawn of Armenian Christianity]. 3d ed.; Venice, 1920.

Allahvertian, H. H. *Ulnia Kam Zeitun Lernayin Avan I Kilikia* [Oulnia or Zeitun, a mountainous town in Cilicia]. Constantinople, 1884.

Amurian, A. *H.H. Dashnaktsuthiune Parskastanum 1890–1918* [The A.R. Federation in Iran 1890–1918]. Teheran, 1950.

Ananun, D. *Rusahayeri Hasarakakan Zargatsume* [The intellectual enlightenment of the Armenians in Russia]. Baku, Etchmiadzin, and Venice, 1913, 1922, and 1926. 3 vols.

Aramiants, Hemayeak. *Depi Kakhaghan* [Toward the gallows]. Constantinople, 1918.

———. *Veratzenundi Yerkunke* [The pains of rebirth]. Constantinople, 1918.

———. *Ankakh Hayastan* [Independent Armenia]. Constantinople, 1919.

Armen, K. *Tigranes the Great, a Biography.* Detroit, 1940.

Armenian National Council of America. *Two Thousand Years of the Armenian Theater: A Digest in English of Professor Georg Goyan's Recent Monumental Work in Russian with Additional Essays in English and Armenian by other Contributors.* New York, 1954.

Armenian Youth Federation of America Central Educational Council. *Armenian Youth Federation of America Program 1949–1950 Blue Book No. V.* Boston, 1949.

———. *Armenian Youth Federation of America Program 1950–1951 Blue Book No. VI.* Boston, 1950–1951.

———. *Armenian Youth Federation of America Program 1951–1952 Blue Book No. VII.* Boston, 1951–1952.

Arpee, Leon. *The Armenian Awakening: A History of the Armenian Church, 1820–1860.* Chicago, 1909.

———. *A History of Armenian Christianity.* New York, 1946.

Aslan, Kevork. *Armenia and the Armenians from the Earliest Times until the Great War (1914).* Translated by Pierre Crabitès. New York, 1920.

Atamian, Sarkis. *The Armenian Community: The Historical Development of a Social and Ideological Conflict.* New York, 1955.

Babayan, Aram, ed. *Hairenik, Hai Groghnere Haireniki Masin* [Fatherland, Armenian writers on the fatherland]. Erivan, 1946.

Barkley, Henry C. *A Ride Through Asia Minor and Armenia.* London, 1891.

Basmadjian, K. J. *Levon V Lusignan Vertjin Takavor Hayots* [Leo V Lusignan, the last king of the Armenians]. Paris, 1908.

Basmadjian, K. J. *Histoire moderne des arméniens.* Paris, 1917.

Bellaud, M. *Essai sur la langue arménienne.* Paris, 1812.

Blackwell, Alice Stone. *Armenian Poems.* Boston, 1917.

Bliss, Edwin Munsell. *Turkey and the Armenian Atrocities.* New York, 1896.

Borian, B. A. *Armenia, mezhdunarodnaia diplomatiia i SSSR* [Armenia, international diplomacy and the USSR]. Moscow-Leningrad, 1928. 2 vols.

Burke, Edmund. *The Correspondence of Edmund Burke.* Cambridge, 1958–1961. 3 vols.

Buxton, Noel, and Harold Buxton. *Travel and Politics in Armenia.* London, 1914.

Chalkhushian, Gr. *Armianskii vopros i Armianskie pogromy v Rossii (Panislamizm)* [The Armenian Question and the Armenian pogroms in Russia (Pan-Islamism)]. Rostov na Donu, 1905.

Chamich, Michael. *History of Armenia.* Translated by Johannes Avdall. Calcutta, 1927. 2 vols.

Cirbied, Jacques Chahan de, and F. Martin. *Recherches Curieuses sur l'histoire ancienne de l'Asie.* Paris, 1806.

Cirbied, Jacques Chahan de, and Mir-Davoud-Zadour de Melik Schahnazar. *Détails sur la situation actuelle du royaume de Perse.* Paris, 1816.

Coursons, Vicomte des. *La Rébellion arménienne.* Paris, 1895.

Cuinet, Vital. *La Turquie d'Asie: géographie administrative.* Paris, 1890–1894. 4 vols.

Darbinian, Artak. *Hai Azatagrakan Sharzhman Oreren (Husher 1890en 1940)* [From the days of the Armenian liberation movement, memoirs from 1890 to 1940]. Paris, 1947.

Der Nersessian, Sirarpie. *Armenia and the Byzantine Empire.* Cambridge, Mass., 1945.

Djanachian, Mesrop. *Patmuthiun Ardi Hai Graganuthian* [History of modern Armenian literature]. Venice, 1953.

Djankulian, H. H. *Hishatakner Haikakan Djeknazhamen* [Memories from the Armenian crisis]. Constantinople, 1913. 4 vols.

Doumergue, G. *L'Arménie, les massacres et la question d'Orient.* 2d ed.; Paris, n.d.

Dzhivelegov, A. K. *Armiane v Rossii* [Armenians in Russia]. Moscow, 1906.

Elisaeus, Bishop of the Armenians. *The History of Vartan, and the Battle of the Armenians: Containing an Account of the Religious Wars Between the Persians and the Armenians.* Translated by C. F. Neumann. N.p., 1830.

Emin, Joseph. *The Life and Adventures of Joseph Emin, An Armenian; Written in English by Himself.* London, 1792.

———. *Life and Adventures of Emin Joseph Emin 1726–1809. By Joseph Emin.* Edited by Amy Apcar. 2d ed.; Calcutta, 1918.

Eprikian, H. S. *Patkerazard Benashkharhik Bararan* [Illustrated Armenian geographic dictionary]. Venice, 1903–1907. 2 vols.

Gabriel, M. S. *Bleeding Armenia: Its History and Horrors under the Curse of Islam.* New York, 1896.

Galemkearian, Grigoris. _Patmuthiun Hai Lragruthian_ [History of Armenian journalism]. Vienna, 1893.

Garnett, David. _The Golden Echo_. New York, 1954.

Garo, Armen [Pasdermadjian]. _Aprevadz Orer_ [Memoirs of past years]. Boston, 1948.

Gharip, Armen. _Hunchakian Matian_ [Hunchakian book]. Second pamphlet: _S.D. Hunchakian Kusaktsuthian Dzragire_ [The program of the S.D. Hunchakian Party]. Beirut, February, 1952.

———. Third pamphlet: _S.D. Hunchakian Kusaktsuthian Dzragire_ [The program of the S.D. Hunchakian Party]. Beirut, March, 1952.

Gismegian, Manoug C. _Patmuthiun Amerikahai Kaghakakan Kusaktsuthiants 1890–1925_ [The history of the Armenian-American political parties 1890–1925]. Fresno, Calif., 1930.

Giuzalian, G. _Hai Kaghakakan Metki Zargatsume yev H.H. Dashnaktsuthiune_ [The enlightenment of the Armenian political mind and the A.R. Federation]. Paris, 1927.

Goodspeed, Edgar J. _The Twelve_. Philadelphia, 1957.

Greene, Frederick Davis. _Armenian Massacres or the Sword of Mohammed_. New York, 1896.

Grousset, René. _Histoire de l'Arménie des origines à 1071_. Paris, 1947.

Hairenik Batsarik Tiv 2 [Hairenik, special issue no. 2]. Boston, 1914.

Hall, H. R. _The Ancient History of the Near East_. London, reprinted 1952.

Herodotus. _History_.

Hobeleanakan Tonakataruthiun I Pars S.D. Hunch. Kusaktsuthian 60 Ameaki [The celebration of the 60th anniversary of the S.D. Hunchakian Party]. San Francisco, 1948.

H.H.D. Amer. Kedr. Komite [Central Committee of the American Branch of the Armenian Revolutionary Federation]. _Vatsunamiak (1890–1950)_ [Sixtieth anniversary (1890–1950)]. Compiled by S. Vratzian. Boston, 1950.

H.H.D. Buro [Bureau of the Armenian Revolutionary Federation]. _Hushapatum H.H. Dashnaktsuthian 1890–1950_ [Historical collection of the A.R. Federation]. Boston, 1950.

H.H.D. Arevmethian Yevropayi Kedr. Komite [Central Committee of the Armenian Revolutionary Federation of Western Europe]. _H.H. Dashnaktsuthiune Yevropayi Metj_ [The Armenian Revolutionary Federation in Europe]. Paris, 1952.

H.H. Dashnaktsuthian Arevmethian Yevropayi Ketronakan Komite [Central Committee of the Armenian Revolutionary Federation of Western Europe]. _H.H. Dashnaktsuthiun_ [A.R. Federation], Paris, 1936.

Harris, J. Rendel, and Helen B. Harris. _Letters from the Scenes of the Recent Massacres in Armenia_. London, 1897.

Horton, George. _The Blight of Asia_. Indianapolis, 1926.

Indjikian, A. M. _Mikael Nalbandiani Kyanki yev Gordzuneuthian Daregruthiune_ [Dairy of the life and work of Mikael Nalbandian]. Erivan, 1954.

Johanissjan, Aschot [Hovhannesian, Ashot]. _Israel Ory und Armenische Befreiungsidee_. Inaugural Dissertation. Munich, 1913.

Jonquière, le Vicomte de la. *Histoire de l'Empire ottoman*. Nouvelle ed.; Paris, 1914. 2 vols.

Kamar-Katiba [Patkanian, Rafael]. *Kamar-Katibai Banasteghtzuthiunke* [The poetry of Kamar-Katiba]. Moscow, 1881.

Karibi. *Krasnaia kniga* [Red book]. Tiflis, 1920.

Kasarjian, Bedros. *Hai Arakelakan Yekeghetsin yev Ir Vardapetuthiune* [The Armenian Apostolic Church and its doctrine]. Paris, 1945.

Kilikia [Cilicia]. St. Petersburg, 1894.

King, L. W., ed. *Bronze Reliefs from the Gates of Shalmaneser King of Assyria B.C. 860–825*. London, 1915.

Kitur, Arsen. *Hai Azatagruthian Djanaparhin* [The road of Armenian liberation]. Beirut, 1949.

———. *Hunchakian Matian* [Hunchakian book]. Fifth pamphlet: *Hunchakian Kelkhavor Tsoytsere* [The major demonstrations of the Hunchakian Revolutionary Party]. Beirut, 1954.

Koriun. *Vark Mashtotsi* [Life of Mesrop Mashtots]. Preface by M. Abeghian. Cairo, 1954.

Langer, William L. *The Diplomacy of Imperialism 1890–1902*. 2d. ed.; New York, 1951.

Lazian, Gabriel. *Demker Hai Azatagrakan Sharzhumen* [Personalities from the Armenian liberation movement]. Cairo, 1949.

Léart, Marcel. *La question arménienne à la lumière des documents*. Paris, 1913.

Leo [Babakhanian, A.] *Grigor Ardzruni* [in Armenian]. Tiflis, 1901–1904. 3 vols.

———. *Thiurkahai Heghapokhuthian Gaghaparabanuthiune* [The ideology of the Armenian revolution in Turkey]. Paris, 1934, 1935. 2 vols.

———. *Ani* [in Armenian]. Erivan, 1946.

———. *Hayots Patmuthiun* [History of the Armenians], Vol. II. Erivan, 1946.

Lepsius, Johannes. *Armenia and Europe*. London, 1897.

———. *Deutschland und Armenia 1914–1918*. Potsdam, 1919.

Levonian, Garegin. *Hai Girke yev Tepagruthian Arveste* [The Armenian book and the art of printing]. Erivan, 1946.

Longuet, Jean. *Le mouvement socialiste international*. Vol. V of *Encyclopédie socialiste syndicale et coopérative de l'Internationale ouvrière*, edited by Compère-Morel. Paris, 1913.

Lynch, H. F. B. *Armenia Travel and Studies*. London, 1901. 2 vols.

M., Y. G. *Thiurkahayots Hin Vadjarakanuthiunn yev Vadjarakank 1740–1890* [Early trade and merchants among the Turkish Armenians 1740–1890]. Constantinople, 1908.

Macler, Frédéric. *La Nation arménienne: son passé, ses malheurs*. Paris, 1924.

Manandian, Hakob. *Feodalisme Hin Hayastanum; Arshakunineri U Marzputhian Shertjan* [Feudalism in ancient Armenia: Arsacid and Marzpan period]. Erivan, 1934.

Manandian, Y. A. *A Brief Survey of the History of Ancient Armenia.* N.p., n.d.

Mandelstam, André-N. *La société des nations et les puissances devant le problème armenien.* Paris, 1926.

Marriott, John A. R. *The Eastern Question.* 4th ed.; Oxford, 1951.

Martuni, Al [Myasnikian]. *Kusaktsuthiunnere Gaghutahayuthian Metj* [The political parties among the Armenians of the Diaspora]. Tiflis, 1924.

Mikaelian, Christopher. *Heghapokhakani Metkere* [Thoughts of a revolutionary]. 3d ed.; Athens, 1931.

Millingen, Frederick (Osman-Seify-Bey). *La Turquie sous le regne d'Abdul-Aziz 1862–1867.* Paris, 1868.

——. *Wild Life Among the Koords.* London, 1870.

Missak, H. *Le Père Ottoman 1644–1676.* Paris, 1903. (A reprint from the *Revue d'histoire diplomatique.*)

Morgan, Jacques de. *History of the Armenian People.* Translated by Ernest F. Barry. Boston, n.d.

Nalbandian, Mikael. *Yerkeri Liakatar Zhoghovadzoy* [Complete works]. Erivan, 1945–1949. 4 vols.

Nalbandian, M. *Andip Yerker* [Unpublished works]. Edited and compiled by Ashot Hovhannesian. Erivan, 1935.

National Congress of Turkey. *The Turco-Amenian Question: The Turkish Point of View.* Constantinople, 1919.

Nazarbek, Avetis. *Through the Storm: Pictures of Life in Armenia.* London, 1899.

——. *The Voice of the Armenian Revolutionists upon the Armenian Problem and How to Solve It.* London, n.d.

Nersessian, M. G. *Hai Zhoghovurdi Azatagrakan Paikare Thiurkakan Bernapetuthian Dem* [The struggle for freedom of the Armenian people against Turkish oppression]. Erivan, 1955.

Nervanian, S. *Heghapokhakanner—Vardan Goloshian, H. Agripasian* [Revolutionaries—Vardan Goloshian, H. Agripasian]. Geneva, 1905.

Nishkian, H. M. *Aratjin Kaidzere Etj Me Karno Zartonken* [The first sparks—a page from the awakening in Erzerum]. Boston, 1930.

Norian, A. *Dervagner H.H. Dashnaktsuthian Gordzuteuthiunits* [Episodes from the activities of the A.R. Federation]. Boston, 1917.

Norman, C. B. *Armenia and the Campaign of 1877.* London, 1878.

Nurikhan, Minas. *The Life and Times (1660–1750) of the Servant of God Abbot Mechitar.* Translated by John McQuillan. Venice, 1915.

Ormanian, Malachia. *The Church of Armenia.* London, 1912.

——. *Azgapatum* [The story of the nation]. Constantinople and Jerusalem, 1912–1927. 3 vols.

——. *Khohk yev Khosk* [Thoughts and talks]. Jerusalem, 1929.

Oshagan, H. *Hai Grakanuthiun* [Armenian literature]. Jerusalem, 1942.

Oswald, Felix. *Geology of Armenia.* London, 1906.

Palasanian, Stepanos, *Hayots Patmuthiun* [History of the Armenians]. Constantinople, 1919.

Parrot, Friedrich. *Journey to Ararat*. Translated by W. D. Cooley. New York, 1846.

Partizuni, *Khatchatur Abovian, Kyanke yev Steghdzagordzuthiune* [Khatchatur Abovian, his life and work]. Erivan, 1952.

Pasdermadjian, H. *Histoire de l'Arménie depuis les origines jusqu'au traité de Lausanne*. Paris, 1949.

Pears, Edwin. *Life of Abdul Hamid*. New York, 1917.

Polozhenie armian v Turtsii do vmieshatelstva derzhav v 1895 godu. [Condition of the Armenians in Turkey before the intervention of the powers in 1895]. Moscow, 1896.

Raffi (Hakob Melik-Hakobian). *Ardziv Vaspurakani* (*Khirimian Hairig*) [The eagle of Vaspurakan (Khirimian Hairig)]. Tiflis, 1893.

———. *Khente* [The Fool]. 3d ed.; Vienna, 1905.

———. *Kaitzer* [Sparks]. Vienna, 1904, 1952. 2 vols.

Rolin-Jaequemyns, M. G. *Armenia, the Armenians, and the Treaties*. London, 1891.

Ruben [Der Minasian, Ruben]. *Hai Heghapokhankani Me Hishataknere* [Memoirs of an Armenian revolutionary]. Los Angeles, 1951–1952. 7 vols. Vols. I, III, and IV are written by Ruben alone. Vol. II is written by Aram-Ruben and contains separate sections by the two revolutionaries Aram and Ruben. Vol. V is by the two revolutionaries Ruben and Yerkat.

Sabah-Gulian, S. *Inknavar Hayastan* [Autonomous Armenia]. Cairo, 1915.

———. *Sotsialism yev Hairenik* [Socialism and the fatherland]. Providence, 1916.

———. *Bareri yev Yezreri Batsatruthiunner* [The meaning of words and terms]. Boston, 1927.

Safrastian, Arshak. *Kurds and Kurdistan*. London, 1948.

Sarafian, Kevork A. *History of Education in Armenia*. La Verne, Calif., 1930.

Sarkissian, A. O. *History of the Armenian Question to 1885*. Urbana, Ill., 1938.

Sarukhan. *Haikakan Khendiren yev Azgayin Sahmanadruthiune Thiurkiayum* (*1860–1910*) [The Armenian Question and the Armenian National Constitution in Turkey (1860–1910)]. Tiflis, 1912.

Seth, Mesrovb Jacob. *Armenians in India*. Calcutta, 1937.

S.D. Hunchakian Kusaktsuthian Fransayi Shertjan [S.D. Hunchakian Party, Branch in France]. *Hushardzan* [Memoria]. Paris, 1930.

Seferian, Mihran M. *Hunchakian Matian* [Hunchakian book]. First pamphlet: *Intchu yev Intchpes Himnevetsav S.D. Hunchakian Kusaktsuthiune* [Why and how the S.D. Hunchakian Party was formed]. Beirut, 1952.

———. ———. Fourth pamphlet: *S.D. Hunchakian Kusaktsuthian Propakant-Karoztchakan Gordzuneuthiune* [The propaganda-missionary activity of the S.D. Hunchakian Party]. Beirut, 1954.

Seropian, Mushegh (*also as* Mushegh Arkyepiskopos). *Mantchesderi Hai*

Gaghute [The Armenian community of Manchester, England]. Boston, 1911.

──────. *Haikakan Meghdsavantje* [The Armenian nightmare]. Boston, 1916.

──────. *Mer Paikare Hai Azatagruthian Ughiov* [Our struggle in the path of Armenian liberation]. Cairo, 1948.

Seton-Watson, R. W. *Britain in Europe 1789–1914*. Cambridge, England, 1945.

Shahaziz, Yervand. *Divan Mikael Nalbandiani* [Archives on Mikael Nalbandian]. Erivan, 1932.

Soc. Dem. Hunchakian Kusaktsuthian Amerikayi Boghokogh Gordz. Marmin. [The executive committee of the protesting faction of the American Branch of the Social Democrat Hunchakian Party]. *S.D. Hunch. Enkerneru Datastanin* [The cause of the members of the Social Democrat Hunchakian Party]. Boston, 1920.

Soc. Dem. Hunch. Kus. Amer-i Sherdjane [Social Democrat Hunchakian Party of America]. *Hunchak Taregirk* [Hunchak Yearly]. Providence, 1931.

──────. *Hunchak Taregirk* [Hunchak Yearly]. New York, 1932.

Soc. Dem. Hunchakian Kus. Kedr. Varchuthiun. [Central Committee of the Social Democrat Hunchakian Party]. *Hisnameak—1887—1937—Sots. Demokrat Hunchakian Kusaktsuthian* [The fiftieth anniversary of the Social Democrat Hunchakian Party, 1887–1937]. Providence, 1938.

Surbezy, Francois. *Les affaires d'Armenie et l'intervention des puissances europeenes (de 1894 à 1897)*. Thèse pour le doctorat. Université de Montpellier, Faculte de Droit, 1911.

Sykes, Mark. *Dar-Ul-Islam*. London, 1904.

Taylor, A. J. P. *The Struggle for the Mastery in Europe 1848–1918*. Oxford, 1954.

Tchobanian, Archag. *Mekertitch Beshiktashliani Gertvadznern U Djarere* [The writings and speeches of Mekertitch Beshiktashlian]. Paris, 1904.

──────. *The People of Armenia: Their Past, Their Culture, Their Future*. London, 1914.

──────. *Mer Grakanuthiune* [Our literature]. Paris, 1926.

──────. *Victor Hugo, Chateaubriand, et Lamartine dans la littérature arménienne*. Paris, 1935.

Teodik. *Amenun Daretsoytse* [Everybody's yearbook]. Constantinople, Vienna, Venice, and Paris. 1907–1929. 19 vols.

Ter-Movsesian, Sahak. *Patmuthiun Hayots Skizben Minchev Mer Orere* [Armenian history from its beginnings to the present]. Venice, 1922–1923. 2 vols.

Thorossian, H. *Histoire de la littérature arménienne des origines jusqu'à nos jours*. Paris, 1951.

Tip U Tar [Type and letters]. Constantinople, 1912.

T-Minasian, Y. *Voskedari Hai Grakanuthiune* [The Armenian literature of the Golden Age]. Erivan, 1946.

Tonapetian, Petros [Vaghinak]. *Hayastan yev Hai Joghovurde Dareri Mit-*

jov [Armenia and the Armenian people through the centuries]. Paris, 1947, 1949. 2 vols.

Tourian, Yeghishe. *Patmuthiun Hai Matenagruthian* [History of Armenian literature]. Jerusalem, 1933.

Townshend, A. F. *A Military Consul in Turkey*. Philadelphia, 1910.

Tunaya, Tarik Z. *Turkiyede Siyasi Partiler 1859–1952* [The political parties in Turkey]. Istanbul, 1952.

Tyler, Mason Whiting. *The European Powers and the Near East, 1875–1908*. Minneapolis, 1925.

Vandal, Albert. *Les Arméniens et la réforme de la Turque*. Paris, 1897.

Varandian, Mikael. *Veradzenvogh Hairenike yev Mer Dere* [The rebirth of the fatherland and our role]. Geneva, 1910.

———. *Haikakan Sharzhman Nakhapatmuthiune* [Introductory history of the Armenian movement]. Geneva, 1912, 1914. 2 vols.

———. *Simon Zavarian (Gidzer Ir Kianken)* [Simon Zavarian, sketches from his life]. Boston, 1927.

———. *H.H. Dashnaktsuthian Patmuthiun* [History of the A.R. Federation]. Paris and Cairo, 1932, 1950. 2 vols.

Vasiliev, A. A. *History of the Byzantine Empire 324–1453*. 2d English ed., rev.; Madison, Wisconsin, 1952.

Vratzian, Simon. *Rosdom, A Biographical Sketch*. Boston, 1950.

Ward, A. H., and G. P. Gooch. *The Cambridge History of British Foreign Policy 1783–1919*, Vol. III. Cambridge, England, 1923.

Y., M. *Enkervaruthiune yev Hai Enkervarakannere* [Socialism and the Armenian socialists]. Cairo, 1910.

Yeramian, Hambarsum. *Hushardzan* [Memoria]. Alexandria, Egypt, 1929. 2 vols.

Yeremian, Simeon. *Azgayin Demker Graget Hayer* [National figures, Armenian men of letters]. Venice, 1913–1931. 10 vols.

Zarhbanalian, Garegin. *Patmuthiun Haikakan Tepagruthian Skezbnavorutenen Mintch Ar Mez* [The history of Armenian printing from its beginnings to the present]. Venice, 1895.

———. *Patmuthiun Hayeren Depruthian* [History of Armenian literature]. Venice, 1932, 1905. 2 vols.

Zartarian, V. G., ed. *Hishatakaran Hai Yerevelineru* [Memorials on some notable Armenians]. Constantiople, 1910–1912. 3 vols.

Zeituntsi. *Zetituni Antsialen yev Nerkayen* [Out of Zeitun's past and present]. Vienna and Paris, 1900, 1903. 2 vols.

ARTICLES

Aharonian, Vardges. "The Armenian Emancipatory Struggle," *Armenian Review*, VI (Winter 1953), 3–21; VII (Spring 1954), 55–60; (Summer 1954), 64–69; (Autumn 1954), 118–121.

Altchutjian, Aram. "Rostome Bakuyum" [Rostom in Baku], *Hairenik Amsagir* [Hairenik Monthly], July 1956–January 1957.

Amurian, A. "Husher Googoonian Arshavakhembits Hovsep Movsisiani (Argam Petrosian)" [Hovsep Movsisian's (Argam Petrosian) memoirs of the Googoonian Expedition], *Hairenik Amsagir* [Hairenik Monthly], February 1934–January 1935.

Ananikian, Mardiros A. "Armenian Mythology," in *The Mythology of All Races*, VII (Boston, 1925).

Andon, Haïr [Megerditchian, Ervant D.]. "Megurditch Portaukalian," *Vasbouragan*, II (March 1941), 2–3.

Aramayis (Ter Danielian). "Sarkis Googoonian," in *Divan H.H. Dashnakt-suthian* [Archives of the A.R. Federation], II (Boston: H.H.D. Amerikayi Kedr. Komite [Central Committee of the American Branch of the Armenian Revolutionary Federation], 1938), pp. 5–25.

Arpiarian, Arpiar. "Hayastan yev G. Bolis" [Armenia and Constantinople], *Nor Kiank* [New Life], II (June 1899–September 1899).

"Ayb U Ben" [A and B], *Droshak*, November 1893, January 1894, March 1894, May 1894.

Beozikian, G. [Shikaher]. "Khesri Tun" [House of the Straw Mat], *Vasbouragan*, II (April 1941), 2–3.

———. "Azatakrakan Sharzhumner Vanum" [Movements for freedom in Van], *Vasbouragan*, II (September 1941), 2–3.

Berberian, Ruben. "Hai Masonnere yev "Ser" Othiake Polso Metj" [The Armenian masons and the "Ser" lodge in Constantinople], *Hairenik Amsagir* [Hairenik Monthly], March 1937–July 1937.

Chuchian, Sahag. "Vaspurakani Vertjin Hariuramiake yev Mer Haire-naktsakannere" [The one-hundredth anniversary of Vaspuragan and our compatriotic unions], *Ardzve Vasbouragan*, XXVII (March–April 1956), 345–347.

Dillon, E. J. "Armenia: An Appeal," *Contemporary Review*, LXIX (January 1896), 1–19.

Dzeruni [Stepan Stepanian]. "Googoonian Khembi Arshavanke" [The expedition of the Googoonian band], in *Divan H.H. Dashnaktsuthian* [Archives of the A.R. Federation], I (Boston: H.H. Amerikayi Kedr. Komite [Central Committee of the American Branch of the Armenian Revolutionary Federation], 1934), pp. 31–86.

Eremian, S. "The Problem of the Decline of Slavery Society and the Rise of Feudal Relations in Ancient Armenia," in *Papers Presented by the Soviet Delegation at the XXIII International Congress of Orientalists, Iranian, Armenian and Central-Asian Studies* (Moscow: USSR Academy of Sciences, 1954), pp. 122–132.

Fenerdjian, A. "Azat Vormnadruthiune Hayots Metj" [Freemasonry among the Armenians], *Hairenik Amsagir* [Hairenik Monthly], October 1954–February 1955.

Ghazarian, Gevorg. "Intchpes Dzenund Arav H.H. Dashnaktsuthiune" [How the A.R. Federation was established], *Hairenik Amsagir* [Haire-nik Amsagir] (November 1925), 7–25.

Giuzalian, Garnik. "M. Portugalian (Mi Etj Heghapokhakan Patmuthiunits)" [M. Portugalian, a page from the revolutionary history], *Vem*, XVI (July–October 1936), 1–29.

————. "Hayots Heghapokhuthiunits Aratj" [Before the Armenian revolution], *Hushapatum H.H. Dashnaktsuthian 1890–1950* [Historical collection of the A.R. Federation 1890–1950] (Boston: H.H. Buro [Bureau of the Armenian Revolutionary Federation], 1950), pp. 14–60.

H., Dz. "Entatsk Sharzhman Hai Heghapokhuthian" [The course of the Armenian revolutionary movement], condensed by Shah-Baze for Teodik, *Amenun Daretsoytse* [Everybody's yearbook], V (Constantinople, 1911), pp. 171–174.

"Hin Teghter" [Old papers], *Vem*, III (January–February 1934), 115–116.

Karon, Heverhili [Sahakian, Karo]. "Pap Alii Tsoytse" [The demonstration of Bab Ali], *Hunchak Taregirk* [Hunchak yearly] (Soc. Dem. Hunchakian Kus. Amer-i Shertjan [Social Democrat Hunchakian Party of America], 1932), pp. 34–52.

Kasarjian, Bedros. "Vov E Shazi Kam Shah Murat" [Who is Shazi or Shah Murat], *Nor Or* [New Day], 1949, December 20, December 23.

Khan-Azat, Ruben. "Hai Heghapokhakani Husherits" [Memoirs of an Armenian revolutionary], *Hairenik Amsagir* [Hairenik Monthly], June 1927–May 1929.

Khatanasian, Yr. "Rostom (Stepan Zorian)" [Rostom (Stepan Zorian)], *Hairenik Amsagir* [Hairenik Monthly] (December 1956), 109–111.

Kurdian, H. "Grakhosakan Ser Anthoni Sherli" [A book review of the biography of Sir Anthony Sherley], *Hairenik Amsagir* [Hairenik Monthly] (September 1936), 170–176.

————. "Israyel Orii Keankin Aratjin Shertjane" [The early years of the life of Israel Ori], *ibid*. (January 1956), 70–78.

————. "Israel Orin Mosgovayi Metj" [Israel Ori in Moscow], *ibid*. (February 1956), 79–80; (March 1956), 72–80.

Lusinian, Nurhan. "Zeytuni Tjakatamarte" [The battle of Zeitun], *Hisnameak—1887–1937—Sots. Demokrat Hunchakian Kusaktsuthian* [The fiftieth anniversary of the Social Democrat Hunchakian Party, 1887–1937] (Providence: Soc. Dem. Hunchakian Kus. Kedr. Varchuthiun [Central Committee of the Social Democrat Hunchakian Party], 1938), pp. 134–146.

Mikaelian, Christopher. "Bekorner Im Husherits" [Fragments from my memoirs], *Hairenik Amsagir* [Hairenik Monthly] (August 1924), 54–62.

Nazarbek, Avetis. "Zeitun," *Contemporary Review*, LXIX (April 1896), 513–528.

Piotrovsky, B. "Excavations of the Urartian Citadel on the Karmir-Blur," in *Papers Presented by the Soviet Delegation at the XXIII International Congress of Orientalists, Iranian, Armenian and Central-Asian Studies*. Moscow: USSR Academy of Sciences, 1954.

Rostom [Zorian, Stepan]. "Aratjin Kailer" [First steps], *Divan H.H. Dashnaktsuthian* [Archives of the A.R. Federation], I (Boston: H.H.D. Amerikayi Kedr. Komite [Central Committee of the American Branch of the Armenian Revolutionary Federation], 1934), 89–91.

Safrastian, A. "Armenian Thought and Literature since 1828," _Asiatic Review_, XXVI (April 1930), 331–336.

Sahakian. "S.D. Hunch. Kusaktsuthian Goyuthian Antsealin yev Nerkayis" [On the existence of the S.D. Hunchakian Party in the past and in the present], _Eritassard Hayastan_ [Young Armenia], 1944.

Sarafian, Vahe A. "Turkish Armenian and Expatriate Population Statistics," _Armenian Review_, IX (Autumn 1956), 119–128.

Sarkiss, H. J. "The Armenian Renaissance, 1500–1863," _Journal of Modern History_, IX (December 1937), 433–448.

"Shahan Tjerpeti Antip Namake Ghukas Katoghikosi" [The unpublished letter of Shahan Tjerpet to Catholicos Ghukas], _Vem_, I (September–October 1933), 134–140.

Shatirian, Martin:

    Sh., M. As dictated to N. Hangoyts. "Hayots Hasarakakan Sharzhumneri Patmuthiunits" [On the general intellectual movement of the Armenian people], _Hairenik Amsagir_ [Hairenik Monthly] (March 1923), 27–39; (April 1923), 50–66.

    Taragir. "Angakhuthian Gaghapare H.H. Dashnaktsuthian Himnadirneri Metainnuthian Metj" [The idea of independence in the thoughts of the founders of the Armenian Revolutionary Federation], _ibid._ (September 1932), 87–103.

Sevian, R. "Yerb E Himnevel Dashnaktsuthiune" [When was the Dashnaktsuthium founded?], _Hairenik Amsagir_ [Hairenik Monthly] December 1936), 57–66.

———. "H.H. Dashnaktsuthian Aratjin Dzragiri Heghinaknere" [The founders of the first program of the Armenian Revolutionary Federation], _ibid._ (February 1937), 71–78.

———. "H.H. Dashnaktsuthian Aratjin Kailere yev Gordzitchner" [Initial tasks and leaders of the A.R. Federation], _ibid._, April 1937–October 1937.

———. "H.H. Dashnaktsuthian Skezbnakan Dzragir-Kanonagire" [The first program-bylaws of the A.R. Federation], _ibid._ (January 1937), 90–99.

Shaginyan, Marietta [Shahinian]. "Khachatur Abovian," _Soviet Literature_ (Moscow, 1945), No. 1, pp. 134–140.

Tahmazian, Gurgen. "Hambardzum Poyadjian (Murat)," in _Hisnameak—1887–1937—Sots. Demokrat Hunchakian Kusaktsuthian_ [The fiftieth anniversary of the Social Democrat Hunchakian Party, 1887–1937] (Providence: Soc. Dem. Hunchakian Kus. Kedr. Varchuthiun [Central Committee of the Social Democrat Hunchakian Party], 1938), pp. 112–116.

Valadian, V. "Sarkis Googooniani Arshavanke" [The Sarkis Googoonian Expedition], _Hairenik Amsagir_ [Hairenik Monthly] (September 1957), 1–9; (October 1957), 23–32.

Vardian, Gegham. "Pap Alii Tsoytse" [The Demonstration of Bab Ali], _Hisnameak—1887–1937—Sots. Demokrat Hunchakian Kusaktsuthian_ [The fiftieth anniversary of the Social Democrat Hunchakian Party, 1887–1937] (Providence: Soc. Dem. Hunchakian Kus. Kedr. Varchuthiun

[Central Committee of the Social Democrat Hunchakian Party], 1938), 124–134.

Vratzian, Simon. "Mi Kani Djeshtumner" [A few corrections], *Vem*, XIV (April–June 1937), 78–82.

————. "H.H. Dashnaktsuthian Dzenunde yev Himnadirnere" [The origin and founders of the A.R. Federation], in *Hushapatum H.H. Dashnaktsuthian 1890–1950* [Historical collection of the A.R. Federation] (Boston: H.H.D. Buro [Bureau of the Armenian Revolutionary Federation], 1950), pp. 61–141.

[Vratzian, Simon]. "Yerb E Himnevel H.H. Dashnaktsuthiune" [When was the Dashnaksuthiun founded?], *Vem*, XXI (January 1938), 112.

Zalian, Mik. "Hairenaserneri Miuthiune" [The Union of Patriots], *Vem*, I (September–October), 113–115.

Zavarian, S. "Hishoghuthiunner Utsunakan Tevakannerits" [Memories from the 'eighties], *Hairenik Batsarik Tiv 2* [Hairenik, special issue no. 2] (Boston, 1914), pp. 3–9.

Index

CPSIA information can be obtained
at www.ICGtesting.com
Printed in the USA
JSHW041037160522
25975JS00002B/154

9 780520 303850